Praise for *The Lion in Autumn*

"[Fitzpatrick is] intent on demystifying the ▓▓▓▓ ▓▓ball coach, moving behind the spectacle of Saturday afternoon to reveal flesh and soul and humanity."   —Buzz Bissinger, *The New York Times*

"[Joe Paterno is] a glorious figure trying to pull his school out of the dark ages and take a stand against those who would exploit student athletes. . . . [Fitzpatrick] provides a picture of a stubborn, aging mortal scared of retirement."

—Bryan French, *Fort Worth Star-Telegram*

"Touching. . . . Fitzpatrick digs beyond the 4–7 record to show the pressures facing Paterno, and to a greater degree, how the coach dealt with the emotions of each mounting loss. . . . The legend may be true, but *Autumn* paints Paterno as a far more complicated figure. . . . The closest we'll come to seeing who Joe Paterno really is."

—Brian Bianca, *The Sentinel* (Carlisle, PA)

"This is not just a book about a football coach. This is a book about an educator and leader going through the most difficult seasons of his career and tasting the ashes of adversity in the autumn of his coaching life. You can feel the emotions and pride of this great man on every beautifully written page. It captures the essence of Joe Paterno as he battles to get Penn State back on top."

—Ernie Accorsi, New York Giants general manager

"With Joe Paterno, it's always been difficult to determine precisely where the man leaves off and the legend begins. Or vice-versa. But in this deftly crafted book we are treated to a thoughtful and articulate examination of the Icon of Happy Valley, set against the detailed backdrop of one of his most taxing seasons."

—Bill Lyon, *Philadelphia Inquirer* columnist

"Even as a proud alumnus of Penn State's hated rival Pitt, I still highly recommend this book!"

—Beano Cook, former University of Pittsburgh sports information director and ESPN commentator

Frank Fitzpatrick has been a sportswriter for *The Philadelphia Inquirer* for twenty-five years. He has been a finalist for the Pulitzer Prize and his numerous awards include first place from the Associated Press Sports Editors in the Best News Story category. He is also the author of *And the Walls Came Tumbling Down: Kentucky, Texas Western, and the Game That Changed American Sports*. He lives in West Chester, Pennsylvania.

THE LION IN AUTUMN

A SEASON WITH JOE PATERNO AND PENN STATE FOOTBALL

FRANK FITZPATRICK

GOTHAM
BOOKS

FOR GENE DOWNS AND RON MAR-ELIA,
Good Friends gone too soon.

GOTHAM BOOKS
Published by Penguin Group (USA) Inc.
375 Hudson Street, New York, New York 10014, U.S.A.

Penguin Group (Canada), 90 Eglinton Avenue East, Suite 700, Toronto, Ontario, Canada M4P 2Y3 (a division of Pearson Penguin Canada Inc.); Penguin Books Ltd, 80 Strand, London WC2R 0RL, England; Penguin Ireland, 25 St Stephen's Green, Dublin 2, Ireland (a division of Penguin Books Ltd); Penguin Group (Australia), 250 Camberwell Road, Camberwell, Victoria 3124, Australia (a division of Pearson Australia Group Pty Ltd); Penguin Books India Pvt Ltd, 11 Community Centre, Panchsheel Park, New Delhi - 110 017, India; Penguin Group (NZ), Cnr Airborne and Rosedale Roads, Albany, Auckland, New Zealand (a division of Pearson New Zealand Ltd); Penguin Books (South Africa) (Pty) Ltd, 24 Sturdee Avenue, Rosebank, Johannesburg 2196, South Africa

Penguin Books Ltd, Registered Offices: 80 Strand, London WC2R 0RL, England

Published by Gotham Books, a member of Penguin Group (USA) Inc.

Previously published as a Gotham Books hardcover edition, 2005

First trade paperback printing, August 2006

10 9 8 7 6 5 4 3 2 1

Copyright © 2005 by Frank Fitzpatrick
All rights reserved

Gotham Books and the skyscraper logo are trademarks of Penguin Group (USA) Inc.

ISBN: 1-592-40239-9

Printed in the United States of America
Set in Meridien, with display in Trajan
Designed by BTD NYC

Men must endure

Their going hence, even as their coming hither;

Ripeness is all.

    —*King Lear* (Act V, Scene II)

INTRODUCTION

JOE PATERNO COULDN'T SLEEP.

That was hardly surprising. Heading into the next afternoon's game with Northwestern, their ninth of the 2004 season, his Nittany Lions were a recipe for coaching insomnia. No matter what he tried, no matter how hard he worked, he just couldn't seem to turn them around.

But the Penn State coach's nature wouldn't permit surrender. And so, sometime before dawn on November 6, a brisk Saturday in State College, Pennsylvania, Paterno decided that rather than twitch around in bed for another hour, he'd review the game plan one last time.

He rose and proceeded down the hall to the den in the modest ranch house that had been his home now for nearly four decades. The four-bedroom house on McKee Street was just a few tree-lined blocks from the northern edge of the university's fifteen-thousand-acre campus, a twenty-minute walk from Beaver Stadium. Its backyard bordered Sunset Park, where even now, fifty days short of his seventy-eighth birthday, the coach would take brisk strolls along its tree-shrouded paths.

Paterno plucked a copy of the game plan off his desk and sat down. How could he squeeze more out of an offense that was by almost any measure his feeblest ever? He'd been pushing the envelope for weeks. For most of his fifty-four years of coaching, Penn State had won with a knock-'em-back simplicity—at times the only variation seemed to be which blocking hole the tailback would run toward. But the game plan he examined now had quarterbacks lined up at wide receiver, tight end, even tailback. There were fullback passes, faked field goals, and flea flickers.

What else could he do? Four weeks earlier, in a home loss to Purdue, his Nittany Lions had run the ball only seventeen times, the fewest ever in the Paterno era. They gained a paltry 18 yards.

By the time the morning sun angled through the den's high windows, he had made several changes. Restless, obsessively prepared, Paterno had performed this same kind of early-morning editing on dozens of Saturdays throughout his years at Penn State. "The will to win is important," he liked to say. "The willingness to prepare is vital." This time, however, he sensed that something in his well-ordered universe was out of place. He just couldn't identify exactly what it was.

Searching, he shifted in his chair and surveyed the room. Everywhere he looked he saw the familiar artifacts of the life he had chosen: the small den in the small house in the small town he had refused to abandon despite dozens of tempting offers; the photographs of his wife, his five children, his fourteen young grandchildren, his countless friends, and the former players who had gone on to the NFL, medical school, even the concert stage; the footballs, plaques, and trophies he had earned by winning 341 games—more than any other coach in history except one—all of them won, as his legion of supporters bragged, the right way.

Then he saw the problem.

Just beneath those elevated windows was a trophy shelf. Long ago, Paterno, a devout Catholic, had placed a crucifix up there, too, perhaps an attempt to ensure that he would not awake one day and find that his long and brilliant career had been a dream. Whenever he worked in the room on sunny mornings, the shadow of that crucifix fell comfortingly upon him.

Recently, though, he'd been so obsessed with redeeming himself and his program that he hadn't noticed the absence of the reassuring shadow. Someone had moved the cross (probably his wife while cleaning). He wondered how long it had been missing. Weeks? Years? Maybe that explained Penn State's baffling fall from its once preordained spot high in the national rankings. He had coached five undefeated teams, won two national championships and four coach-of-the-year awards, led his teams to thirty-one bowl appearances. But in the last five years, his teams had lost more often than they'd won. He needed to change his luck.

So he climbed up on a chair and reached for the trophy that now obscured the crucifix. It was the Timmie Award, which the Washington (D.C.) Touchdown Club had presented him in 1986 as its Coach of the Year. It was a twelve-pound, silver-plated depiction of an adolescent football player standing on a solid wooden base, and as he held it in his hands it seemed heavier than he had remembered.

Suddenly, the trophy slipped from his grasp and, like one more well-aimed arrow of misfortune, tumbled toward his head.

It clipped the scalp behind his left ear and he staggered. He braced himself to prevent a fall and muttered something angrily in that whiny Brooklyn accent he had never lost. Carefully stepping down, he pressed a hand against the fresh wound. The blood was flowing now, warm and plentiful. He was cut, not badly, but deep enough to ensure a hospital visit.

As he woke his wife to drive him to Penn State's Health Center, where they would sew eleven stitches behind his ear, he knew that the damn sportswriters would find out. He could imagine the next morning's headline in the *Centre Daily Times*: PATERNO INJURED BY FALLING TROPHY WHILE TRYING TO MOVE CRUCIFIX.

No one's going to believe this, he thought.

Actually, anyone who had been following Paterno and his Penn State football team in 2004 would have found it perfectly plausible. In the midst of another troubling season, he had been reaching for some spiritual comfort. Instead, he got smacked in the head by his glorious past.

That early-morning mishap explained a lot about Joe Paterno in 2004.

After nearly thirty-nine years as Penn State's head coach, he remained restless, curious, devoted, competitive, and superstitious. His luck had been bad almost since the moment a Minnesota receiver had grasped a desperate fourth-down pass against his second-ranked team in 1999. And as his persistent but loving critics pointed out at every opportunity, he was, in many ways, a fragile old man.

By the fall of 2004, Paterno's age and the deflated status of Nittany Lions' football had combined to create an unusually volatile atmosphere in State College. Troubling questions tumbled through central Pennsylvania's crisp autumn air like falling leaves. Would the old coach yield to reality and bow out gracefully? Or would he stubbornly hang on until he keeled over on Beaver Stadium's Kentucky-bluegrass sideline? Could so powerful a figure ever be persuaded to step aside? Or at least agree on a successor? If so, who might that be? His son Jay? Coordinators Tom Bradley or Galen Hall or someone from outside the program like Rick Neuheisel or Kirk Ferentz? Would Paterno at least reveal his plans at some point? And what would happen to the university's donations, applications, and prestige if he left? Or, worse, if he continued to lose?

There were no easy answers. Paterno's résumé was bulletproof. Time, tenure, and testimonials seemed to place the coach beyond the normal reach of authority. He had been at Penn State since 1950, when the Lions ran a Wing-T and played before crowds of fifteen thousand on a dusty field next door to Rec Hall. He had been head coach since 1966. In addition to the 341 games and the two national championships, he'd won nearly universal admiration for the classy program he'd built, one that had graduated eighty-six percent of its players and sent nearly three hundred of them to the NFL. His passion, intelligence, and commitment had helped transform an obscure agricultural college into a multifaceted Big Ten research institution, one that attracted topflight students and professors, deep-pocketed donors, and national respect. He'd rejected law school, countless NFL offers, and even politics to remain at the university.

In the process, he had become a national icon, the antidote to all that was toxic in college sports. He was "JoePa," Penn State's greatest asset. "Joe Paterno," former Penn State president John Oswald once said, "is a university president's dream." He was a towering figure in American sports, a Pennsylvania folk hero as solid and immovable as Mount Nittany itself.

But this unprecedented Penn State slump that began in 2000 and lingered on like a bad dream for five seasons now had eroded Mount JoePa's reputation. Losing had pulled back the curtain on Paterno's wizardry, revealing him to many as a stubborn, aging mortal. His supporters still outnumbered his detractors by a wide margin, but the gap was narrowing every day. Students, alumni, donors, fans, and sportswriters urged him to step aside. For the good of the football program. For the good of Penn State. For the good of Joe Paterno. Some of Paterno's more powerful foes had begun, according to the *Wilkes-Barre Times Leader*, "letter-writing campaigns, secret meetings in dark, smoke-filled rooms, even boycotts of the traditional post-home-game pasta dinners at the Paterno home."

"I agree that Joe has more than earned the right to go out on his terms, but there comes a point in all of our lives when you look in the mirror and say, 'It's time,' " a major Penn State donor told the paper. "Besides, and I know this is going to sound disrespectful, people aren't coming to that stadium every week because our library is rated number one in the nation. That's nice and all, but we'd still like to beat Michigan."

In the autumn of 2004, Happy Valley, long the capital of college-football optimism, had become a different place. A half century of certainty had been replaced by doubt. There had been no Big Ten titles since 1994, no nonconference road wins since 1999, just one bowl game in the last five years, and very few mentions on ESPN, unless it was some hand-waving ex-jock poking fun at Paterno's age. Even the huge crowds at Beaver Stadium had shrunk lately, down by four thousand a game.

The moral superiority Penn Staters had long felt about their pristine football program was crumbling too. While the team's graduation rate remained remarkably high, there had been so many disturbing off-the-field incidents involving players in 2003 that at times it was hard to distinguish Penn State from an outlaw program. At least eleven Nittany Lions had run-ins with the law that season. Worse, Paterno sometimes seemed willing to excuse, perhaps even hide, their transgressions.

"Penn State football is supposed to matter, as much as anything in sports can," said Ryan Jones, a '95 grad, early in the 2004 season. "We boast proud traditions and a coach and a program that still stand for things most coaches and programs don't. But we're not relevant anymore, and life was a little bit better when we were."

Most fans, their pride stung no less than the coach's, wanted assurances that the Penn State tradition would be reborn. If Paterno could do it, all the better. But if, as many now were convinced, he could not, then significant change was essential. And at Penn State, significant change could only mean one thing.

The detractors had hoped he might walk away when his contract expired after the 2004 season. But the previous May, at his request, the coach received a four-year contract extension, a deal set to run through his eighty-second birthday in 2008. The new contract virtually guaranteed that no one was going to tell him when to retire. Armed with that formidable club, Paterno could laughingly shrug off inquiries about his plans. He was not, he said, "ready to be buried."

The extension was, depending on one's view of Paterno, either a nice gesture or a national embarrassment.

"It's disappointing," said Paul Morrison, one of the first Nittany Lion Club boosters to call publicly for a coaching change. "I just haven't seen the performance on or off the field for the past handful of years. I was hoping to see a change of direction, someone new with more youth and energy."

"I know where I am and I think that if the day comes when I feel like I'm not able to do the job or the game's passed me by or I can't get up with a lot of enthusiasm . . . I don't have to stay in coaching," Paterno said. "I can get out of it. But I don't feel that way right now."

As the new season dawned, the apparently unbridgeable gap between what many alumni and fans felt was necessary and what was actually possible was wider than ever. That bred frustration, which led to more angry letters, e-mails, and radio-talk-show calls.

"I think, honestly, Joe has to realize at some point that he needs to kind of hang things up here and try to leave while he can still have some kind of good reputation," Skip Dreibelbis, a former Penn State player, said on a State College postgame radio show, where the coach's detractors tended to gather. "Because if things continue this downward spiral that they're in, what's going to become of Penn State football?"

Paterno's supporters were, if not as persistently noisy, just as passionate. Their fortress was the State College Quarterback Club, a hardcore group of local loyalists who had been conducting casual weekly lunch meetings with the coach for decades.

"He deserves to be handled differently than anyone else," said Jim Meister, the club's president. "He put Penn State on the map. No matter where you are, if you mention Penn State, people will say, 'Isn't that where Joe Paterno is?' "

That renown tinges the debate with sadness. No one enjoyed watching Paterno tarnish his image, even if he insisted he was unaffected by it all. But what do you do when a legend falters?

"Years ago," Paterno said, "when I came home crying that somebody called me a Wop, I said 'Mom' "—he pretends to be crying—" 'they called me a Wop.' She said, 'Sticks and stones will break your bones but names will never hurt you.' All of that is fine. As long as they don't call me a Wop in the paper, I'm all right."

That was about the only thing they didn't call him. Long college football's most revered figure, the aging coach was becoming the butt of jokes. And not just in Pennsylvania. In Biloxi, Mississippi, a reader wrote that city's *Sun-Herald:* "More ugly rumors out of the Big Ten: allegations Joe Paterno once gave a recruit a free stagecoach." From *The Miami Herald*'s Greg Cote came: "Did you notice last week? Poor Paterno coached the entire game with his left blinker on." A Toronto newspaper had initiated a "JoePa Award," to be presented annually "to those whose reputations are sullied by hanging around too long."

He was at the heart of a tempest. And with each defeat the rain fell harder, the wind blew stronger. Had Paterno, an English-literature major at Brown more than a half century earlier, not been consumed by his team's failings, he might have recognized how much he had come to resemble Lear, Shakespeare's aging, befuddled king. Tarnished by time, confounded by his rivals, beset by the rising cries of critics, enmeshed in a controversy involving an heir, he was an increasingly tragic figure moored on the storm-wracked heather of his legend.

Four or five years ago, as Paterno tells the story, he ran into an eighty-two-year-old Penn State fan who had enjoyed a long and successful career as a corporate CEO.

"Never retire," he told the coach.

Recently, Paterno saw the man again.

"Damn it," he said to the coach now. "You took my advice."

Throughout this late-life ordeal, Paterno could still laugh at himself. He liked to say that was because he had no ego. One of his favorite stories on that topic concerned his father, Angelo, a lawyer who had died of a heart attack in 1955.

"I have not been an ego guy. I never had an ego," he said. "When I was a kid, a junior in high school, I got my picture in the *Brooklyn Eagle*. I'm sitting there in my room looking at my picture and my dad said, 'Keep looking at that picture and that's the last time you'll ever have your picture in the paper.' I've never forgotten that."

It was a nice story. But no one gets to be as successful as Paterno without an ego. It was true he didn't live in a big house, or drive a Mercedes or buy expensive Italian suits. But wasn't it egotistical to demand so much from players and himself? And to get it? Paterno might not be self-conscious, but he certainly is self-aware.

"Joe's ego is like Dean Smith's," said Patrick Reusse, a *Minneapolis Star-Tribune* columnist. "It's not an in-your-face kind of ego. It's more a sideways ego. But in the end it's still a huge ego."

Now that ego was badly bruised.

A few years earlier, he had seemed ready to wean himself gradually from the daily grind of his job. Maybe he'd cut back in this area or that, have one last great season and then walk away to become a kind of coach emeritus, one who, upon request, injected himself into recruiting, fund raising, or public relations for the university. Instead, the embarrassments of 2003 persuaded him he needed more, not less, involvement. So Paterno began to reimagine himself.

"I felt we weren't very good and I hadn't done a very good job," he said. "So I had to sit back and say, 'Hey, do you want to stay in this thing? If you want to stay in it, you'd better get off your backside and get to work again.' "

Before the 2004 season, he shuffled his coaching staff, bumping longtime offensive coordinator Fran Ganter into an administrative post and replacing him with Galen Hall. He altered lifetime routines. He more closely monitored his players' performances and academic progress. He got more involved in the play calling. At times, he frantically—maybe even desperately—pushed his players, his staff, and himself. He nagged and challenged them all in practices that were more physically grueling than any Penn State senior could recall.

It was all quite taxing for a man of seventy-seven, even one so unusually fit and energetic. But that's how he always handled adversity, with a hitch-up-your-pants, plant-your-feet-in-the-ground determination. That was the Brooklyn street swagger in Paterno, the cocky self-assurance that toughened, and sometimes obscured, his more familiar intellectual side.

"Over the years, every time things started getting a little rough, he'd always be one of those guys who thrived on it," said Tim Curley, Penn State's athletic director. "The rest of us would get gray hair and go crazy and he's not like that. He's so competitive he seems to welcome the challenge."

He had watched Bear Bryant die in 1983, just a month after that legendary coach quit at Alabama, and it frightened him. So, in the words of *Centre Daily Times* sports editor Ron Bracken, who has known and covered Paterno for decades, he kept "hitting the reset button on his retirement clock."

Every five years or so, he'd look around at his wife and children, or his wife and grandchildren, at the growing costs and commercialization of college sports, at the increased recruiting competition and media demands, and he'd talk about retirement.

"I don't want to hang around too long," he said. "I'll probably coach another four or five years." That was in 1973.

He forecast his imminent departure again in 1978, in 1982, in 1986, in 1989, in 1997, and in 1999. In 1990, he had predicted that by

2000, he'd be sitting in the Beaver Stadium stands, "second-guessing a coach who doesn't throw the ball enough."

He was rightfully proud of the record he had amassed, the lives he had changed, the acclaimed program he had constructed. Still, he had regrets.

"I can remember things that happened twenty years ago in football games," he said once, "but I can't remember what my kids did."

Maybe he also thought about the books he hadn't read, the places he'd never seen, how nice it would be to sit on the beach near his summer home in Avalon, New Jersey, with a Jack Daniel's and a *New York Times* and not have anything to worry about.

And yet he couldn't walk away. He couldn't even settle on a scenario in which that might be possible.

Tommy Bowden, the son of Bobby Bowden, the seventy-five-year-old Florida State coach who had passed Paterno's record-setting victory total, recognized the symptoms. He grimly predicted that either his father or Paterno "will die on the field, I'm sure."

But for all his game-day miseries, when practice resumed each Monday, he would be miraculously revived. Standing out there on those skinny legs, wearing a plain gray sweatshirt, khaki pants, and black football cleats, Paterno was as energetic, as cranky, as meticulous, as vocal, as involved as ever.

Sometimes, despite increasing evidence that it would be unlikely for this diminished Penn State program, he mused about having one last unbeaten team. There had been at least one in every other decade he had been head coach. Sometimes he hinted that he'd like to name an assistant head coach and then gradually hand the reins to him, just as Rip Engle had done for Paterno. Sometimes he suggested that before departing he just wanted to get Penn State football back on track.

His lifelong passion to succeed—"a maniacal need to be first," his brother termed it—long ago trumped his other interests. Now it was too late and he was too proud to admit it. He had invested so much in Penn State football that to leave it in this state, despite all he had accomplished, would be a tacit acknowledgement of failure.

"If you think that I am going to back out of it because I am intimidated, you are wrong," he said as the season began in 2004. "If you think I am going to stay when I think I am not doing a good job, you are wrong. Those things have to develop and have to evolve. Right now, I think we can get this thing done and do a good job. We obviously have to recruit some people. We have to recruit some skilled people. I have said that before. I don't want to hang around here and pull Penn State down. . . . I could walk out of this thing. I could call and tell you today I am going. What does it mean to me? It doesn't mean a thing to me. What impact does it have on the program, the coaches, and is it the best thing for Penn State? They are the things that I think about all the time. It has nothing to do with Joe Paterno."

No, even with a battered ego, a fraying historical reputation, and a bloodied head, Joe Paterno couldn't leave.

"I know of several old friends who have called Joe and said, 'Look, nobody is going to make you leave. But for God's sake, why not get things lined up for when you do decide to do it?' " said one longtime Penn State insider. "Joe doesn't want to hear it. He just cuts those people out of his life."

Matt Millen, the former Penn State star who now is the Detroit Lions general manager, experienced that very thing. "Two years ago, I called him and said, 'You know, Joe, it really isn't my business, but you should name a successor,' " said Millen in 2003. " 'It doesn't mean you have to retire.'

"He told me, 'Millen, you're right—it isn't any of your business.' "

He was going to turn his program around—even if it killed him.

CHAPTER 1

THE WHISTLE that officially began the 2004 season blew at precisely 10:00 A.M on March 27, its shrill cry careening around cavernous Holuba Hall like the shriek of a wounded bird. From the outside, the enormous corrugated-steel practice facility, just a short distance from Beaver Stadium, resembled a warehouse. Inside, its 118,000-square-foot vastness was dark and drafty, the dreariness enlivened only by the garish green Astroturf that carpeted its floor.

On this first day of spring practice, Joe Paterno prowled up and down that artificial surface. Hunched at the hips, head constantly tilted forward, dark eyes focused on the exercising players stretched out at his feet, he resembled a hawk waiting to swoop down on unsuspecting prey.

Wearing his usual practice uniform—gray sweatshirt, khakis, black football cleats over white tube socks—the coach frequently barked and snapped in a manner that, depending on the player, could irritate, intimidate, infuriate, or amuse.

But as familiar as this agitated figure might have appeared to his team that morning, the old man was not the same coach who just four months earlier had been humiliated by Penn State's season-ending 41–10 loss at Michigan State. The seventy-seven-year-old Paterno had, out of desperation, reinvented himself.

Bruised and battered during that nine-loss season, he had spent the last few months deconstructing Penn State football. He was going to demand more, inspire more, discipline more. He was going to discard some philosophies that no longer worked and adopt a few new ones.

"You forget to do the things that got you there," he would explain. "You stop paying attention to the tiny details. Now I've got to get back to those things. It's like starting over. I've got to prove a couple of things and I think it's going to be interesting to see if I can do it."

His team had gotten its first glimpse of the changes a month earlier.

The 2003 Nittany Lions had been as bad off the field as on it. Inside the program, there was a hope that with the end of that dreadful season might come an end to the extracurricular trouble as well. Paterno certainly intended that to be the case.

Then, sometime around 4:00 A.M. on February 7, near the end of the Alpha Phi Alpha fraternity's "Black Ice" dance and skate party at Penn State's Greenburg Ice Pavilion, a fight broke out. Like a sprawling barroom brawl from an old Western, it went on for more than ten minutes and eventually involved fifteen to twenty people. Among them were three key players, defensive linemen Matthew Rice and Ed Johnson and quarterback/wide receiver Michael Robinson.

Robinson, the central ingredient in Paterno's football plans for the upcoming season, had been knocked into the rink's glass trophy case during the fight. The junior was cut so badly behind his left ear that he needed twenty-four stitches to close the wound. No charges were ever filed, but Paterno suspended Johnson and Rice for summer practice. Robinson, whose role in the melee the coach deemed "not as aggressive," was put on probation.

"They were wrong. They were in a fight," Paterno told reporters. "We've taken care of it."

That sentiment was for public consumption. Privately, Paterno fumed. He quickly summoned his team to a meeting. He told them he wouldn't put up with that kind of thing this season. They were going to discover a lot of changes when they returned to the field the following month. Either they'd work harder and behave better or they wouldn't be running out of the Beaver Stadium tunnel with him next September 4 for the season-opening game with Akron.

"He told us, 'That's it,' " said senior quarterback Zack Mills. " 'Next incident, you're gone.' He was tired of it happening every other week. He's serious. . . . The margin for error is gone."

All rules would be strictly enforced. No long hair, cornrows, beards, or mustaches. Players struggling in class or late for meetings would jeopardize their playing time.

The athletes, many of whom had been so dismayed by the 3–9 season that they were considering transfers, welcomed the new spark they saw in their old coach.

"We needed Joe to put us in our place," said tight end Isaac Smolko.

So even though, at this first spring workout, the players' outfits were relatively casual—navy-blue shorts, white T-shirts, spikes, and helmets—the atmosphere was surprisingly intense for March.

"He wants to coach like he coached in the past, when people were scared of him," said Levi Brown, an offensive tackle. "I don't think people have been scared of him lately."

Players had been accustomed to Paterno's whiny complaints and his obsession with details. Many of them, though, had begun to tune him out. While they respected his accomplishments, and were in awe of his reputation, they couldn't help but occasionally see him as a grandfatherly figure, a hopelessly outdated old man who sputtered furiously—comically sometimes to them—at their mistakes and constantly referenced long-gone players and coaches.

Now, with his postbrawl crackdown and his vow of zero tolerance, their views began to change. Almost immediately, defensive linemen Johnson, Lavon Chisley, and Tamba Hali got rid of their cornrows.

"[After] a three-and-nine season, a lot of people might say, 'It's over. We should leave. Some people should get out of here,' " explained Hali. "But if you have guys still here, trying to work . . . showing our dedication, that's more togetherness right there. . . . If anything is going to help us get back on track, we want to do that."

Paterno's message came through so loud and so clear that it even filtered down to some of the Pennsylvania high school players Penn State was recruiting.

"Paterno is cracking down on everything now, he wants his program run his way," Dan Lawlor, a fullback from Mechanicsburg who signed with the Nittany Lions, told a reporter. "He's doing everything he can to help it recover."

A. Q. Shipley, a defensive tackle from Coraopolis who also wound up at Penn State, said that in his talks with Paterno, the coach had "come across real strict. You can just tell it's his way or no way."

Paterno needed more than discipline. He needed a new Penn State paradigm.

While college football was getting faster and flashier all the time, Paterno's teams often appeared as out of fashion as their famously stark navy-and-white uniforms. Right or wrong, the perception was that the Nittany Lions were mired in the past. Was it any wonder so many hip-hop-generation recruits, even in Pennsylvania, were looking elsewhere?

"The teams that play us know what we're going to run," star running back Larry Johnson had said after a 2000 loss to lightly regarded Toledo, a bitter postgame analysis that inflamed the "Joe Must Go" movement. "They can pull out the tapes from '92 or '93, and we run the same offense. Same plays, same offense. . . . Sometimes, I don't even know the play and I can guess what's coming. The system is too predictable. It's been around too long."

If Paterno couldn't produce evidence of positive change in 2004— on and off the field—the tumult surrounding his age and abilities would ratchet up considerably. That was why a near-palpable sense of urgency surrounded him.

He had always been fanatical in his devotion to his job. "He goes and goes and goes until it's time to go to bed," his brother George once said. As he aged, that passion grew uncontrollably, like kudzu, until it choked out almost everything else.

"There isn't anything in my life anymore except for my family and football," Paterno said. His wife of forty-two years offered a similar assessment, though adding "walking" to his short list of passions.

A year ago, however, he had hinted that he was nearing a point when he might begin to relinquish some duties to assistants. While he remained remarkably involved in every detail of football and recruiting, Paterno, mentally at least, had seemed ready to relax his grip.

But sometime during those long winter walks around town or on Sunset Park's bicycle and jogging paths, Paterno convinced himself that what was required was more, not less, dedication. At his age, with his detractors howling, he didn't have time for long-range solutions. So changes, drastic changes, had to be tried. And they had to be tried fast.

Extracurricular demands had long been a burden and a drain on the time he could devote to the players and coaching. Now he began to think of ways to ease that load, perhaps by creating a new position in the athletic department for someone who could handle the requests, the phone calls, and the paperwork.

"One of the problems that you get the longer you're in it: The more friends and kids, and people who count on you," Paterno had said earlier, "and your time away from coaching gets more and more significant. People have funerals, [former] players have kids who need a hand, the whole band of people you're involved with stretches. Every year it stretches a little bit more. That's when you start to get swamped. You keep thinking it won't hurt here, it won't hurt there. You wake up one morning and you have a crappy organization."

By the time spring practice began, there were whispers around State College about Paterno's "Grand Experiment II." This master plan allegedly was not at all like its famous predecessor, in which Paterno outlined his plans to marry academics and athletics. This experiment was all about restoring the luster to his program.

"We had to get the whole program back into a little different mode," Paterno said of his off-season contemplations. "You've got to figure out how you're going to get this thing done so you can protect the coaches and make sure the university has the ability to continue the kind of tradition we've had. You have an obligation to make sure the kids you recruited have some success. All of that was in my mind when I decided I was going to give it a shot. And once I made that decision, I wasn't going to go about it halfhearted. I was going to bust my butt."

Continued football difficulties could be devastating to Penn State. Too much losing could adversely affect more than the school's athletic reputation. Alumni contributions, political support, and student applications all rode on the back of football success.

So in the run-up to spring drills, he further limited his access— and that of his assistants and players—to fans and reporters. He stopped walking to his office each morning and evening to save time. His wife told interviewers that he was "preoccupied, distracted."

"There's more getting up in the middle of the night and writing ideas down," Sue Paterno said of her husband. "More going to work at one or two in the morning. If something goes through his mind, he can't sleep."

Had outsiders been able to observe him they would have seen a man who, despite having a contract about to expire, was not ready to quit. Quit? Hell, he was so excited he could hardly sleep. He made mental lists of problems that needed addressing. And given his 2003 team's rap sheet and woeful statistics, they were lengthy. Eleven Penn State players had been cited or arrested. On the field, the Lions' lone victories had come at home, against three perennial weak sisters, Temple, Kent State, and Indiana. Those teams' combined win–loss record was 8–28.

Paterno believed his last team had lacked heart and character. They hung in games until adversity arrived and then, typically in the fourth quarter, folded. Penn State had blown late leads to Nebraska, Northwestern, and Ohio State in 2003. They drew close to Minnesota, Wisconsin, and Purdue but extinguished themselves late in those losses.

Though he remained convinced physical conditioning was not a major reason why the 2003 Lions collapsed, he had his players lift more in the winter, run more in the spring.

"He wants to see who are the guys who are going to step up and make plays in the clutch, when you're tired, fatigued, sweating, breathing hard, because that's what it's going to take to win those fourth quarters," junior center E. Z. Smith said.

The needs of their legs, arms, and torsos addressed, he turned to where he felt the real problems existed—in their hearts and minds.

"I don't think we've been tough enough mentally in the clutch," Paterno said.

He had been disappointed with some of his now-departed players, particularly guys like Tony Johnson and offensive tackle Chris McKelvey who were constantly in his doghouse and didn't seem to care. The locker room lacked leaders. There had been few wise elders for the underclassmen to turn to in tough times. As a result, bad easily made the leap to worse.

"We had a lack of leadership," conceded kicker Robbie Gould. "Seniors didn't want to take that role. This year, there's guys that want to get it done and show the young guys how it's supposed to be done."

Penn State hadn't elected permanent captains in five years, but now Paterno felt this youthful 2004 team would need them. The coach discussed his plans with the players. He told them two of his favorites, fifth-year seniors Mills and linebacker Derek Wake, would be ideal. Not surprisingly, the two strong, silent types were selected.

"We've run the gamut," said wide receiver Gerald Smith, discussing the new captains' personalities. "In the past, we've had guys who, just because they were seniors, acted like leaders, jumping around and yelling. But in the back of your mind you're thinking, *What have you done? You haven't done anything.*"

The team assembled before Paterno that morning in Holuba Hall was a remarkably young one. Of the ninety-seven names on its spring roster, only fourteen were seniors in their last year of eligibility. That reflected an off-season purge of sorts, one that was further evidence of this new Paterno.

Traditionally loyal to veterans, often criticized for sticking with seniors over apparently more gifted underclassmen, he had decided Penn State would go with youth in 2004. He urged several fifth-year seniors to leave the team and a few, including offensive lineman Nick Marmo and linebackers T. C. Cosby and Tim Johnson, did so. At least two other players, linebacker LaMar Stewart and center Dan Mazan, already had decided to transfer.

That meant more time to work with freshmen. Most freshmen had difficulties adjusting to college life. Many were away from home for the first time. There were the pressures of dorm life and school-work. And Paterno knew his ways took some getting used to.

"Kids coming out of high school just aren't prepared for it," said Robinson. "Coach will say something to reporters that's meant for you. In meetings, you'll think he's talking about somebody else but he's really talking about you. He'll yell things at practice and you're not sure how to take it."

Three of the Penn State players on the field with Paterno that morning were freshmen whose high school classes hadn't even grad-uated yet. Linebacker Dan Connor, offensive lineman Greg Harrison, and defensive lineman Elijah Robinson had accelerated through their senior years so they could enroll for the spring semester and partici-pate in spring drills.

Connor, Pennsylvania's outstanding scholastic defensive player the previous fall, had taken an extra load of core courses at Strath Haven High to finish early.

"One thing I don't need to be doing is getting lazy, developing bad habits," he explained to the *Philadelphia Daily News*. "I can avoid that by going up there and getting a jump on things. . . . It looked like they might need help [at linebacker]. If they needed me to play in Septem-ber, I didn't want to go through the whole freshman thing, getting ac-climated and trying to fit in football. This way, I get that taken care of. I'll know my way around, have classes already done, and it will be easier."

Paterno was ambivalent about the trend. A sentimentalist by na-ture, he hated to see youngsters pass up things like senior proms and senior weeks at the Shore—even though most managed to squeeze in those activities anyway.

"It's their last year in high school," he said, "and it should be such a good time. . . . If I had my way, we would have freshmen ineligible.

That is the way I would look at it. Let [the NCAA] come in and give us eight to ten more scholarships and have freshmen ineligible. I would prefer that."

In his mind, Paterno was mildly optimistic. Penn State's strength would be its sophomores and juniors, players who would be at their peaks in '05 and '06. They would be supplemented by a class of freshmen recruits that *Sports Illustrated* ranked twelfth best in the nation. And that was before Pittsburgh-area quarterback Anthony Morelli (rated the third-best high-schooler at that position in the U.S.) decided to rescind his verbal commitment to Pitt and come to Happy Valley.

Morelli's February 5 decision illustrated some of the benefits and drawbacks to Penn State recruiting. Paterno remained a first-rate closer. His charm, his legend, his commitment to academics could sway almost any recruit's parents. But his reputation for rigidity, and the uncertainty his age created, often worked against him.

Rival coaches for years had been persuading recruits that the Paterno era might end at any time. "All these years when everybody was telling kids [not to go] to Penn State because Paterno won't be there, about seven hundred of those [coaches] are gone," Paterno had said.

A six-four, 212-pounder, Morelli originally had been the Lions' second choice. Paterno wanted Chad Henne, from Wilson High, in West Lawn, Pennsylvania, Kerry Collins's alma mater. The feeling was mutual. But Henne, who ended up at Michigan, told those around him he had not been impressed with quarterbacks coach Jay Paterno, and the head coach wouldn't promise him that he'd play as a freshman.

It brought to mind the situation with Tony Dorsett, who, as a phenomenal high school running back in western Pennsylvania in 1972, had expressed a desire to play at Penn State. Paterno told him he would have to sit and learn for a year behind John Cappelletti. Dorsett went to Pitt instead and on to a Hall of Fame career with the Dallas Cowboys.

"I never tell a kid he'll start, no matter what," Paterno said.

What also drew Henne to Michigan was the knowledge that nearly every Wolverines quarterback in the last two decades had made it into the NFL. "What's Penn State done with its quarterbacks?" asked Henne's coach at Wilson, Jim Cantafio, who also coached Collins.

Henne ended up starting for the Wolverines and helping them win a Big Ten championship and a Rose Bowl berth.

In the meantime, Morelli had verbally committed to Pitt, apparently convinced the Paterno era was ending. But on a January 24 visit to Happy Valley, when the coach persuaded him he'd be around at least another four years, Morelli got on board.

The indecision Morelli exhibited was typical. For the last few years, conversations among recruits about Penn State football had increasingly been dominated by concerns about the coach's status. Just that morning, in fact, a bizarre rumor was wending its way through Internet chat rooms and radio talk shows. It claimed Rick Neuheisel, the former Colorado and Washington coach, would be hired as a graduate assistant and, eventually, become Paterno's successor.

Paterno laughed it off. "I'd have to call him up and give him directions to State College," he said of Neuheisel, a close acquaintance. The coach blamed the speculation on the Internet, even though this man who still didn't use a cell phone or a computer admitted he knew nothing about the technology. ("What the hell do I know about downloading music?" Paterno once said when a player had been accused of that popular campus offense. "I can't download a jar of peanut butter.")

He enjoyed this time of year. With no travel, few media obligations, and the absence of in-season pressures, it was a time when he could focus on teaching. But concerns about the health of student athletes had led to recent limits on just how much teaching he could do. After NCAA medical personnel discovered that injury rates among football players were higher in the spring than during the season, guidelines were tightened. New NCAA rules restricted the number, length, and nature of the spring drills.

Schools were limited to fifteen days of practice, which could take place anytime within a twenty-nine-day period. On three of those days, contact was banned and the only protective equipment a player could wear was a helmet. Tackling was prohibited on four of the remaining twelve days, and on five others it was permitted no more than fifty percent of the time. The workouts could go no longer than four hours a day, including meeting time, and twenty hours a week.

That left just three days—including the April 24 Blue-White Game—when live scrimmages could take place.

"I'm comfortable with the new rules," Paterno said. "But we can't cut back any more. If we do, we might as well eliminate coaching altogether. The game will simply be about recruiting."

At the news conference marking the start of spring workouts, Paterno had drawn snickers from the assembled reporters when he said one of his big worries in 2004 would be tackling. Penn State's defense, though terribly inconsistent in 2003, particularly against the run, was deep in returning talent.

Junior cornerback Alan Zemaitis led the Big Ten with eighteen pass breakups and the team with four interceptions. Safety Mike Guman, one of just two senior defensive starters, and hero back Calvin Lowry were well above average. There were several young and talented linebackers, including sophomore Paul Posluszny, Tim Shaw, J. R. Zwierzynski, Connor, and converted fullback BranDon Snow. And the line had a host of returning veterans in Hali, Johnson, Chisley, Rice, Scott Paxson, and Jay Alford.

It was the offense, as Paterno and everyone else at the news conference knew, that needed serious help. The previous season, Penn State had ranked 103rd nationally in total offense out of 117 teams in Division I-A.

In 2003, Paterno had alternated Mills and Robinson at quarterback—getting little efficiency from either. Asked last November who would be his starter in 2004, he irritated both players when he said the job would be won in the spring.

Mills, who would be a fifth-year senior, felt the position should have been his. He had been sensational at times as a freshman, most memorably coming off the bench to lead the Lions to the stirring comeback victory over Ohio State that made Paterno college football's winningest coach. But shoulder and knee injuries, offensive-line troubles, and a lack of capable wide receivers had diminished his production and made the native of Ijamsville, Maryland, a favorite target of frustrated fans.

"I just look at it as just another thing I have to deal with," said Mills of his battle for playing time with Robinson. "It's part of the job. It's part of the responsibility."

Robinson, a junior from Richmond, Virginia, was more athletic, explosive, and versatile, with the ability to play wideout, running back, or even safety. Paterno persisted in saying he "may be the best all-around football player in the country." But he had serious flaws as a quarterback, not the least of which was his passing accuracy.

Robinson completed less than forty-five percent of his passes in '03 and had the same number of interceptions as TD passes (five). Mills was barely better, with six touchdowns and five interceptions.

"My passion to win would help me swallow my pride and play receiver or tailback," Robinson said. "But the only thing that would totally satisfy me would be to be the quarterback."

While neither appeared capable of single-handedly transforming the sputtering offense, they clearly were the most threatening weapons Penn State possessed.

"[Robinson] and Zack Mills are going to carry this football team," Paterno predicted. "I hope we can keep those two kids healthy."

So that spring he and his staff began to devise an attack designed to keep opponents off balance. Both QBs frequently would be used simultaneously. Each would get plenty of snaps. Each would line up as a slot receiver from time to time. Robinson might even run the ball from the tailback position.

"We are going to try to use him [Robinson] in a lot of different ways," predicted Paterno. "He can throw the ball. He can run the ball. He can catch the ball. As a wideout he would be a great blocker. As a running back, he can break tackles."

What continued to make Robinson appealing as a quarterback was Penn State's offensive line. The unit, which figured to consist of Smith, Brown, Tyler Reed, Charles Rush, and Andrew Richardson, had been dreadful in '03. That helped explain the lack of production from the tailbacks.

While it was widely known as Linebacker U., Penn State also had an incredibly successful tradition at tailback: Cappelletti, Lenny Moore, Lydell Mitchell, Curt Warner, Blair Thomas, D. J. Dozier, Curtis Enis, Ki-Jana Carter, Larry Johnson. But in 2003 Robinson, with 107 rushes, had carried the ball more often than either of the top two returning tailbacks, sophomores Austin Scott and Tony Hunt.

As a senior at Allentown's Parkland High School, Scott had set three spectacular single-season state records—3,853 rushing yards, fifty-three touchdowns, and 322 points. But his freshman year had been disappointing. Though fans continually clamored for the phenom to play, particularly when it became clear the '03 season was another lost cause, Paterno used him sparingly. Privately, the coach felt Scott hadn't grasped the offense quickly enough and that he had deficiencies as a pass-catcher and blocker. Scott ran the ball one hundred times in '03 for 436 yards and five touchdowns.

Hunt, from Alexandria, Virginia, carried it just thirty-four times for 110 yards and one TD. Another 2003 freshman tailback, Rodney Kinlaw, tore up a knee in practice that September and was redshirted.

Paterno hoped Robinson's versatility as a runner and passer would overcome some offensive shortcomings. But what he really wanted was for him to become Mills's big-play wide receiver. That was the Nittany Lions' most obvious weakness. The five leading pass-catchers from a year ago were gone, not that anyone but their opponents would miss them. Lions receivers had dropped twenty-four catchable balls in '03, missed blocks, and run the wrong routes often.

Tony Johnson, who had a team-high thirty-two catches, was gone. Maurice Humphrey (thirty), expected to be a gamebreaker, had been expelled from school following aggravated-assault charges. Speedster Ernie Terrell had left to run track full-time. Junior Kinta Palmer, a ballyhooed recruit from South Carolina, had been buried on the third team for some unexplained reason. And Josh Hannum would soon transfer to Division III Ursinus. That left senior Gerald Smith as the top returnee, and he had managed just fifteen catches the previous season. Neither Terrance Phillips nor Terrell Golden would worry too many defensive coordinators.

Paterno hoped that by employing the dangerous Robinson as a wideout from time to time, he could dissuade opposing defensive coordinators from stacking eight players in the box, and maybe earn some breathing room for Hunt and Scott.

"Last year, our wideouts were horrible," Paterno said. "They were confused at times, they didn't run routes the same way twice in a row. The quarterbacks got a lot of [criticism], but most of the time, it was not their fault."

Winning seasons and bowl appearances had been the norm for decades in State College. This prolonged slump had arrived as unexpectedly and mysteriously as the Black Death struck medieval Europe. In the disbelief and panic that ensued, scapegoats were easy to find.

A few believed Paterno's downfall was predestined the moment the Nittany Lions abandoned the East for the Big Ten. Ostensibly the move into the storied midwestern conference populated mostly by large state institutions looked like a perfect fit. Penn State, despite its location, had always been more midwestern than northeastern in its culture and outlook. But the move greatly increased the football schedule's degree of difficulty on a week-to-week basis. And, maybe more significantly, it invited schools like Michigan and Ohio State into places where Paterno had enjoyed nearly exclusive recruiting rights. Penn State games against Big Ten opponents were broadcast throughout the region and high school stars from Pennsylvania, New Jersey, and Maryland had begun signing more frequently at Iowa, Ohio State, and especially Michigan.

More spiritually inclined Penn State supporters, however, were convinced the decline began just after the university decided to add a new level onto Beaver Stadium's south grandstands. Those new seats, they believed, angered the football gods by forever obscuring the fans' view of Mount Nittany, the sacred symbol of Penn State.

Others pointed to the Minnesota game on November 6, 1999. On that Homecoming Saturday, LaVar Arrington–led Penn State was 9–0 and No. 2 in the national polls. Trailing, 23–21, with 1:22 left, and facing a fourth-and-16 situation at the Lions' 40, Minnesota quarterback Billy Cockerham heaved a Hail Mary pass downfield. The ball bounced off a Gopher's wide receiver and a Penn State defensive back but was caught by a diving Arland Bruce, a senior who had fourteen previous career receptions. As time expired, Minnesota kicker Dan Nystrom made a game-winning 32-yard field goal. Its national-championship hopes dashed, Penn State lost its remaining three games that season and twenty-six of its next forty-eight through 2003.

But perhaps the most logical theory was the most mundane. After the '99 season, longtime defensive coordinator Jerry Sandusky had retired. If nothing else, the loss of a man who had been at Paterno's side for thirty-one seasons prompted a major shift in staff responsibilities.

Paterno responded to Sandusky's departure somewhat oddly, eliminating the coordinator titles. He named defensive backs coach Tom Bradley the "coach in charge of defense." He gave Ganter the same distinction with the offense, in addition to an "assistant head coach" designation. Also, the coach's thirty-five-year-old son, Jay Paterno, previously the tight-ends coach, took charge of the quarterbacks before the 2000 season and was handed additional play-calling responsibilities. As for his own role, Paterno reconsolidated some of the offensive duties he had grudgingly yielded.

When those moves resulted in losing seasons in 2000, 2001, and 2003, the offensive staff became the focus of discontent. Even as Paterno prepared to run his 2004 squad through spring drills, fans were griping about the offense on the local radio sports-talk station, 970-AM, and in letters to the *Centre Daily Times* and student-run *Daily Collegian*.

Jay Paterno became a lightning rod for much of that dissatisfaction. The program's critics, especially those reluctant to criticize Paterno, blamed his son for many of the difficulties—poor quarterbacking, subpar recruiting, dismal play-calling.

An online poll conducted among visitors to *PSU Playbook*, a Web site for Nittany Lions fans, posed this question: "Is Jay Paterno the biggest obstacle Penn State faces?" There were 249 votes: Eighty-five percent said yes, fifteen percent said no. The respondents' biggest fear was that Paterno was grooming his son, who had been a walk-on quarterback at Penn State and later an assistant at James Madison, Virginia, and Connecticut, as his successor.

"A lot of people have said I've been hanging around long enough so that I can turn the job over to Jay," Paterno would say. "That's not fair to Jay and it put a lot of heat on him, I think unfairly. It's awfully tough to have your kid follow you. A couple of guys have tried that and it hasn't worked that well. If, when the time comes, they want to consider him, that's one thing. But it's awfully tough."

Paterno was extremely loyal to his entire staff. Being a Penn State football assistant was practically a lifetime job. Sandusky had worked with him for thirty-one years, Ganter thirty, Dick Anderson twenty-five.

◆   "You have to look at the track record of this place," Paterno said. "We don't go jumping around, getting rid of people, bringing people in . . . it's just not my style."

That wasn't to say there were no internecine staff disputes. Conflicts between strong-willed men were inevitable, even in Happy Valley. Paterno's nature was to nag, prod, and interfere. As a young aide to Engle, he had precipitated many arguments himself. "At meetings," he said of those early days, "I was a damn loudmouth."

But while two coaches jawing at each other on the sideline during a 10–2 season might appear merely to be a difference of opinion, it was seen as a deep-rooted problem after losing records in three of the last four years. Fans and sportswriters had begun to note how often Penn State coaches openly disagreed. Ganter and Jay Paterno frequently appeared to be at odds on play calls. Communication—from the coaches' box, to the sideline, to the huddle—often broke down, causing on-the-field confusion and delay-of-game penalties.

"Paterno says he wants another national championship run," wrote Neil Rudel in the *Altoona Mirror*. "Most fans would settle for getting the field-goal unit out without having to waste a time-out."

Despite being constantly in the TV cameras' focus, Paterno himself often jumped on assistants himself during games. Afterward he would make excuses. And even though Paterno saw Robinson as one of the nation's best players, the staff couldn't seem to agree on a consistent role for him.

So Penn State supporters constantly called for another staff shakeup. And whether it was as a response to that outcry or not, Paterno eventually gave it to them.

●   ●   ●

On February 17, in a vaguely worded athletic-department news release, it was revealed that Ganter was being moved to a new administrative position, associate director for football operations. Galen Hall, 61, a one-time Penn State quarterback when Paterno was Engle's quarterbacks coach, would be brought in to take his place for the 2004 season.

In addition, Mike McQueary, another ex-Lions quarterback who recently had been a graduate assistant, would now coach the maligned wide receivers. He replaced Kenny Carter, whose departure to become Vanderbilt's running backs coach was widely seen as a bone to the program's critics. McQueary also would become the recruiting coordinator, a role previously held by Jay Paterno.

It was a lot to digest. Ganter, whose son was currently one of Penn State's backup quarterbacks, and whose wife, Karen, had died suddenly of a brain aneurysm in 2002, had long been seen as Paterno's successor. Had he been sacrificed to the team's offensive problems? Or did the move make sense? Whatever the answer, his job shift further obscured Penn State's post-Paterno future. If Ganter, the most obvious choice, wasn't going to be the Nittany Lions' next coach, who was?

At a February 18 news conference, Curley indicated that the former assistant coach would help ease his growing workload, supervising camps and clinics and acting as a marketing liaison. Ganter was close enough to the coach that he could handle a lot of his more personal responsibilities, become an intermediary between Paterno and his ex-players.

"I knew the job was good for Penn State football, but I didn't know if it was good for Frannie. Frannie was the only guy who could make that decision," Paterno would explain. "We certainly didn't want to push him into it in any way, even though in the back of my mind I felt this was something that would be helpful to the whole program. . . . It's going to be kind of strange not being down on the sideline arguing with him every once in a while."

In what sounded like an indictment of the old staff, Ganter said, "We agonize over game plans, down and distance and tendencies, and all of that kind of us stuff. [Hall] is a terrific game coach. . . . [He is] a guy who can see what's happening quickly and make game adjustments as the game is going on."

Hall's hiring as offensive coordinator—though technically he was "running-backs coach/in charge of offense"—was equally intriguing. His résumé included both Penn State credentials and success as an offensive architect elsewhere. But it also contained a scandal, something squeaky-clean Penn State typically shunned.

Hall had been the offensive coordinator on a pair of national-champion Oklahoma teams in the 1970s and later was a successful head coach at Florida. He had since worked in virtually every professional league—the NFL (with the Dallas Cowboys as running-backs coach in 2002), NFL Europe, the XFL, and the Arena Football League.

In 1989, however, Hall had resigned at Florida after admitting he had violated NCAA rules by supplementing the pay of two assistant coaches by $22,000 and by arranging transportation to court for a player so that the athlete could face child-support charges.

Already, early in the spring, questions were raised about how Hall and Jay Paterno would divvy up the signal calling. Could a new, strong-willed coach with so much experience peacefully coexist with the boss's son?

"Jay will call certain plays in certain situations, and Galen will call most of the game with some input from [offensive-line coach] Dick Anderson," Paterno said. "When we get into certain situations, Galen turns it over to Jay and vice versa."

If that weren't unwieldy enough, the elder Paterno would be reinserting himself more forcefully into the play-calling process. And, of course, he would retain veto power over anything in the game plans Hall and his son devised.

"I don't care if God were making the calls, I would have a couple disagreements with Him," Paterno said.

The revamped staff seemed to catch Paterno's fever. They attacked their spring duties with zest.

"It seems like we have a rookie coaching staff," said E. Z. Smith. "They're hungry. They want to win. They're eager to teach us. Everybody has enthusiasm. Nobody is out there just going through the motions."

That included Paterno himself, who at one point in the spring became a victim of his own renewed focus on discipline.

The large *S* in the middle of the team's locker-room carpet has traditionally been off-limits. Anyone who stepped on it had to do ten push-ups. One day in the spring, during another impassioned speech, Paterno inadvertently tread on it three times.

"Instead of having him do thirty push-ups, we made a deal and let him do thirty sit-ups. He did them in front of the whole squad," said E. Z. Smith. "When you have a coach who is seventy-plus years old and won't take a shortcut, what kind of excuse do we have? We don't have any ground to stand on if he's not taking a shortcut."

CHAPTER 2

CENTURIES AGO, in the broad valley now dominated by the campus of Pennsylvania State University, the Susquehannock Indians named the mountain that rolled so gently across the southern horizon Nita-Nee—barrier against the elements.

For Penn State, a rural agricultural college transformed by football and postwar demographics into a forty-two-thousand-student megaversity, Mount Nittany, which lent its name to the school's athletic teams, has remained both a practical and a symbolic great wall. Two thousand feet high, it frequently shields State College and neighboring hamlets from harsh storms. More significantly, though, it separates the uncertain world beyond from a place that those here call, without a trace of irony, Happy Valley.

The image of Happy Valley as a Brigadoon in the hilly heart of Pennsylvania was enhanced by its physical and cultural isolation. "To the kids that come to school here," said Gary Grey, an ex–Penn State linebacker and now a visiting business professor, "this is an out-of-the-way Disneyland." It's as if on arrival, students and professors squeezed through a crack in the natural universe, emerging into a locale as pure and pristine as it was picturesque. The problems of Philadelphia, Pittsburgh, and Harrisburg were too remote to matter. There was no crime or grime in Happy Valley, no corruption or cynicism.

Actually, until the middle of the nineteenth century, there was nothing much at all in Happy Valley but a few farms and a foundry. It wasn't until the tumultuous years before the Civil War, when the concept of land-grant learning institutions began to take shape, that this pastoral locale started its slow transformation into the university town where a man named Joe Paterno eventually would plant himself.

The story of Penn State began in the 1850s when America, founded by a learned elite in the cities and towns along its Atlantic coast, was developing a more democratic character as it expanded relentlessly westward. The frontiersmen and farmers populating the vast new territories were confronted constantly by vexing challenges. Soil needed to be replenished. Rivers needed to be bridged. Children needed to be educated. The private colleges of the East, which produced classically trained aristocrats fluent in Latin and Greek, offered little practical help with their daily problems.

According to Michael Bezilla, author of *Penn State: An Illustrated History*, the "elitist character [of schools like Harvard and Yale] clashed with the democratic values of the young republic." That split generated a movement to establish schools where agriculture and the technical sciences would be emphasized.

In 1855, Pennsylvania established the Farmers High School in remote Centre County, where the Nittany and Penn valleys converged. A local farmer, James Irvin, donated the two hundred acres. His land was ideal for agricultural work and studies, since most of its trees already had been cleared to feed the nearby Centre Furnace.

Even for the sons of farmers, Centre County was an isolated setting. The school was surrounded by Allegheny Mountain peaks and forests thick with maple, beech, ash, and hemlocks, and the nearest rail station was twenty-two miles away. Many students who journeyed there faced long stagecoach trips to the school after disembarking from trains in nearby towns. (Even three quarters of a century later, the college's president, Edwin Sparks, called the location "equally inaccessible from all parts of the state." And well into the 1990s, long-distance travelers to State College had to fly into Harrisburg and then journey ninety miles northward along a mountainous, two-lane road.) The site's primary benefit, as far as anyone could tell initially, was that it was situated near Pennsylvania's geographical center.

In 1857, Congressman Justin Morrill of Vermont introduced legislation to create a nationwide system of rural colleges. Under his proposal, the schools would be endowed by revenue from the federal government's sale of western land. To provide settings for these institutions, states would be granted thirty thousand acres for each of their U.S. senators and congressmen.

While the measure passed initially, it eventually was vetoed by President James Buchanan. A Pennsylvania Democrat, Buchanan was beholden to the South, where the land-grant system was seen as an overextension of federal power. The measure languished in the overheated, pre–Civil War political climate until, in 1862, with the hostilities under way and the South seceded, it was passed and signed by President Lincoln.

Pennsylvania's legislature designated the Farmers High School as the state's land-grant institution. Soon renamed the Agricultural College of Pennsylvania, it grew, slowly but steadily, through the decades—eventually accepting women in 1872. In 1874 its name was changed again, to the Pennsylvania State College.

There was little time for sports in the intensely structured life of work and study in that early era of Penn State history. Devotees of certain athletic activities, such as the cricket-loving students from the Philadelphia area, played among themselves when opportunities arose. School-sponsored athletics did not yet exist, and various social clubs and extracurricular organizations arose to fill the need.

Sometime in the 1880s, a group of Penn State students formed a football club. The new sport, a rough-and-tumble hybrid of soccer and rugby, had spread west from the East Coast's private institutions, where it had first gained popularity. Penn State's club was led by a student-captain, George Linsz, because paid coaches were considered a violation of the prevailing amateur standards. On November 5, 1887, the football club played its initial game, at Bucknell, scoring a 54–0 victory over a squad from that college in nearby Lewisburg.

A five-hundred-seat grandstand was erected in 1893 to accommodate spectators at the on-campus field where the football team practiced and played. With increased popularity came increased competition. Soon schools were eschewing some of the long-accepted guidelines of amateurism in their desire for victories. Penn State hired its first paid coach, George Hoskins, the school's director of physical training, in 1892.

Students at the college, whose enrollment in the 1894–95 school year had reached 221 (roughly the size of the village that had grown up around it), began to take notice. Football games increasingly became occasions for excitement and expressions of school spirit. In developing its football traditions, Penn State, like schools elsewhere, looked to the precedents set by Yale, Harvard, Penn, and Princeton, then the big leagues of college sports.

When Penn State's baseball team traveled to New Jersey for a game in 1906, junior H. D. "Joe" Mason was captivated by Princeton's tiger mascot. Returning to campus, Mason fired off a letter to *The Lemon*, a student publication, suggesting Penn State adopt a lion as its symbol. The choice would be appropriate, he stressed, because mountain lions had roamed the nearby hills as recently as the 1880s. Mason's suggestion caught on instantly. And since the most prominent of those mountains was Mount Nittany, its name quickly was appended to *Lions*.

Playing the kind of East-dominated schedule that would remain a fixture through the Paterno years, the Nittany Lions teams were up and down through the first few decades of the twentieth century. But then, as now, the alumni demanded victories. When Bob Higgins's team went 2–8 in 1931, with five shutout losses, the outcry was tremendous. "No boy wishes to become part of an institution which is a target of jokes and ridicule," wrote Charles Heppenstall, a nineteenth-century Penn State player, in a letter to the *Alumni News* that year.

Even then, debates raged about the nature of the program. Across the nation, football's excesses, as detailed in the scathing 1929

Carnegie Report on American College Athletics, were widely understood though still largely unregulated. While some schools adhered to the amateur concept, others ran barely disguised professional operations. In the absence of any binding national guidelines, Penn State vacillated between the two models.

In 1900, its board of trustees had authorized scholarships for athletes who had been at the school at least a year, making Penn State one of the first colleges to do so. Later, responding to various criticisms from reformers or boosters, the number would be reduced or raised again.

Penn State football provided one of the incidents those opposed to big-time football liked to reference. In October of 1902, Andrew Smith played for the Nittany Lions in a 17–0 loss at the University of Pennsylvania. He apparently played well enough to impress his opponents, because two days later he was practicing with Pennsylvania's team in Philadelphia. He played three more games for Penn State before transferring to Penn. Smith earned all-American status at Penn in 1904, then dropped out of school.

"We go out after men for the sake of baseball and football, offering all sorts of inducements," said W. H. Andrews, the chancellor of Allegheny College, not long after Penn State had beaten that Pennsylvania school's team, 50–0, in 1904. "It isn't a thing unknown among us for a man to go from the football team of one college to the football team of another in midseason. Scholarships are offered to promising players. Professionalism is winked at."

Eventually, in response to the Carnegie Report, Penn State did away with all athletic scholarships, a move that pleased some alumni but angered others who saw it as an unnecessary overreaction.

In a 1935 interview with the *Daily Collegian*, former coach Hugo Bezdek observed that Penn State might be tilting too heavily toward the amateur model. "[Penn State] should cast off its Simon-pure pretensions and bring back scholarships," Bezdek said. President Ralph Hetzel quickly rejected the suggestion.

Scholarships would be reinstated fifteen years later, in part because even then Penn State saw football as a valuable revenue-producer. In 1927, thirty million college-football fans bought $50 million worth of tickets. In the aftermath of World War II, with the GI Bill flooding campuses with returning veterans, those numbers jumped significantly. Competing colleges began to view football as a means both to make money and to attract the new breed of everyday students.

Penn State's student population soared to 10,200 in 1946, with more than half of them returning veterans. A year later, eighty percent were vets. Temporary dormitories, labeled "Veterans Villages," were constructed on the east end of the campus to accommodate the mad rush.

With thousands more students, and in many cases their families, on campus, attendance and interest increased for the football games at fourteen-thousand-seat Beaver Field. In 1946, the Nittany Lions attracted five-figure crowds to all their home games for the first time ever. And with postwar victories over nationally recognized teams like Navy, Pitt, and Washington State, demand stayed strong. In 1949, the trustees decided to more than double the size of the facility, expanding its seating capacity to twenty-nine thousand.

Higgins's last two Penn State teams, in 1947 and 1948, went 9–0–1 and 7–1–1. The '47 team, without any scholarship players, earned a No. 4 national ranking and a berth in the Cotton Bowl, where the Nittany Lions tied Doak Walker's SMU Mustangs, 13–13. When Higgins retired following the '48 season, he was replaced by assistant Joe Bedenk. After a strife-filled 5–4 record in 1949, Bedenk agreed to step down so long as he could remain an assistant.

The college was then undergoing another major transformation. Although it had been an exclusively agricultural school in its first two decades, Penn State's academics had remained second rate. They were, according to Bezilla, "inferior to [those] found at many private colleges and universities. . . . Too many members of the Penn State community considered their school worthy of competing on the gridiron or the gymnasium floor with the likes of Penn or Syracuse or Ohio State but inferior to those institutions by almost every academic standard."

That perception began to change in 1950, when Milton Eisenhower, the future U.S. president's younger brother, became Penn State's president. Eisenhower had a more aggressive, wider vision than his predecessors and set about to upgrade the college's reputation, both academically and athletically.

He believed that with successful athletics and increased funding from the state legislature, Penn State could expand its profile nationally. He had seen it work at his previous school, Kansas State, and at many of the public institutions in the Big Ten. He hired talented professors, authorized athletic scholarships, and immediately began lobbying politicians, cleverly beginning what would become a long-standing tradition of providing them with game tickets. In 1951, Penn State provided 150 athletic scholarships and 50 grants for room and board. Recipients, however, were required to meet the same academic standards as other students.

As to who would replace Bedenk, it was clear Penn State was going to follow the prompting of the student-run *Daily Collegian*, which urged administrators to find "a big-time coach for a big-time college." The man eventually selected was a native Pennsylvanian, an ex–coal miner who longed to return to one of those charming small towns where he had cut his coaching teeth.

When he was hired to coach Penn State in the spring of 1950, Brown's Charles "Rip" Engle was forty-four years old and prematurely gray.

Despite his 28–20–6 record at the Providence school, Engle had often felt like an interloper at the elite eastern institution, with its urban campus and a student body comprised primarily of the sons of wealthy New Englanders. He had grown up dirt poor in Elk Lick, a glorified mining patch near southwest Pennsylvania's border with Maryland. He dropped out of school early and went to work in the mines, moving up from mule driver to mine supervisor by the time he was nineteen.

"That mule," he later said, "taught me how to work."

Engle was a careful, meticulous, and frequently glum man. "Rip's not happy unless he's sad," said longtime Syracuse coach Ben Schwartzwalder. He tired of mining quickly, particularly the dirt and grit that were its unavoidable residue. Eventually, he left to return to school, enrolling at nearby Western Maryland College. Stronger and more world seasoned than his peers, he starred there in basketball, baseball, and football. After graduating in 1930, he took a job as a teacher and football coach at Waynesboro High School.

Just nineteen miles from the Gettysburg battlefields, Waynesboro was a charming town of pretty churches and Victorian homes in the fertile farming heart of south-central Pennsylvania. Twenty years later, Engle would still talk lovingly of the area to Paterno, describing its rolling hills, tree-lined streets, and the handsome red farms whose barns had floors "clean enough to eat off."

His Waynesboro teams were spectacularly successful. They went 86–17–5 and won conference titles in eight of eleven years before Engle, somewhat reluctantly, took an assistant's job at Brown in 1942. Two years later he assumed the top job. In six seasons there, his best team, by far, had been his last. The 1949 Bruins finished 8–1, thanks in part to the play of a skinny-legged senior quarterback from Brooklyn.

(Seven years later, the Ivy League would be formed, primarily as a means of reining in the influence of football at the member universities. The demise of Penn's program, which had regularly attracted some of the state's best players as well as crowds of more than sixty thousand to its Franklin Field, would help Penn State enormously.)

Engle accepted the Penn State job late, just as 1950's spring practices were beginning. He was hired with the understanding that he would keep its staff—Bedenk, Al Michaels, Jim O'Hora, Tor Toretti, Frank Patrick, and Earle Bruce—if the university would consider a certain number of academic exceptions for football recruits. "Engle argued that most institutions that wanted winning football teams made concessions in regards to the academic standing of potential athletic recruits," wrote Bezilla.

It worked. Penn State would win. And football would introduce America to Penn State.

The new coach also got the authority to hire an additional assistant. Engle approached two of his Brown aides, Gus Zitrides and Bill Doolittle. Both turned him down. While still at Brown, Engle had asked that school's graduating quarterback to help him tutor his freshman successor in the Wing-T offense. Hoping to install the same offense for a Nittany Lions program that had run and coached the Single Wing exclusively, he asked the young New Yorker to accompany him west.

He had been planning on applying to law school, but after considerable thought, Joe Paterno said yes.

One of the corporate sponsors of Penn State football in 2004 was MBNA, the giant credit-card company. Students work out at the MBNA Fitness Center on campus, and before every home football game, workers in MBNA booths lure fans to sign up for cards with free Penn State T-shirts, hats, and towels. It is a connection hardly worth mentioning in relation to Paterno except as an indication of just how long the coach has been in State College.

We can no longer imagine a world without credit cards. They've existed for generations, growing in significance, number, and use with each passing year. But credit cards haven't been around forever. Only since 1950. That year, on May 13, Diners Club introduced the first one.

And thirteen days later Paterno came to Happy Valley.

An edgy, argumentative, intellectually curious New Yorker, he was, unlike Engle, hardly ensnared by the region's charm. State College was a "hick town," he said, and he quickly told the head coach to "start looking around for another coach, because I'm getting out of here."

He would stay, of course. So long that his distinctive face became, along with Mount Nittany, the central-Pennsylvania landscape's most prominent feature.

All that was a long way in the future in the spring of 1950. It took time for Paterno to overcome his culture shock and recognize State College's unique assets—idyllic location, hardworking and friendly residents, small-town innocence. Eventually, he melded the virtues of this almost mythical Happy Valley into Penn State football, infusing his program with an aura of middle-American propriety.

The attributes generations of sportswriters admiringly tagged to his program read like something from *The Boy Scout Handbook:* Nittany Lions were always successful on the field, academically proficient in the classroom, hard workers, sticklers for the rules, humble in victory, sportsmanlike in defeat. In short, Penn State football should be as untainted as the famously unadorned uniforms its players wear.

As Paterno's career moved forward, the atmosphere he created increasingly served as a counterpoint to the excesses of college sports. His teams had never been sanctioned by the NCAA. "Penn State is the poster child for doing it right in college sports," NCAA president Myles Brand would say in 2004.

In the late 1990s, when the national average for graduating football players was barely over fifty percent, Penn State graduated eighty-six percent. Ex-players praised him for opening their eyes to a world beyond football. Mike Reid, for example, a defensive tackle who was one of Paterno's first and fiercest all-Americans, went on to become a concert pianist, a juxtaposition that struck no one as odd in Happy Valley.

"How many football coaches majored in English Literature at an Ivy League school?" retired Penn State athletic director Jim Tarman, a Paterno friend since 1950, asked. "When he sits up half the night, as he did for years, doing Xs and Os for the next day's practice or next Saturday's game, he always listens to opera. I think the fact that he has such a broad range of interests is one of the reasons our football program has been different."

Far from being hamstrung, his Nittany Lions managed to capture two national championships (1982 and 1986) and, were it not for the quirkiness of the college-football ranking system, probably should have won a few more. In 2001, Paterno passed Bear Bryant as the sport's all-time winningest coach. He already held the record for most bowl victories and appearances. He has had five unbeaten teams, at least one in each decade from the 1960s through the 1990s.

He further burnished his saintly image in 1997 when he and his wife, Sue, a former librarian, donated $3.5 million to Penn State to be used to endow teaching positions and scholarships at the school, and to support two building projects, one of them a new library that now bears their name. Penn State, its professors will tell you, is the only university where the football stadium is named for a school president and the library for the football coach.

Since 1999, however, with his teams losing more often than they win, his critics have been bolder in portraying him as a controlling coach with an irritatingly pious attitude. They note the secrecy with which he shrouds his salary, practices, locker-room access, players, and even his family. Though there is no evidence to support their claims, some of them also whisper that Penn State may have avoided NCAA sanctions only because its isolation has discouraged the kind of intense big-media scrutiny that has turned up scandals at places like Colorado and Minnesota, Alabama and Miami.

Some also see a coach whose teams remained overwhelmingly white long after the influx of African-American players in the 1960s and 1970s changed college sports. Many elite black athletes have not wanted to spend their college years in bucolic State College. Criticism from some blacks put Paterno's recruiting practices in the spotlight. In recent years, he has lured many more African-American recruits, but State College still remains a difficult sell to urban youngsters.

More problematic for Paterno's Happy Valley myth has been the increasing off-the-field trouble. Has college football moved so far to the dark side that even the players Penn State recruits must succumb? Has Penn State lowered its standards? If so, why hasn't the change been reflected in more victories? If not, then why all the arrests and suspensions?

Through it all, Paterno and others have continued to portray Penn State as a shining example of college sports, trumpeting their high graduation rate and commitment to academics.

"You have to decide what kind of program you want to have," said athletic director Curley. "We've played against other student athletes that just wouldn't have been academically successful here, and they may have beaten us. But we're very proud of that. I think it is the right model. I believe it's the right paradigm for college athletics."

Paterno was introduced to Penn State with a short two-column story and photo halfway down page three of the May 27, 1950, edition of the student-run *Daily Collegian*.

The Saturday-morning headline offered no indication of the news's ultimate significance:

PATERNO, BROWN GRID STAR, ### ADDED TO FOOTBALL STAFF

A *Providence Journal* sportswriter, Barney Madden, praised Paterno's intelligence to the unidentified *Collegian* reporter who wrote the story. "He is the guy who made Brown's offense go," said Madden. "You'll like Paterno."

In the photo, taken while he was at Brown, Paterno had thick black hair and a cockiness so evident that it nearly burned through the page. Without his trademark glasses, he was squinting beneath dark brows as he cocked his right arm to throw an unusually fat football.

Surrounding the Paterno story in that day's *Collegian* was evidence of the kind of small-town, small-time atmosphere the coach was entering. Page one's top headline referred, in long-outdated terms, to the college's spring carnival, "Large Crowds Throng Gay Midway." There was a story about a Poultry Club picnic on page two. Gabardine raincoats were on sale at Pennshire for $15.95. And the newspaper's biggest advertiser was Chesterfield cigarettes.

Paterno had promised his parents he would go to law school. While still at Brown, he'd taken the law boards and, according to brother George, "finished in the top ten percent nationally." His father, Angelo, who had passed the New York state bar as an adult, planned to start a practice in Long Island and hoped his son might join him there. He'd been accepted to Boston University's law school during his senior year.

When he told his mother, Florence, he would be coaching instead, she nearly passed out. His father was more understanding. Even when he learned his son's salary. Paterno, who also would be a part-time physical-education instructor, earned $3,600 that first year.

"I never made any real money," the elder Paterno advised his son. "But I'm doing what I want to do. That's more important than money. If you like coaching, stay with it."

He appeased his parents by telling them he would try coaching for a year. If it didn't work out, he'd go to law school. That option stayed in his head for more than a decade. "Until I got married," he said, "probably every time I lost a football game, I thought, *I'm going to law school.*"

On their 342-mile drive to State College, Paterno, always curious, pumped Engle for information about his plans, about rural Pennsylvania, and about the new head coach's philosophies.

Paterno remembered them stopping in Westminster, Maryland, (though Westminster would have been far past State College for anyone traveling from Providence, and it's likely the actual visit occurred later). He said they visited Western Maryland College, where Engle had played for a former Penn State coach, Dick Harlow. Engle now sought the older coach's advice.

"He told Rip to go get himself a great running back," Paterno said. "He said a great running back is somebody [who] when you put him in the secondary three times, you got two touchdowns."

Paterno's uneasiness had intensified on the long ride west. All the cows and the wide-open spaces made for an alien landscape. He couldn't imagine being here long. He would be going back to Providence soon anyway, to pick up his diploma at Brown's June 9 graduation. Maybe he'd just hang around there all summer and then start law school. Yeah, he could see himself in Boston before the leaves turned next fall. Instead, Paterno quickly discovered that his interest in football was at least as strong as his passion for the law.

"One of the reasons I felt like I wouldn't stay was that I really felt I was cheating myself not going to law school," he said. "I thought my dad was upset because I wasn't going to law school. When I got into the coaching and liked the coaching, I thought, *Gee this might not be a bad idea.*

"I said to Rip, 'How do I coach? What's it take? Is there a course, something like that?' " Paterno recalled. "Rip handed me film. He said, 'I'm going to give you three reels of film every day'—in those days we had sixteen-millimeter film—'and I want you to chart every single play on both sides of the football.' When I was done, he'd give me three more reels. I did that all summer. I finally started to realize what the game is all about. And I came back, and he said, 'What do you think? Are you going to be all right?' and I said, 'You know, I may be the best coach ever.' "

But initially he wondered what appeal State College could possibly have for a literature major who read Virgil, Shakespeare, and Camus and who had traveled here with his opera and classical-music records. The town's population was twenty-eight thousand. There wasn't much to do socially except go to the movies. "It was," Paterno said, "a cemetery."

"The pace was so different from what I was used to," he said. "The whole culture was different. You couldn't get a drink. And the only place you could get a plate of spaghetti was a place called the Tavern. It cost half a buck and they had celery in the sauce. There were things I was used to that just weren't available."

Pennsylvania's archaic blue laws meant State College's movie theaters couldn't even open on Sundays (an edict that remained in effect until 1955). On the day he arrived, the choice at State College's theaters wasn't promising: *The Fighting Kentuckian*, with John Wayne, was playing at the Nittany, *Samson and Delilah* at the Cathaum, and *No Sad Songs for Me*, a Margaret Sullavan tearjerker, at the State.

It was for the most part a cultural wasteland, its appeal undetectable to those raised in the more cosmopolitan cities of the Northeast. Years later, when *New York Herald-Tribune* sports editor Stanley Woodward traveled to State College to interview his fellow New Yorker, he joked that to get there "you swung the final ninety miles through the trees."

Paterno spent his first night in a spare bedroom at the Engles' home on Woodland Road, in the same College Heights neighborhood where he would one day raise his own family. The following morning he walked the few blocks to Beaver Field. The campus adjoining the stadium was growing rapidly. Penn State had twelve thousand full- and part-time students in 1950. Tuition was $200, something of a bargain since it cost $600 a year to educate one student at the school that same year. The gap was made up by the increasingly compliant legislature of a state then still rolling along on its coal and steel wealth.

When he got to Beaver Field, he didn't find anything to write home to Brooklyn about. The old facility wasn't much more than grandstands, mostly metal but some wooden and rickety. It was surrounded by a few brick ticket booths. Players changed in an adjacent water tower. Penn State football had attracted an average of only 20,708 fans to its four home games in 1949 (a figure that would dip to 17,259 in the first season of Engle/Paterno.) The total contributions from alumni—to the entire university, not just athletics—amounted to less than $71,000.

Paterno stayed with the Engles until, at the coach's request, he moved into the dormitory where Penn State's football players occupied two floors. He was supposed to be their monitor, but he so disliked the experience that when he became head coach he insisted football players live among the general student population.

The following year, he moved in with Steve Suhey and his new wife, Ginger. That planted Paterno a little more firmly into the Penn State community. Suhey had been an all-American guard there before graduating in 1947. And Ginger was the daughter of Bob Higgins, the college's football coach from 1930 through 1948. Several of their sons would later star for Paterno teams and one, Paul, would become a university trustee. And in 2005, Steve Suhey's grandson, Kevin, would be a freshman on a Paterno team.

"Through them I was fortunate enough to meet some younger people," Paterno recalled. "We had fun. You found out you didn't have to get a good plate of spaghetti. After a couple of beers, it all tastes the same. And I got to like the people. And I liked coaching."

Before the 1952 season, defensive line coach Jim O'Hora and his wife, Bets, moved into a new home, and partly to help defray expenses, they asked Paterno to live with them. He stayed with them even after the O'Horas moved to another house and wouldn't depart their extra bedroom until 1961.

As a single man, he was unusual among Engle's assistants. A photo of Penn State's 1953 staff shows Paterno, standing in the snow without his trademark glasses, as the only aide without a spouse. Marriage was of little importance to someone with his ambitions. Paterno and the rest of Engle's staff enjoyed an unusual closeness. The married couples included Paterno in their off-the-field rituals, even before he was married.

"Thursday nights we used to say, 'The hay's in the barn,' and we'd go out and relax," he said. "We worked hard but on Thursday nights we wanted to spend a little time with the family. So we would take the wives to one of the coaches's houses and we'd have a couple drinks and then we'd go out and get something to eat. We'd go downtown to the Tavern or Duffy's, different places."

Still, the native New Yorker's frequently abrasive style annoyed some of the older, more low-key members of Engle's staff. He had, in his late brother's words, "a rage to win." That trait, coupled with his natural drive and impatience, frequently made him an irritant.

But those early colleagues also recognized Paterno's coaching gifts—his ingenuity, detail-oriented mind, and an uncanny ability to convince people that his was the best way. Engle put him in charge of quarterbacks and gradually, throughout the 1950s and 1960s, began delegating more and more responsibility to his protégé.

That didn't leave Paterno much time for a social life, not that he could have conducted much of one from his quarters in the O'Horas' bedroom. Finally, in 1961, O'Hora suggested it might be time for the then thirty-four-year-old coach to do something about that. He took Paterno aside and offered him some Irish advice.

"You know, Joe, when my dad came over from Ireland, my cousins used to come over, and they needed a place to stay," O'Hora said. "So my cousins would come over and they'd be here three or four months, and my dad would say, 'Sean, you've been here three months, it's about time you find yourself a lady and get on with your life.' Joe, you've been with us [almost ten] years."

Paterno took the hint and rented an apartment a few blocks away from the O'Horas. Shortly afterward his relationship with Sue Pohland, a brainy student from Latrobe, Pennsylvania, blossomed. One of their first dates took place at a lecture by literary critic Leslie Fiedler. In May of 1962 they were married.

"Sue's a German girl but she turned out to be a good cook," he said. "When Mom found out we were going to get married, she said, 'A German girl? Where are you going to eat?' "

By then Paterno had become enamored of Penn State and State College. And the feeling was mutual.

"When I came here, I was a little bit of an egghead but I was accepted," he said. "A guy by the name of Phil Young, who was one of the foremost Hemingway guys, he and I used to argue all the time about Hemingway. I never thought he was as good as Phil thought. And we used to go downtown and sit around and argue about things like that. We'd go to faculty clubs. I wasn't looked down on as a dumb football coach. They were accessible. The town was small. You know the thing about this place is if I get on the phone with my staff and said we want to meet in fifteen minutes, everyone can be here. They don't have to worry about the bridge going up. They don't have to worry about the tunnel being crowded. I mean, it's a great place to live."

He liked the players and the students too. In 1966, when the fires of social activism ignited many other campuses, student-government president Robert Katzenstein described the typical Penn State student as "passive, conscientious, law abiding, and [socially] ultraconservative." Paterno had his own description. "They weren't snooty like at Brown," he said.

Apparently forgetting his own initial misgivings, Paterno frequently scolded players who complained there was nothing to do in the remote mountain borough.

"Nothing to do?" he would begin, making an argument that probably didn't sway too many coal-region linebackers. "I suppose there was nothing for the Romantic poets to do in the Lake Country of England either?"

Married and with a growing family, Paterno desperately craved a head-coaching job. He had turned down offers to become an NFL assistant, but in 1962 interviewed for the head position at Yale. Yale approached him again in 1964, by which time Paterno had become "assistant head coach" to Engle. This time the Ivy League school made him an offer.

He decided to stay at Penn State because Engle, then sixty, informed him he'd be retiring soon, and university administrators assured him he'd be given every opportunity to succeed his longtime boss.

After the Nittany Lions finished 5–5 in 1965, Engle stepped down and Paterno, offered $20,000 a year, took over at last.

CHAPTER 3

SPRING PRACTICE concluded with the 2004 Blue-White scrimmage on April 24, an azure-blue Saturday in State College.

Perched in a booth high above the Beaver Stadium field, like some football god bemusedly observing his creation, Paterno was analyzing the scrimmage's action for the university's radio network. The headphones that comically engulfed much of his head were larger and provided more padding than some of the old leather helmets he had worn as a quarterback at Brooklyn Prep. Dressed in his standard game-day uniform of a blue blazer, blue oxford shirt, brightly colored tie, and khaki slacks, Paterno looked relaxed. After today's game, his one period of relative calm was about to begin.

Summer workouts wouldn't start until August. He could squeeze in a few weeks with the family in Avalon. The only real demands the coach had this summer, beyond his usual fretting and obsessive preparations, were the frequent trips in a university jet to schmooze with donors, alums, and recruits and a few speaking appearances at football camps.

While it remained large in the eyes of fans and the media, the dreadful 2003 season had receded farther and farther into Paterno's seldom-used rearview mirror. A new cycle of football loomed, one filled, if not with spectacular promise, at least with a little of the old optimism.

"We're going to be OK. I don't think we're gonna be a great team," he said in what was an almost annual refrain. "Not this year. Maybe in two years. But we'll be OK."

Paterno had ascended to the stadium's radio booth after the lengthy news conference that always preceded this annual scrimmage.

"God almighty, all you guys here for a spring practice," he said after taking his seat in a room packed with reporters. "I'm flabbergasted. I guess sometimes I forget how much interest there is in Penn State football."

It quickly became clear that football wasn't the media's primary interest on this day. The Penn State press corps's relationship with the coach had changed, soured in fact, during the unprecedented spate of trouble in 2003. Now, the sportswriters wanted to know what steps Paterno would be taking in the future to prevent these off-the-field embarrassments from reoccurring.

"Can't we just talk about football?" he pleaded at one point.

Occasionally Paterno the broadcaster was distracted, by a visitor to the booth, a sudden recollection, or the spectacular vista of the unspoiled Allegheny Mountains framing the horizon, their foothills dotted with silver-topped silos and picture-book barns.

"What a beautiful day," Paterno gushed in the midst of play-by-play man Steve Jones's description of a pass attempt, sounding more like a first-time visitor to rural central Pennsylvania than someone who had spent fifty-four years here. "Look at the cows. And the farms."

Far removed from the disaster that was the previous season, he seemed to be enjoying himself. He told stories about his father and about Engle, the silver-haired mentor who had lured him to State College.

But he had plenty to say about the game as well. Paterno called a player who fumbled a "knucklehead." He booed the White squad's decision to punt. He jokingly suggested a defensive back who had permitted a wide-open receiver to score "ought to be shot." He seemed to know every player's father or grandfather, not surprisingly, since many had been on his squads over the years. He mocked the job he had done in 2003. And when the stadium's giant TV screen showed two of his former players in the crowd, NFLers Brandon Short and Brad Scioli, he good-naturedly chastised the latter.

"Put your hat on straight, Scioli," he yelled, as if the baseball cap-wearing Indianapolis Colts defensive end were standing for inspection in front of him. "You look like an Italian gangster."

For all the fun he was having, though, Paterno's grasp of radio was nearly nonexistent. He hacked frequently into his mike, forgetting the "cough button" and drowning out Jones's words. From time to time, focusing on the details of his players' execution, he appeared to forget he was on the air. After a blown coverage or a missed block, you could hear him mumble, in that undiminished nasal twang, "Awwww, for cryin' out loud, that's just terrible."

Paterno's listeners certainly didn't mind. Alumni and those rural Pennsylvanians for whom big-time sports meant Penn State football relished this rare candid glimpse of a man who increasingly wrapped his program in secrecy. Those people hardly expected a coaching legend to suddenly reveal himself as an accomplished broadcaster. Many Penn State supporters, however, did expect that he continue to be a competent coach. And following the dismal seasons that had marked a strangely troubling new millennium at Penn State, some insisted he no longer was.

Paterno was offering no indication that the 2004 season might be his last, even though his five-year contract was due to expire at season's end. "I'm an idealist, I'm a romantic, and I'm a little bit of a corn-ball," Paterno had said in March, "but I'm not naive—I understand human nature. There's nothing that's always exactly the way you want it. I've got to understand people are going to say, 'Hey, you're in it too long.' "

Freshman players said he had assured them he would stay through their four years. He told reporters he still felt fresh and motivated.

"I've got a lot of reasons to retire," he said. "I have five children, (14) grandkids, and a young, active wife. It isn't a question of ego or games won. I've always wanted to have an impact. I'm a teacher. You wake up every morning feeling good, looking forward to it. When I lose that, I'll know."

• • •

As Paterno the radio analyst casually dissected the scrimmage, a nearby press-box television, tuned to that day's NFL draft, unwittingly provided an ongoing commentary on the current state of his program.

Seventeen years ago, Penn State had defeated Miami for the school's last national championship. That 1987 Fiesta Bowl triumph over the trash-talking Hurricanes, whose success was clouded by talk of academic difficulties and legal problems, was, in retrospect, a last stand. Penn State's pristine image, represented by its stark uniforms, its exemplary graduation rate, and its intensely moralistic coach, temporarily had stalled the arrival of what looked to some like a new, frightening sports order.

Now, the face of one Miami star after another flashed on the press-box TV, smiling images that seemed to mock their school's long-ago conquerors. In all, a record six Hurricanes were selected in 2004's first round. Miami, despite—or perhaps because of—an outlaw image it had never shed, continued to hold a spot near the top of college football's heap.

Penn State, meanwhile, by almost any comparative standard, had slipped badly. The draft's first round would be completed without a single Nittany Lion being picked. So would the second round. Midway through Round Six, on the following day, just one had been selected, cornerback Rich Gardner, a third-round choice of the Chicago Bears.

There were many reasons. Paterno simply wasn't recruiting as much talent these days. And the NFL-caliber players that did play at Penn State were often hidden from the scouts because of Paterno's obsession with secrecy.

A day earlier David Kimball, a little-known backup Penn State kicker in '03, had shocked NFL Combine observers with an awesome display. Quickly, he went from being a virtually unknown commodity to a seventh-round pick of the Indianapolis Colts. A league personnel director told *The Milwaukee Journal-Sentinel* that such surprises involving Nittany Lions were typical: "[Penn State is] the toughest place in the world to get information."

Scouts, who generally had unlimited access to other big-time programs, were hamstrung by Penn State. They could attend practice only one week during the fall and another in the spring.

"I've talked with a lot of players around the league and they really believe Coach Paterno's policies hurt them in the draft," said ex–Penn State running back Eric McCoo, who has played with the Bears and the Eagles. "At most other places, there are a lot of times when scouts can watch you practice. And sometimes he can get in one of his bad moods and not let them in at all. That probably hurts recruiting. Players want to go where they have the best shot of being seen."

When the scrimmage ended, Paterno took the elevator down to field level. There, nearly lost amid the towering herd of exiting players, he roamed around near the tunnel for an instant, as if momentarily unsure of where he fit into this chaotic scene. Quickly, though, he regathered himself, sought out Hall and, with a look of pure relish, began discussing what he had seen.

Another season, his 39th, now dominated his horizon, a view as appealing as the cows and barns he had glimpsed from the radio booth. Paterno had determined to confront it with all the zeal and dedication he had managed to smuggle into his late seventies, all the single-mindedness that marked his previous thirty-eight.

No beer is sold in Beaver Stadium. So for Penn State students among the crowd of forty thousand, the Blue-White Game was merely a brief interruption from a more entrenched weekend ritual—drinking.

For some, it wasn't even an interruption.

"A lot of students went out to the parking areas around Beaver Stadium and just partied and never went into the game," said Penn State police chief Tom Harmon. "I don't know if [nice weather means] they drink more, or just spend more time outside, where they're more likely to get caught. But it was a busy spring weekend, and the incidents were primarily alcohol related."

Paterno insists his players remain typical Penn State college students, and in this regard at least, they were. A year earlier, several, including wide receivers Tony Johnson and Maurice Humphrey, starting center E. Z. Smith, quarterback/wideout Michael Robinson, defensive linemen Matthew Rice and Ed Johnson, offensive lineman Tom McHugh, and punter Jeremy Kapinos, had gotten themselves into alcohol-related trouble. At Penn State, and virtually every other American college, alcohol has assumed a role of frightening significance.

"For a lot of students, college is one big party with a $19,000-a-year cover charge," said Murray Sperber, author of *Beer and Circus: How Big-time College Sports Is Crippling Undergraduate Education*.

In State College, the partying on autumn weekends typically begins on Thursday night and continues unabated until the NFL games end on Sunday. In between, alcohol washes over the campus like a great tsunami of trouble.

"I think there's got to be some kind of effort to make young people understand that some of the problems we have are alcohol related," Paterno said. "It's one thing to have a beer with your father . . . my father would bring out a bottle of wine. It's another thing when these kids are going berserk."

Because Pennsylvania restricts the sale of liquor and wine to state-run stores, there are only three places to buy it in State College. That was not a deterrent. Since 1997, according to Graham Spanier, Penn State's president and a longtime advocate for altering the collegiate binge-drinking mentality, sales at those three stores has increased by more than $5 million.

Late on a Friday or Saturday night, on bar-pocked College or Beaver avenues, or along any of the cross streets filled with fraternity houses and subdivided homes, sleepy State College resembles Pottersville, the Sodomesque alternate version of Bedford Falls in *It's a Wonderful Life*. Students, drinks in hand, pack the porches of apartment houses. Others line up outside popular bars like the Rathskeller, Mad Mex, or the Lion's Den. The raucous din from within those establishments leaks out onto the sidewalks. There it melds into the menacing yowls of wandering packs of inebriated students careening loudly through the streets. Some scream "WE ARE . . ."—a cry that other packs immediately answer with ". . . PENN STATE!" Often the verbal jousting has a harder edge. On homecoming weekend, ten days before the 2004 presidential election, tipsy Bush supporters' night-

long chants of "Four More Years!" were met by their equally inebriated political rivals' "Ten More Days!" On the November night before
the unbeaten Pittsburgh Steelers and Philadelphia Eagles met, the opposing cries were "E-A-G-L-E-S! EAGLES!" and "Phil-ly Sucks! Phil-ly
Sucks!".

It is a recipe for trouble. Alcohol-related arrests marred countless
football weekends. In 1998, during the town's summer Arts Fest,
thousands of students and other young people poured out of the bars
and gathered on Beaver Avenue. Soon, the unruly crowd had blocked
traffic. Some residents of the high-rise apartments along the street began throwing cups and cans at the revelers, who returned fire. Soon,
three dozen streetlights had been ripped down, store windows had
been smashed, and cars damaged. Two police officers were injured in
the melee.

"We all have a pretty good understanding of what the problem is,"
said Spanier. "The solutions continue to elude us, at least at a level that
would make a marked change in student behavior. We feel there is
modest progress and we've had some successes, but all of the stars are
not yet properly aligned. And it's an interesting social question as to
whether they ever can be, given the culture in our society and in university communities generally."

That culture had threatened to swallow Paterno's team and reputation in 2003.

The volume of player turmoil—everything from a purported bicycle theft to sexual assaults—was unprecedented at Penn State. As a
result, Paterno found himself on the defensive most of the year, dis-
tracting him from his coaching duties and delighting those who saw
him as unbearably self-righteous.

The trouble actually began toward the end of 2002. That November 12, in the midst of the week between Penn State victories over Virginia and Indiana, a female student charged that Anwar Phillips, a
redshirt freshman cornerback, had sexually assaulted her at an on-
campus apartment.

One month later, following a private Judicial Affairs hearing, the
university suspended Phillips, who had played in every game that

season, for two semesters. But the next semester was not scheduled to begin until mid-January, and three weeks later, on New Year's Day, Phillips played in Penn State's 13–9 Capital One Bowl loss to Auburn.

When the arrest and suspension became public in March, Paterno and the entire athletic department came under heavy fire. While university officials contended the athletic department had been notified of Phillips's punishment before the bowl game, no one has ever been certain if Paterno also knew.

"Based on the information we had at that time, we felt it was approriate that he could participate in the game," said athletic director Curley.

The criticism and questions mounted until, on April 10, Spanier released a statement indicating students facing suspension would no longer be allowed to participate in university activities. The president insisted a miscommunication was to blame for the Phillips incident and noted the policy had subsequently been altered to make sure athletic directors learned immediately of any action against a Penn State athlete.

For his part, Paterno refused to answer questions about Phillips. "What happened, happened," Paterno said. "I have very little control over it." When questions persisted at a subsequent news conference, he lost his temper. "That's nobody's business but mine," he said. "It's not the fans' business, and it's not yours."

Phillips eventually was acquitted of the charge and rejoined the team early in the 2003 season. But the questions for the coach continued. After the acquittal, he urged the media to apologize to the player for publicizing the incident, a suggestion that a *Centre Daily Times* editorial met with a resounding rejection.

What also may have contributed to Paterno's unusual behavior during the Phillips case was the criticism he had attracted four years earlier after jumping to another troubled player's defense.

In 1998, quarterback Rashard Casey and a friend were accused in an assault on an off-duty police officer in Hoboken, New Jersey. He, too, would later be acquitted. "I get crucified for [defending] Ahmad Collins," Paterno said in '03, confusing Casey with Andre Collins, a

Penn State star from that same era. "He sued the city of Hoboken and got a big award, and none of you guys ever published that."

Regardless, the handling of the matter, and what was seen as the use of a loophole to permit Phillips to play, struck many as an indication that Paterno and Penn State were no longer the bastion of ethics they claimed to be. When a bowl game was at stake, even they were willing to abandon the moral high ground. All the trouble involving players that followed the next season only helped reinforce that perception. What did the critics want Paterno to do? He insisted he tried to detach himself from the punishments.

"I have nothing to do with what the university does," Paterno said, claiming he would not intervene on behalf of any player. "I get notes. I've never wanted to be in a position where people thought as a football coach I had something to do with what decisions were made. [From] the university president right down through the RA [resident assistant]—they've never had a telephone call from me. I don't believe in it."

In the summer of 2003, E. Z. Smith, the gregarious son of a North Carolina high school coach, was cited twice in one week for underage drinking. Paterno suspended him from the team for a year. McHugh was removed, too, after being cited for public drunkenness and harassment for allegedly hitting a woman. Kapinos was cited for underage drinking and disorderly conduct. And after the season, just weeks before the Blue-White Game, Robinson, Rice, and Johnson had been involved in the ice-rink brawl.

Given the team's shortcomings at wideout, the 2003 incident that may have had the most negative impact on Penn State football occurred when Humphrey, the team's second-leading receiver in 2003, was expelled for assaulting two female students. A player with game-breaking potential, he was convicted but avoided a jail sentence by serving time in an alcohol-rehab center.

"Losing Maurice Humphrey was a disaster for us," Paterno said in 2004, when his offense again proved remarkably inept. "I don't think people realize that."

Times had changed. Increasingly, it was clear that even the

fortress of secrecy that was Penn State football had glass walls. The good-natured mischief of 1966 was now front-page notoriety.

"Yeah, we have more distractions, but that doesn't mean I have more misbehaved kids," Paterno said. "I can go back to a couple guys in the seventies who drove me nuts. The cops would call me, and I used to put them in bed in my house and run their rear ends off the next day. Nobody knew about it. That's the way we handled it."

In 2002, State College police arrested 2,357 people for alcohol-related incidents, 559 for drunken driving. Among those, as their coach pointed out, only the football players were likely to turn up on the evening newscasts.

Early on the morning of October 16, 2003, during Penn State's bye week, campus police spotted Tony Johnson, a senior wide receiver who is the son of Penn State assistant Larry Johnson, driving erratically. A university police officer said the car twice swerved across a center line. Tests revealed Johnson's blood-alcohol level to be 0.136, far above Pennsylvania's legal limit of 0.08.

Four days after Johnson's arrest, during his weekly news conference, Paterno appeared to excuse the behavior.

"It will get all blown out of proportion," he said, "because he is a football player. But he didn't do anything to anybody."

Asked if he planned to suspend the player, he stuck his foot farther into his mouth. Paterno said he would do so "just because I have to send a message to the squad that it is inappropriate to be out in the middle of the week having a couple of drinks."

Officials from groups like Mothers Against Drunk Driving were outraged, believing Paterno was trying to downplay the dangers of drunk driving. The coach quickly made a rare public retreat.

"Being a friend of the family, I probably rationalized a little bit about Tony's decision, but not in the sense I felt he was not guilty of what he did," Paterno explained. "I apologize to anybody out there who thinks that I in any way have any misconceptions about the dangers of DUI."

There was a part of him that felt guilty. He had recruited these youngsters to his team and then, because of other demands on his time and efforts, removed himself from their day-to-day lives. They weren't bad kids. Some of them just needed a little more guidance, a little more discipline.

"I have a handful of kids that are immature jerks who have been spoiled by their families," Paterno said. "They're not bad kids, and they're going to be all right, but sometimes you'd like to have a baseball bat to wake them up."

Paterno would get a wake-up call of his own in the summer before the 2004 season when Kevin Baugh, a receiver and kick returner on his 1982 national championship team, was murdered. Baugh was stabbed to death on August 22 in a Massachusetts park during what police there described as an argument over drugs. It was revealed that Baugh, forty-two, had struggled with addictions for years. He had died penniless and, according to some accounts, a crack addict.

The news, coming so soon after their season of public sinning, stunned Penn State's football family. In his new role, Ganter took dozens of calls from Baugh's former teammates asking if they could help, looking for answers.

"He was so well liked," said Ganter, "so well thought of."

Baugh had been drafted by the Houston Oilers but never played in the NFL. He bounced around from job to job until he came back to Penn State in 1993 to work on a master's and perhaps take a position as a graduate assistant on the football staff.

Baugh told Paterno he'd had problems with drugs in the past but had overcome them. Nothing was immediately available, but with Paterno's blessing, he accepted a similar position in Utah. Things didn't work out there, and according to newspaper accounts, his instability and drug dependence mounted. Not long before his murder, desperately seeking a change, he and his wife had planned to return to Pennsylvania and look a for a coaching job.

When Paterno heard the news of Baugh's death and thought of all the problems his most recent team had encountered, he immediately wondered if he should have responded differently when the ex-player had come looking for a job a decade ago.

"I'll be very frank with you," Paterno said. "To this day, I think I could have done something else. Now I knew he was getting involved in some things he shouldn't have been getting involved in. . . . He and Kenny Jackson and Maurice Williams all came up here together and were three of the best skill people we ever had. It's very difficult for people to understand that these guys don't have it all made because they get a scholarship and are playing on a football team. They can't imagine all the problems in their lives. Kevin had a broken family. He was trying to take care of his sister. He was trying to take care of a lot of things that he didn't have the resources for. I think the NCAA has to realize that there are some kids who, when they decide to go to college and play football, they're forsaking some responsibilities."

On May 13, 2004, Penn State stunned its alumni, its students, and much of the nation when it announced in a bland news release that Paterno had signed a four-year contract extension.

All those who had calculated that Paterno would walk away when his contract expired after the 2004 season scratched their heads. The aging coach already was struggling mightily. He would be eighty-two when the extension expired. What were they thinking?

The reaction nationally was split between those who thought it ridiculous ("Penn State president Graham Spanier doesn't appear too far removed from the cuckoo's nest," Stephen A. Smith wrote in *The Philadelphia Inquirer*) and those who thought it a noble way to permit Paterno to walk away when he wanted ("Penn State did the right thing. . . . [It] showed a resolve few schools possess these days, in the face of widespread disapproval," said Brad Rock of the *Deseret Morning News*).

"At Penn State," Spanier later explained, "winning isn't every-thing. . . . People are so proud of the academic achievements of our athletes and the integrity that our coaches bring to the program, there's more tolerance here for having a bad season than you would find in most any other school."

When he finally commented publicly on his extension, Paterno insisted it wasn't a big deal.

"It's not like the roof is ready to cave in. . . . We've got a lot of work ahead of us, but I'm not like the secretary of defense [Donald Rumsfeld] these days, where I don't know what's going to happen."

As the summer continued, the old Paterno style began to surface more frequently. At a July 24 leadership conference in Harrisburg, he showed off his revived swagger to 650 people.

"I'm talking to you after a 3–9 season," he said, "and I'm just as cocky as I was after coming off a 12–0 season."

During an appearance at an August booster-club dinner in Valley Forge, just outside of Philadelphia, hundreds of Penn State grads and supporters lined up for his autograph. Normally autographs were an irritant to Paterno, but this time the coach accommodated everyone.

"He had a great summer," said Curley. "We traveled the state, did a lot of speaking engagements. And he was fired up. Everyplace we went there were great crowds and [autograph] lines that were like an hour long. If anything, hard as it might be to believe, he did even more than normal. He seemed more energized and enthused and positive than any other year I can remember."

In fact, his off-season efforts, aimed at renewing himself and his program, had been so focused that his famed tunnel vision had intensified. Paterno's cultural myopia was a running joke among those closest to him. His family recalled the night when the coach returned from a black-tie dinner in the Clinton White House. They asked him who he had seen there.

"I sat beside this guy, Nick Cage."

The famous actor? he was asked.

"I don't know," said Paterno, "he just said his name was Nick Cage."

In late August, during the final preseason news conference, Paterno was asked for his opinion on the previous day's NCAA ruling concerning Southern California wide receiver Mike Williams. Williams, who had sought to enter the NFL draft, had just been barred from returning to USC, which was being ranked as the nation's No. 1 team in preseason polls. The story led ESPN's *Sports Center* and was on page one of sports sections everywhere.

"I have no idea whom you are talking about or what you are talking about," Paterno replied. "So I can't answer that. I don't know."

There just wasn't time for ESPN, MTV, and movie stars. He, and everybody else in the program, had work to do. Throughout spring practice and preseason camp, he had been concerned only with devising ways to best use Robinson's talents, with finding a reliable tailback and a couple of wide receivers, with improving the special teams that had performed so poorly in 2003.

He had declared his assistants off-limits to the media until after the season. He didn't even want his players interviewed. Heather Dinich, the *Centre Daily Times* Penn State beat writer, had asked to talk to twelve players over the summer and had been granted interviews with two. And while Paterno hadn't told anyone yet, once the season started, he planned to stop attending the traditional Friday-night media cocktail sessions that long had been a popular staple of his regime.

The refocused Paterno was on display in August when Jim Moore, a *Seattle Post-Intelligencer* columnist, escorted a team of Little League baseball players to Penn State. The Washington youngsters, who were competing in the Little League World Series in Williamsport, fifty-three miles away, had asked to see where Paterno and his team were practicing.

"There he was," Moore later wrote of their encounter, "wearing those same big glasses I'd always seen on TV. Then all of a sudden, the man I was excited to meet turned into a raving lunatic. 'Get them out of here! Get them out of here!' he screamed to [Penn State sports information director Jeff] Nelson. 'Get them the hell out of here! Next time I'll . . . ' I didn't catch the end of his threat because the photographer and I were hurriedly whisked away, so as not to further disturb a disturbed icon, even though we did nothing to disturb the icon in the first place."

According to Moore, Paterno later apologized and visited with the Little Leaguers. But the episode was another indication of the emotional investment the coach was making in the 2004 season.

As he flew around that summer—to supporters-only dinners in Philadelphia, Pittsburgh, and Hershey, to speaking engagements, and to football banquets in talent-rich areas of South Carolina and

Virginia—Paterno heard the same questions: Mills or Robinson? Can Penn State get back on top? Are you thinking of retiring?

He wished all those worried fans could see how well things were going, how excited he was on the eve of another season, how even the weather had been cooperating with his grand plan.

"I think overall we had a good preseason," Paterno said on August 27. "I'm a little disappointed in a couple of kids, but I think overall we did about as well as we can expect. The weather has been good. We've had fairly hot weather, but not that oppressive humidity or hot weather where you can't get a lot of work done because kids just run out of steam. . . . We were able to get outside more often than we have in other years because when it rained, it rained at night and we didn't get a lot of rain during the day."

For Paterno at least, the sun was shining again in Happy Valley. Even if all those critics and sportswriters were too blind to see it.

Among all the extraneous happenings in the world he had missed that summer were *Sports Illustrated*'s preseason rankings. The magazine, whose worshipful writers over the years had been greatly responsible for Paterno's deification, had Penn State an almost unthinkable No. 50. That sobering news might have concerned the naysayers. But not Paterno. He was feeling fresh again. The kids were buying into the changes. The new staff was working out well. The Nittany Lions would surprise some people this season. And then watch out in 2005.

All that talk he had heard about fans threatening to give up their season tickets unless Paterno was replaced was nonsense. Someday soon they were going to be the hottest tickets in college football again.

Didn't they realize it was Penn State football, not Paterno, that was going places?

CHAPTER 4

WHAT YOU NOTICE FIRST about Joe Paterno is how out of place he appears in central Pennsylvania. After more than a half century in the picket-fence borough of State College, he still resembles a New Yorker who can't find his way home.

Penn State's head coach is the area's single most significant and revered resident. Centre County citizens adore him and are proud that he has settled and succeeded in their midst. Yet in many ways Paterno has never been fully assimilated into their community. In attitude, demeanor, and spirit, he remains an outsider. The thick New York accent, with its constant contractions, its dropped *g*'s, and whiny assuredness, is far too clipped and urban for him ever to be mistaken as a native. A *Washington Post* profile a quarter century earlier described his voice as "full of hero sandwiches and screeching El trains."

Paterno's taste in clothes—blazers, oxford shirts, understated plaids, ties on the sideline—also identify him as an interloper in a section of Pennsylvania where many consider hunting jackets fashion statements.

His slightly hunched, corner-boy swagger further betrays his city roots. So do his interests: Literature, the opera, and Italian food are not attractions indigenous to the region. Occasionally, he'll take note of the green, rolling hills that surround State College and remark, as if observing the landscape for a first time, "Geez, isn't it beautiful up here?" But the long walks he likes are opportunities for contemplation, not nature loving.

To the friendly, accommodating, slow-moving Pennsylvania German natives, the coach's impatient, direct, argumentative nature—"excessively focused and serious" is how his late brother once described it—often seems grating, excessive, foreign.

Paterno, as generations of players will tell you, is extremely verbal. Watch him on the sideline. As he roams nervously throughout games, his mouth rarely stops. He talks with and yells at whomever he happens to be near—assistant coaches, players, officials. Away from the field, he flatters and jokes with waitresses, fans, cops, neighbors, and parents. And he's accumulated a sizable collection of stories that he'll retell at the slightest provocation.

One of the few times when anyone can recall the coach being silent for an extended period also marked the moment when he might have come closest to abandoning his profession.

On a September 23, 1967, bus ride back from Annapolis, Maryland, Paterno arrived at a psychological crossroads. After just eleven games as the Nittany Lions' head coach, all the plans and dreams he had formulated in sixteen seasons as Rip Engle's assistant were evaporating in a haze of mediocrity. His best coaching attributes—competitiveness, a fierce drive, a need to excel—had turned inward and were devouring him.

Normally, during long postgame journeys, he would rehash the game with the other coaches. That day, his hair disheveled, his mood sour, Paterno stared aimlessly out a window near the front of the bus for most of the 150-mile trip. What provoked the gloomy silence was the team's 23–22 loss to Navy earlier that Saturday. Paterno had been embarrassed. "The shabbiest game I'd ever been a part of," he later called it.

With fifty-seven seconds left in the Nittany Lions' season opener at Navy–Marine Corps Memorial Stadium, Midshipman Rob Taylor had caught a 16-yard touchdown pass. Taylor's catch was his school-record tenth of the game. Penn State's defense had surrendered 489 yards to smaller, less-talented opponents.

Paterno's record as head coach was 5–6. Maybe he had made a

mistake. Maybe he should have listened to his parents and gone to law school. Maybe he didn't belong at Penn State.

"I was having my doubts," said Paterno of that trip. "We were terrible."

Back in Pennsylvania, there had been some grumbling. Fans moaned about Paterno, questioned his credentials. He had never been a head coach before and it showed. He had come in with a bunch of big ideas and lots of talk. But where were the results? Look at what happened when the Nittany Lions played the big boys in 1966. They had lost to Michigan State, 42–8; to UCLA, 49–11; and to Georgia Tech, 21–0. Now 1967 had begun with a loss to Navy. Maybe he wasn't the right man for the job. Maybe he was meant to be an assistant.

His players weren't thrilled either. Dennis Onkotz, one of a talented group of sophomores Paterno had recruited before his first year, wondered why he and the rest of the outstandng defenders from the previous season's freshmen team stayed on the bench while Navy rolled up close to 500 yards. Cocaptain Bill Lenkaitis said those early players "weren't real crazy" about Paterno's perfectionist demands. "If he didn't like the way we were practicing," said Lenkaitis, "he'd make us start practice over."

The practices that followed the loss at Navy were painful—particularly for some of the upperclassmen. Paterno, it turned out, was thinking like Onkotz. In the silence of that bus ride from Annapolis, he had rejected the thought of quitting and instead formulated a strategy. He was going to put aside his penchant for playing upperclassmen and turn to his younger, more talented players.

"We had some really good young players. We had some sophomores—in those days, freshmen were not eligible—that were good players," he recalled later. "And I said to myself, 'You'd better find out [about them], Paterno.' "

So he gave youngsters like Onkotz, linebacker Jim Kates, defensive tackle Steve Smear, and defensive back Neal Smith more repetitions that week, much to the annoyance of the junior and senior starters. His reasoning that week was as much practical as philosophical. He knew he'd need more depth Friday night in Miami, where the forecast for the game against a University of Miami team, ranked No. 1 in the preseason by *Playboy*, called for hot and muggy conditions.

"Because I was worried about the heat . . . we went to Pittsburgh and stayed at a hotel," he said. "We worked out at the Moon Township High School, got on the plane . . . went to the hotel in Miami the day of the game. We stayed in the hotel, got on an air-conditioned bus, went out on the field, and nobody knew how hot it was."

As the game in the steamy Orange Bowl wore on, Paterno began inserting more and more sophomores. Midway through the second quarter, there were six of them on the Nittany Lions' defense. And they played spectacularly, limiting Miami to just 69 yards rushing in a 17–8 triumph. It was a reprieve for Paterno and a major turning point for his program.

"If we lost that game, I probably would have told some people here that they needed to start looking around for a new coach," he said. "I was thinking about law school."

Despite the victory, more difficulties with his team followed the Miami game. That night two Penn State players were having a beer in the airport bar—a violation of the coach's guidelines—when Paterno spotted them. He booted one off the team and suspended the other. Later, Lenkaitis and quarterback Tom Sherman met with the coach and suggested he might have overreacted to their teammates' indiscretion. They warned of a brewing players' revolt unless he relented.

Paterno stood his ground. Eventually, the players' hard feelings eased as victories helped them gain a new respect for their coach. After a blocked punt cost Penn State a 17–15 loss to UCLA a week later, the Nittany Lions would go unbeaten the remainder of the season.

"There comes a time when you know that things have got to change," Paterno would say of the Miami game and its aftermath, "that something has got to be done differently. And you've got to have the guts to do it or you're just another guy."

The seven straight victories to conclude the 1967 season earned 8–2 Penn State a Gator Bowl matchup with Florida State. Paterno was revved up for his first postseason game as head coach. During the five weeks between the final regular-season game and the December 30 contest in Jacksonville, he made major changes in his offense and defense and pushed his players relentlessly.

Glenn Killinger, a former Penn State all-American and himself a college coach, attended a Paterno practice that week.

"I was real proud of myself and asked Killy what he thought," said Paterno. "He said, 'Joe, you're working them too hard.' He had watched fifteen minutes and he could see that. And he was right."

Penn State led 17–0 at the half but tired badly after intermission. But it was a controversial coaching decision, as much as his players' weariness, that sparked the Seminoles' comeback.

Spurning a field goal, Paterno had his team go for it on a fourth-and-1 at his own 15-yard line early in the third quarter. The Lions' failure to make that first down revived the Seminoles. They scored two touchdowns before the quarter ended and tied the game on a 26-yard field goal with fifteen seconds left.

Curiously, given the label he would later acquire as being too conservative, Paterno tried to portray his unusual fourth-down decision as a harbinger of the bold moves that Nittany Lions fans could expect in the future. "That may be the best thing I ever did for Penn State football," he said.

It was difficult to disagree. Penn State would win its next twenty-three games, a remarkable streak that firmly planted the program in the national consciousness.

Confidence and heart, Paterno believed, were as important to success as talent. And whenever a team loses a game it ought to have won, it sheds some of the bravado winners require. Suddenly, an unseen vulnerability works its way through a losing locker room like a virus. The only known cure is victory.

That's why 1967's season-ending success was so important to the futures of both Paterno and Penn State football. The winning streak, the bowl invitation, the No. 10 ranking in the final polls, had instilled and hardened in them a confidence they'd been lacking. Once he felt it, and once he got his team to feel it, Paterno knew this gifted Penn State football team was headed for glory.

"Football basically is a morale game," he told fellow coaches in a speech in 2002. "You play with your heart. You play with your mind. If you've got morale, then you've got a chance to win. If you've got the right kind of people, then you've got a chance to win. . . . At least, if you've got morale, then you have a chance to play as well as you can."

Joined in 1968 by legendary linebacker Jack Ham and tackle Mike Reid, who was recovered from a knee injury that had sidelined him in '67, Penn State's defense would become overpowering, yielding just 106 points in ten regular-season games. And its offense, led by tailbacks Charlie Pittman and Bob Campbell, tight end Ted Kwalick, and quarterback Chuck Burkhart, would average 34 points a game. These '68 Nittany Lions would be Paterno's first great team, their perfect season—the first of five he would experience. They would win ten straight regular-season games and beat Kansas, 15–14, in a wildly exciting Orange Bowl. It was Penn State's first season without a tie or loss since 1912.

It also marked the beginning of something else: the legend of Linebacker U.

Ham, a quiet sophomore from Johnstown, Pennsylvania, joined juniors Onkotz and Kates in what would be a spectacular unit. Ham had been an unremarkable lineman at Bishop McCort High School until, before his senior year, the six-foot 165-pounder was shifted to linebacker. He played well that year but was still too small to attract much major-college attention. Virginia Military Institute indicated it might be interested if Ham went for a year's toughening-up at Massanutten Military Academy, a Virginia prep school.

"It was a good experience, football-wise," said Ham of his year in Virginia. "But I realized pretty quickly the military life wasn't for me and ruled out going to VMI."

Smear had been his high school teammate and he recommended Ham to Penn State's coaches and the university to Ham. Paterno and assistant George Welsh were impressed by a film from one of Massanutten's games—they liked Ham's quickness, his toughness, and particularly his football instincts. Fortunately, because one high school senior had changed his mind at the last minute about coming to State College, there was a scholarship still available.

"Even then, though, none of us had any idea what a tremendous player we were getting," Paterno would say.

It didn't take them long to find out. When Ham showed up at spring practice after the 1967 season, Paterno immediately started him at outside linebacker in his 4–4–3 defense.

There had been other great Nittany Lions linebackers before Ham, Kates, and Onkotz—in particular, W. T. "Mother" Dunn, a turn-of-the-century star with an unfortunate nickname; Bob Mitinger, an all-American from the Engle era; and Dave Robinson, who played mostly end at Penn State before becoming an all-NFL linebacker with Vince Lombardi's Packers. But Ham and Onkotz were at the head of what would become a virtually nonstop assembly line of superb Penn State linebackers turned out by Paterno and Jerry Sandusky. Sandusky, a former Penn State player, would be hired as a defensive assistant in 1969 and remain on Paterno's staff until his retirement in 1999.

Among those who went on to play in the NFL were Kurt Allerman, LaVar Arrington, Ralph Baker, Bruce Bannon, Greg Buttle, Andre Collins, Shane Conlan, Ron Crosby, John Ebersole, Keith Goganious, Jim Laslavic, Lance Mehl, Matt Millen, Rich Milot, Ed O'Neil, Scott Radecic, Brandon Short, and John Skorupan.

Sandusky, who became the defensive coordinator in 1977, eventually wrote a book on the subject, *Developing Linebackers: The Penn State Way.*

The linebackers, Sandusky said, "had to be outstanding athletes in the defensive scheme we played."

But football judgment was equally as important. Penn State wanted those who played the position to process instantly what they saw developing in front of them. Opposing coaches liked to say that while any good linebacker would read a play, *then* react, Penn State's would read *and* react instantaneously.

"Coach Radakovich [Dan Radakovich, who was in charge of the linebackers until departing after the 1969 season] and the other coaches had a saying back then," said Onkotz. "They said, 'If you're going to make a mistake, make it at full speed.' Basically, in the four-four we played, it was the job of the defensive linemen to keep people off us. We had people like Reid and Smear who did that very well, so we just had to run around and hit people."

Uncovering outstanding linebackers was, as Sandusky noted, merely a matter of identifying strong, quick, and mentally agile players. And neither he nor Paterno hesitated in moving gifted players to the position. Former quarterbacks, in particular, made good linebackers. Both Onkotz and O'Neil played the position in high school. (Both also would return punts at Penn State.) Arrington had been a high school running back, Buttle a tight end. And Charlie Zapiec was a star offensive lineman for the Nittany Lions before Paterno switched him to linebacker, where he became an all-American.

Paterno would achieve a measure of historical infamy, though, while recruiting Jim Kelly, the future NFL Hall of Fame QB, by suggesting the western-Pennsylvania schoolboy should be a linebacker. Kelly, headstrong even then, decided to go to Miami instead.

"I'd probably be a bartender in East Brady, Pennsylvania," Kelly said while recalling the incident before his Hall induction in 2002. "I would have been a good linebacker, but not a Hall of Fame candidate. I wasn't fast enough."

Paterno would explain that the criticism he's taken ever since for making that suggestion might be unfair. It came, he said, during a year when Penn State also was recruiting Dan Marino, Todd Blackledge, and Jeff Hostetler, all of whom, along with Kelly, would be part of the greatest quarterback draft in NFL history in 1984.

"I had an assistant named J. T. White who was recruiting Kelly," Paterno recalled. "He knew we were close with Blackledge and Hostetler and he asked me what he ought to tell Kelly if we signed both those other quarterbacks. I said to tell him if he came here and couldn't beat out those guys, he could play linebacker."

Penn State's arrival as a national power occurred midway through the 1968 season when it avenged the previous year's loss to UCLA with a 21–6 victory. Like so many other games that season, this one turned on the play of the linebackers. Ham blocked a punt and Kates returned it 36 yards for the game's first touchdown.

That nationally televised win ignited something in Penn State and its fans. Students back in State College poured into the streets that night in a spontaneous celebration. And the next two weeks, for victories over Boston College and Army, near-record crowds packed every corner of Beaver Stadium.

Paterno's Nittany Lions, who had a pair of freshman running backs named Lydell Mitchell and Franco Harris waiting in the wings, concluded the 1968 regular season by rolling over Miami (22–7), Maryland (57–13), Pitt (65–9), and Syracuse (30–12). They earned a No. 3 national ranking and a spot opposite sixth-ranked Kansas in what would be a memorable Orange Bowl.

During that Orange Bowl week in Miami, Paterno enjoyed his first serious exposure in the national spotlight. He and Kansas coach Pepper Rodgers bantered constantly with each other and with the assembled sportswriters at news conferences. For the first time, fans all across the country were introduced to the concept of the Penn State coach's Grand Experiment.

In an era when the best-known college coaches were the gruff Woody Hayes and the taciturn Bear Bryant, Paterno was a refreshing change. Far from being a burly, cliché-spouting jock, he appeared instead to combine the brains of a professor, the principles of a priest, and the personality of an entertainer. And, in what was a confirmation of his comments following the 1967 Gator Bowl, he also won points for daring when the game was on the line.

Kansas, with left-handed quarterback Bobby Douglass, fullback John Riggins, and halfback Donnie Shanklin, had built a 14–7 lead in the fourth quarter. The Jayhawks had an opportunity to run out the clock but Reid twice sacked Douglass to force a punt with 1:16 remaining in the game. When Smith tipped the kick, Penn State took over at midfield.

Paterno was ready with a decoy play he had been thinking about all week. He told Campbell to run a deep post pattern. He wanted Burkhart to overthrow him. That likely would lure Kansas into thinking the Lions were impatient. Then, on the next play, the quarterback could dump off a little screen to Kwalick underneath the coverage.

But Campbell broke free of safety Tommy Anderson on the play and Burkhart heaved it.

"I knew I had thrown a good pass because you can always feel that," Burkhart said later. "But on the other hand, they've got a prevent defense working on Bobby, who doesn't exactly run a 4.4 40."

Just as the public-address announcer was revealing that Shanklin had been named the game's MVP, Campbell caught the ball. The 47-yard connection gave Penn State a first down on the Kansas 3 with under a minute to go. The Jayhawks sent in an extra linebacker, Rick Abernethy, for their goal-line defense. While no one noticed until four plays later, no Kansas defensive back ever left the field.

Two off-tackle runs by fullback Tom Cherry produced nothing, perhaps because it was 11 on 12. On third down, Paterno called the "scissors" play. Burkhart was to fake a handoff to Pittman, then give the ball to Campbell on a reverse. But Kansas, with the extra defender, had managed to penetrate so deeply on the play that the quarterback didn't want to risk a handoff. Instead, he kept the ball and skirted around the left side of the Jayhawks line for a touchdown that moved the Lions within a point, 14–13.

Recalling how dissatisfied he had been after the Gator Bowl tie with Florida State a year ago, Paterno immediately signaled that, on what would be the game's final play, Penn State would go for two points.

On the sideline, Reid bent his head in prayer. Other players held hands or looked skyward. When Burkhart's pass for Kwalick was knocked down, Kansas supporters swarmed onto the field to celebrate what they thought to be a notable bowl victory. They failed to notice that in the middle of the chaotic scene in their end zone an official was waving a white flag above his head. On the conversion try, umpire Foster Grose finally had noticed the twelfth Kansas defender. The illegal-procedure penalty gave Penn State a reprieve.

"I don't think there was a doubt in anyone's mind that we would score," said Burkhart.

This time, running right at Kansas all-American left end John Zook behind Zapiec, Campbell carried it into the end zone and the Nittany Lions had a 15–14 triumph.

Now it was Penn State's turn to celebrate and they did. Players were still sky high when the team bus returned them to the Ivanhoe Hotel. There, many retreated to their rooms to watch the game, which had been blacked out in Miami and was being televised on a delayed basis by a local station.

When Lou Prato, then a Pittsburgh telecaster and now the director of the Penn State All-Sports Museum, and his wife got back to the hotel, they noticed that, unlike the previous nights, there was live music in the lobby. It was Reid, a concert pianist and future Grammy winner.

"Mike was a unique guy," said Onkotz. "He was such a great football player but his first love was music. That was clear even back then. Guys relaxed in different ways, but for Mike it was always the piano. I can remember him sitting and playing at some of the oddest places and times."

As impressive as Penn State's 11–0 season had been, in the end it was good enough only for a No. 2 ranking in the final national polls. Big Ten champ Ohio State, 10–0 after defeating USC in the Rose Bowl, was declared the national champion.

In Paterno's mind, the national perception that Eastern football was inferior had hurt his team. Privately, he was disappointed.

"The sportswriters and sportscasters heaped all kinds of praise on us," he said, "but couldn't quite bring themselves to credit us—or any college in the East—with having a great football team."

After the 1969 season, Paterno's disappointment would turn to anger.

The team that Paterno gathered around him moments before the opener of the 1969 season—ironically, another game at Navy—was almost certainly the best he would ever coach. The prospect of guiding all that talent helped explain, in part, why he had turned down a serious off-season offer to coach the Pittsburgh Steelers.

Ten starters returned on defense. Three of them, Reid, Onkotz, and Smith, would earn all-American honors that season. Reid, in fact, would win the Outland Trophy as the nation's top interior lineman. Ham would be an all-American in 1970. The unit would hold opponents to single digits in scoring seven times in 1969, allowing 90 points in eleven games, a meager 18 in the last four.

On offense, Pittman returned and became an all-American, even though he shared time with sophomore Mitchell. Harris backed up Don Abbey at fullback. Kwalick was gone but sophomore Dave Joyner, a future all-American himself, anchored a strong offensive line. Burkhart provided senior experience at quarterback.

Their only close calls that season came in two road victories—17–14 at Kansas State on October 4, and 15–14 at Syracuse two weeks later. Penn State ended its regular season November 29 with a 33–8 victory at North Carolina State. The Nittany Lions were 10–0 and ranked third at the time.

Two weeks earlier, Paterno's team had voted to accept an Orange Bowl bid. It wasn't a casual decision. Though he hadn't done so the year before, the coach this time asked his half-dozen or so black players for their preference among the southern cities that hosted New Year's bowls. Mitchell, Harris, Pittman, and the others had reservations about Dallas, in part because of President Kennedy's assassination there a little more than five years earlier. They preferred Miami.

Paterno informed his team of their preference and also let them know that he believed Ohio State, then No. 1 and the defending champion, would be their chief competition for a national title. Since the Rose Bowl's contract with the Big Ten and Pac-Ten meant the Lions couldn't possibly face the Buckeyes, his players passed up a possible Cotton Bowl date with either Texas or Arkansas and opted again for Miami's Orange Bowl.

"We all had had a good time there the year before," said Onkotz. "There was no way we could have known it then, of course, but it turned out to be a big mistake. That was the last time Joe let his players decide which bowl they were going to."

The decision backfired when Michigan upset Ohio State on November 22. Texas then assumed the polls' top spot, unbeaten Arkansas became No. 2, and Penn State No. 3.

Those rankings set up a dream matchup—for everyone but Paterno and Penn State, that is. Texas and Arkansas were set to play each other in their regular-season finale, December 6 in Fayetteville. ABC television commentators, like former Oklahoma coach Bud Wilkinson, either unconcerned or unimpressed that Penn State also was undefeated, ballyhooed the Southwest Conference matchup as "the Big Shootout" for the national championship.

The game generated so much national hype that President Nixon, a huge football fan who had been a backup lineman at Whittier College decades earlier, helicoptered into Arkansas to watch it in person. Texas won, 15–14. Afterward Nixon went down to the Longhorns' locker room and handed coach Darrell Royal a plaque declaring the Longhorns national champions.

Nixon's premature action might merely have been a shrewd political move designed to bolster his new Southern strategy. If so, it had the opposite impact in Pennsylvania, where Paterno and Penn State supporters were furious. The politically astute Nixon had taken that into account. After honoring Texas, he quickly announced that he would present a plaque to Penn State in honor of its unbeaten streak, which by then stood at twenty-nine.

Privately, Paterno suggested a place where the president could store the plaque. Publicly, he released a statement that said his team "would be disappointed at this time . . . to receive anything other than a plaque for the number-one team." Four years later, while delivering a commencement address at Penn State, Paterno revealed how much Nixon's snub had upset him. "How could the president know so little about Watergate in 1973," he said, "and so much about college football in 1969?"

But Ohio State's loss and Nixon's public pronouncement had put Penn State in a powerless position. All the Nittany Lions realistically could hope for was that Texas would lose to Notre Dame in the Cotton Bowl while they defeated Missouri in the Orange Bowl.

Unfortunately, before they stifled Missouri, 10–3, in Miami, intercepting seven Terry McMillan passes in the process, Texas beat the Irish, 21–17. There was virtually no chance that those voting in the poll were going to reverse the Nos. 1 and 2 teams after those results, but Paterno lobbied anyway.

"I don't like to keep pushing this thing," Paterno said after the Orange Bowl, "but I still think we have as much right to number one as Texas or anybody else. Why should I sit back and let the president of the United States say that so-and-so is number one when I've got fifty kids who've worked their tails off for me for three years?"

His words, of course, were in vain. Texas was No. 1 in the final voting, Penn State No. 2, Southern Cal No. 3, and Ohio State No. 4.

"Sure we wanted to be number one, but it really wasn't that big a deal," says Onkotz, who now works with a financial-investment firm near State College. "The media wasn't nearly as big back then, so you didn't hear about it all the time, the way you would now. And, to be honest, we were all so busy. I was a biophysics major, so I had a lot of classes that took a lot of time and work. I didn't have a lot of time to think about who was number one."

Years later, even after Penn State had won two national championships, Nixon's call still angered the coach. "The bloodcurdling nerve!" he wrote in his 1989 autobiography. ". . . Nixon *favored* us with an honor that any idiot consulting a record book could see that we had taken for ourselves, thank you, without his help."

He began to promote a postseason play-off system. Like so much of what Joe Paterno has proposed for college football over the years, his suggestion was seen as thoughtful and constructive. And then it was ignored.

CHAPTER 5

LESS THAN TWENTY-FOUR HOURS before Penn State's September 4 season opener, and much to the relief of the sweltering thousands who had assembled in Beaver Stadium for the Friday-night pep rally, the oppressive heat that had shrouded State College finally yielded to more comfortable weather.

The heat had not wilted these Penn State fanatics, twenty thousand of whom seemed a tiny gathering as they huddled together in a corner near the 107,282-seat stadium's south end zone. Almost all were wearing some item of apparel bearing the Nittany Lions logo—a chiseled but unthreatening feline whom the school's sports-information staff jokingly called "the chipmunk." Like religious pilgrims, they had brought along relics and icons—lucky seat cushions, lucky jerseys and hats, lucky buttons that read PENN STATE PROUD, YOU'RE IN LION COUNTRY OR WE ARE . . . PENN STATE!

Further evidence of their fidelity was evident in the hundreds of lumbering RVs, plastered with Nittany Lions paw prints and decals, that were parked in the vast lots outside. Though this was merely a rally in advance of the next day's 3:30 P.M. game against Akron, some fans had conducted tailgate parties nonetheless. At a few of the more extravagant affairs, life-size cutouts of Paterno ("Stand-Up Joes") were propped up among the living guests, positioned as carefully and lovingly as figurines in a Christmas creche.

These loyalists, drawn long ago to the program Paterno had pushed to prominence, paid dearly for their devotion. Since 1971, five years after Paterno became head coach, Penn State's season-ticket holders have had to make sizable annual donations to the Nittany Lion Club for the privilege of purchasing tickets. For a $5,000 contribution, each club member was entitled to as many as fourteen seats (at an additional $46 a game in 2004). To upgrade location, a larger donation was required. In all, eighty percent of Beaver Stadium's capacity was controlled by club members, their annual seat-rights contributions totaling nearly $10 million to the university.

Such spend-to-spectate schemes suggested that Penn State, too, had become the kind of money-driven football program Paterno had once sought to tame. Here and virtually everywhere else that battle had been lost. College football was a $5 billion business fed by television, corporate sponsors, and frenzied boosters.

In the late 1960s, when Paterno first revealed his Grand Experiment—an attempt to produce football success *and* educated, well-rounded players—Beaver Stadium held 46,284 fans. His initial game as head coach, against Maryland on September 17, 1966, drew only 40,911. But the Nittany Lions' combined record of 30–2–1 from 1967 through 1969 sent demand spiraling and created three decades of nearly nonstop stadium expansion. Its capacity rose to 57,538 in 1972; 60,203 in 1976; 76,639 in 1978; 83,770 in 1980; and 93,967 in 1991.

Then came the most recent project, the $94 million expansion that added the Mount Nittany–obscuring, 11,500-seat upper deck, plus sixty luxury suites atop the east grandstands. A ten-year lease on one of those fourteen-foot-by-thirty-foot boxes initially cost between $40,000 and $65,000, not including the price of tickets. Five-year leases were even more expensive per season. (But, thanks to a favorable IRS ruling, without which college football would be hard put to exist in 2004, up to eighty percent of the cost of those suites was tax deductible as a charitable contribution.)

Paterno's program generated enough annual revenue to pay for itself and contribute an additional $12–$16 million to support the university's other twenty-eight sports. In 1999, counting the Nittany Lion Club donations, football had produced close to $35 million in revenue.

By 2004 the fans' largesse had become a double-edged sword for Paterno. While their money permitted him a massive recent upgrade in football facilities, it also gave the ticket-holding investors a significant voice. The coach had long been able to reject demands from boosters and alumni. "We are happy to accept their money," he once said, "but we don't want their two cents' worth."

That attitude was fine when Penn State was ranked in the top ten every year. But many ticket holders now resented having to pay thousands of dollars a year to watch a sub-.500 team lose at home to Toledo, as the Lions did in the 2000 opener. As the dissatisfaction with Paterno broadened, a tiny minority of boosters threatened to withhold future contributions unless the coach stepped down. University officials acknowledged that athletic giving had leveled off since 2001, just about the time the current slump was getting under way. Nearly $20 million had been donated that year. By 2003, the figure had dipped to $18 million.

Now, heading into a tough 2004 schedule that, realistically, didn't promise much relief, they remained concerned. While most of those then gathering in State College for the Akron weekend weren't yet aware of its existence, the athletic department was already one year into a five-year, $100 million fund-raising drive, "Success With Honor: A Campaign for the Penn State Way." Publicly, it was billed as a way to fund more athletic scholarships, coaches' endowments, more advising, plus upgrades to its sports-medicine facilities. Privately, some administrators and fans saw the effort, which would be revealed to the public the following month, as insurance against more lost games and more lost donations.

"They'd better get it while they can," said a 1970 graduate.

The pep-rally crowd included alums, parents of football players and band members, as well as those whose only connection to the university was a lifetime's allegiance to Paterno's teams. Most had come from the big cities along the eastern seaboard and from the tiny communities surrounding State College. All day, long lines of cars, SUVs, and pickup trucks had moved relentlessly into the tiny college town like armies of ants en route to a picnic spill.

Each football weekend, visitors spent roughly $4 million in and around State College. Hotel rates more than doubled, with rooms at the university-owned Penn Stater going for well over $200 a night. Then there were the busy bars and restaurants, the crowded souvenir shops, and the long lines at stadium concession stands.

Some had come to Beaver Stadium on foot: students who resided in nearby dormitories, including the newly arrived freshmen who were getting their first live taste of Penn State football; the returning alums who stayed in downtown apartments and hotels; the big shots in the Nittany Lion Inn, a handsome campus hotel just a short distance down Park Road; and those who had come from a 5:00 P.M. women's volleyball match in Rec Hall, parading en masse behind the school's Pep Band as it made its noisy way down Curtin Road.

In the twilight, Penn State's campus, described in the football media guide as "picture-postcard perfect," dripped with nostalgia. Older couples strolled arm in arm along the grassy quad, beneath rows of stately elms and willows. Students and graduates shared cocktails on the patios of elegant Greek Revival fraternity houses. Parents took their blue-and-white-clad youngsters on sentimental journeys through classroom buildings and dormitories.

The university's columned structures, its broad lawns, tree-lined paths, and small-town charm brought to mind all those impossibly earnest 1930s movies about college life that Paterno, who had grown up watching them, called "cornball stuff." Even the campus buildings appeared to have been named by a sentimental but unimaginative screenwriter—Old Main, Rec Hall, Agricultural Hall. Outside one, a small brick building near the heart of the campus, a row of people waited in line. The Creamery's 110 flavors of ice cream—including the perennially popular "Peachy Paterno" and "JoePa-stachio"—were made on the premises, in part from milk supplied by Penn State's 175-cow dairy herd. On warm football weekends like this, the Creamery sold as many as eight thousand cones a day.

The lovely campus evoked a welcoming atmosphere that had become one of Penn State's most valuable assets. Paterno, in fact, was a partner in Pinnacle Development, a local company that capitalized on Happy Valley's charm. Pinnacle had recently constructed the Village at

Penn State, a $125-million, university-affiliated retirement community. Despite entrance fees that initially ran as high as $250,000, its communities, with syrupy names like Tradition Point and Homecoming Ridge, appealed to golden-aged graduates. Many of those dewy-eyed alums had been specifically targeted by Pinnacle, which had purchased the rights to Penn State's name, logo, and alumni-marketing network.

Paterno's national profile had helped the university create a powerful marketing machine. That night's pep rally, for all its seeming innocence, was in reality a vehicle to bolster Penn State football traditions in a troubled era. The new, fast-paced video that would be debuted at the rally ("One Hungry Pride"), the scores of fresh-faced cheerleaders, the corporate-sponsored calendars handed out to attendees, the Blue Band, even Paterno's appearance, were all part of a massive sales pitch.

A year earlier, school officials had hired Guido D'Elia, a Pittsburgh marketing executive, to find new ways to sell football, along with men's and women's basketball. The hiring hinted at what had become a major topic in athletic administration meetings: Now that Penn State could no longer guarantee an annual bowl appearance to its supporters, how did they sustain interest, attendance, and donations?

D'Elia, with Paterno's blessing, already had injected loud music, fast-paced videos, and a more aggressive, contemporary style into Penn State's traditionally conservative approach. "He throws a lot of ideas out there," said Curley, "and some of them stick."

D'Elia was a high-energy urban hipster set down in a football culture that didn't welcome change. He wore shirtsleeves and jeans instead of blazers and khakis, sold with noisy videos instead of staid mailings, and tried to integrate a Luddite head coach into a wired era. The fact that the frenetic D'Elia did not fit the Penn State mold indicated just how desperate the situation was.

When Paterno had talked about starting the season with a Friday-night pep rally, D'Elia jumped at the suggestion. That kind of emotion-charged, feel-good gimmick was more important than ever to maintain a positive and generous attitude among the university's 440,000 living alumni, many of whom had made it clear that they wanted to see change.

• • •

Sponsored by Sheetz, a Pennsylvania-based convenience-store chain, and promoted all week on Web sites, radio stations, and newspapers, "Penn State Football Eve" was a resounding success.

School officials had expected eight to ten thousand fans. But by the time Paterno and his hundred-plus players arrived in two large buses, there were twice that number in the stands.

Finally, after the video had been shown, the cheers shouted, and the players introduced, Paterno took the microphone from radio broadcaster Steve Jones's hand and addressed the crowd with the fervor of a revivalist preacher. This would be his official 2004 debut. Feeling born again in his coaching life, he was going to proselytize.

He began, as he often did, with a literary allusion, quoting from the title character's speech before the Battle of Agincourt in Shakespeare's *Henry V.* "If we are marked to die, we are enough / To do our country loss; and if to live, / The fewer men, the greater share of honor."

The quotation's precise meaning in this context lost to perhaps all but himself, Paterno followed that by instantly transforming himself from intellectual to inciter. Gone was the caution that marked his tentative news conferences.

"Where else would you get this kind of turnout for a team that was three and nine last season?" he screamed. "Nowhere! You are the greatest fans in college football. . . . Tomorrow, with over a hundred thousand people here, I want every single one of them helping this football team get back where we want Penn State football to be. We want to be right on our way to the Rose Bowl. We want to be on our way to another national championship!"

Before the enthusiastic buzz he created had subsided, Penn State's football team had marched out of the stadium and reboarded the buses. They would be making the short trip down Route 220 to the Toftrees Hotel and Resort, a golf-course inn where they spent the nights before home games. Although Paterno didn't believe in athletic dorms because he felt players ought to be fully integrated into the university's life, the Friday nights before football games were different. All the alcohol-fueled noise made dorm-room sleeping nearly impossible.

"I'd much prefer to have them sleep in their own rooms, but how do you accomplish that?" he said. "On a college campus? It's impossible. We play at twelve o'clock. We have three thousand students that don't wake up until twelve-thirty. Maybe if we were drawing three hundred people or so you could. But how can they get a good night's sleep when you have parties and unsupervised people coming in and out?"

The coach was not on either bus. He preferred to sleep at home, which was only 1.4 miles from the stadium. So as the rally concluded with sparkling fireworks exploding loudly in the artificial-light-bleached sky, he walked through the parking lots and up onto Park Road.

Then, flanked by the stillness of the dark university on one side and the soft glow of his College Heights neighborhood on the other, he headed toward home.

By 8:30 A.M. Saturday, along busy College Avenue, Paterno was ubiquitous.

The Student Book Store, the leading independent merchandiser of Penn State and Paterno paraphernalia, already was packed. Inside, life-size Paterno cutouts ($39.95) were being sold to fans dressed for a game that was still seven hours away. The coach's familiar face—its long Roman nose, dark eyes squinting intently behind tinted glasses, pursed lips, all topped by that dark thicket of hair—could be seen on three-foot-tall JoePa bobble-heads ($349), on JoePa Christmas ornaments ($6.95), on JoePa masks ($6.95), and JoePa afghans ($59.95). Norm Brown, the shop's manager, said business had been down the last few seasons, but that today, with a new season's optimism so tangible, it was picking up again.

In the lengthy breakfast line outside the nearby Corner Room restaurant, some fans had on T-shirts that expressed their devotion to Paterno. Others wore "True Blue" buttons.

"True Blue" was, in part, a reaction to all the anti-Paterno talk of recent years. Founded during the off-season by a pair of Penn State students, Jon Apperson and Justin Casavant, its principle aim was to eliminate the negativity and apathy that were becoming so apparent at home games. That trend had begun with the odd sound of Beaver Stadium boos during the stunning 2000 loss to Toledo. The college community was as dismayed by the booing as by the loss. When more boos and more defeats followed, posters bearing the inscription WE BE-LIEVE, printed on a blue background, began appearing in doorways and windows all around town, hopeful stars in a darkening sky.

"I figured it was OK to get upset, to second-guess Joe, but . . . we needed to do something to show our support," said Rob Schmidt, the general manager of State College's WBUS-FM, the radio station that distributed the signs. "The signs are our way of saying that we believe everything will be all right."

The new negativity was distressing for many in Happy Valley. The University Faculty Senate, at the urging of Scott Kretchman, the school's NCAA faculty athletic representative, responded with an antibooing resolution. It encouraged Beaver Stadium fans to "reduce or eliminate" boos and tasteless cheers like "Bullshit!" or "Ohio State sucks!", to refrain from cheering when opposing players were hurt, and to applaud good play on both sides. When the ridiculously naive guidelines were read over the loudspeaker system at a game later that 2000 season, they were, not surprisingly, met by even louder boos.

(Curiously, Penn State's decline had helped with fan decorum elsewhere. At University of Pittsburgh home games, students had once delighted in chanting "Penn State Sucks! P-E-N-N-S-T Sucks!" even when their team wasn't playing its longtime rival. Now the derisive cheer had virtually disappeared. "We said it because they [Penn State] were good," Pitt student Tim Murphy told the *Daily Collegian*. "But now they do suck, so we don't do it anymore.")

Still, it was true that during the Nittany Lions' mediocre new millennium, the level of excitement at Beaver Stadium had been greatly reduced—despite crowds that rarely fell below a hundred thousand. The notable exception had been the near delirium that accompanied the Saturday Night Massacre of Nebraska on September 14, 2002—a 40–7 Penn State triumph that briefly revived the glory.

"[We] were just kind of talking about the atmosphere, and how we might have the quietest hundred thousand fans in the nation," said True Blue's Apperson of his motivation. "If you had an atmosphere as close to [the Nebraska game] as possible for every game, it's certainly gonna be a weapon."

True Blue wanted all fans, but in particular the twenty thousand or so students who attended each game, to adhere to three principles: "1. Wear Blue. 2. Be early and rowdy. 3. Stay to the end."

Now, in the hours before the Akron game, as spectators gathered along a stadium-entrance walkway to greet the Lions on their arrival, a True Blue member in white hard hat and a blue No. 11 Penn State jersey led them in raucous cheers.

"Let's Go, baby! Remember, We are . . . PENN STATE."

At just about that time, after having parked his car in the driveway of his mother's Cape Cod house on nearby Park Road, athletic director Tim Curley was making the short walk to the stadium.

He had grown up in this house, across the street from the old Beaver Field. He played football at Penn State in the 1970s, then began working as an administrative assistant to Paterno. By 1993, he had risen to AD. Now at fifty, he was a member of Paterno's Palace Guard, those Penn State employees and trustees who owed their loyalty—not to mention their jobs—to the coach. One local sportswriter that summer expressed the widespread view about Curley and President Spanier when he wrote that they were "seemingly puppets sitting on Paterno's knee—and there's no question who pulls the strings."

Curley's morning walk spoke volumes about the professional but unpretentious atmosphere Paterno had created. Though it was a sweltering September 4, the AD wore a tie and an oxford shirt. He exuded a buttoned-down contentment. And why not? He was working in his hometown. For his alma mater. He could park at his mom's house. And why should he ride to the game in a limo or park in a reserved spot when he could walk?

That was all so State College. So Penn State. So Paterno.

Over his left arm, Curley carried what had become the most essential element of the Paterno-era Penn State uniform—a blue blazer. Like so many other traditions at the school, the fondness for blue blazers could be traced back to the coach. He was absolutely fanatical about players and athletic-department staff dressing professionally. His obsession, friends said, dated back to his early days as a Brown student.

Ever since he had worn a sweater to a fraternity party and been humiliated, he rarely was caught underdressed. A blue blazer had been a staple of his tastefully conservative wardrobe. And though his recent game attire often included a blue windbreaker in its place, Paterno seldom went more than a day or two without donning one.

The "Penn State Blazer" had become so embedded in the college's culture that it frequently was awarded as a prize at university golf tournaments or fund-raising events. You could buy them in several College Avenue clothing stores. Jack Harper's Young Men's Shop offered a limited edition of a thousand "Penn State Navy Blazers" at $295 each. Distant alumni could custom-fit their own by purchasing a set of nine brass buttons, engraved with Penn State's official seal. The buttons sold for $129.98 in the university's bookstore.

So it wasn't at all surprising that when a police escort deposited the buses carrying the football team at its stadium entrance ninety minutes before the Akron game, Paterno emerged with a blue blazer slung over his left arm.

His face betraying nothing, the coach, eyes down, walked by himself down the tunnel and into the locker room. The senior captains, quarterback Zack Mills and linebacker Derek Wake, came next, followed by the rest of the team.

It was 2:05 P.M. The buses had arrived fifteen minutes behind schedule because Paterno and the coaches had kept the team longer at the Lasch Building. The revamped coaching staff wanted to make sure players understood what was at stake. The 2003 disaster was over, Paterno told them. It was time they all ran into that stadium and carried Penn State back to its rightful place in the football universe.

"He reiterated a lot of positive aspects," linebacker Paul Posluszny would say of his coach's pregame talk. "He said we had put in all that work and that now was the time to reap those benefits. He reassured us that we could play this game. He said we are Penn State and only great football players come out of here."

Paterno and the players eventually drifted onto the field for warm-ups. The coach found his Akron counterpart, J. D. Brookhart, at the 32-yard line. Brookhart, in his first year at the Ohio school, had been Pitt's offensive coordinator for the past seven seasons and the two men had met often in the past.

As his team lined up to stretch and loosen up, Paterno walked among the rows of young men, patting their padded shoulders, or pulling them closer to him for a private word of pregame encouragement.

Paterno then shook referee John Carson's hand and thrust an arm around the official's shoulder in a gesture of reconciliation. Paterno had made national headlines two years earlier when, after a 42–35 loss to Iowa, he chased Big Ten referee Dick Honig into a Beaver Stadium tunnel, grabbed him by the shirt, and complained about two controversial calls. The old coach had criticized the officiating frequently the last few seasons, and increasingly carped at officials from the sideline. In doing so, he had earned himself the belated reputation of a referee baiter.

At the opposite end of the field, Akron players were also going through warm-up routines, occasionally glancing up at the huge crowd that was building around them. Soon, both teams retreated to their locker rooms for final instructions.

Penn State players were buoyed by a season-opening optimism. They were ready to win this game and begin to make up for the indignities of last year. Just before 3:30, Paterno called them together for a few final instructions and the Lord's Prayer. This was the best part of the week for him.

"To gather a team around you just before a big game," Paterno once wrote, "to look at grown men huddling close to each other with tears in their eyes, each one taking the hand of another on each side until everybody and every soul in that room is connected, each pledging to give and to expect the best, each becoming part of all the others—to look into those strong faces that say, *If we can only do it today*—to be there is to see and touch and be touched by people who have joined a cause that they have made bigger then themselves. If they can do it here, they will be able to do it anywhere."

Then he led them to the mouth of the tunnel that opened onto the southern end of the stadium. He stood motionless as the emotionally charged players hopped in place behind him, slapping each other on their shoulder pads, their collective shouts joining into an eerie, anticipatory chant.

Just as they appeared to be approaching a frenzy, Paterno raised his right arm and began to jog toward the field. The signal released the blue-shirted swarm behind him and soon the coach was overtaken by charging Nittany Lions. The delighted fans, having waited more than nine months for this sight, arose with a thick, throaty roar.

Paterno felt exactly as he had at the start of his fifty-four other Penn State seasons. Excited. Upbeat. A little nervous. There was just one difference. He had never wanted to win any more than he did right now. Not so much to quiet the critics, but for his own peace of mind. For Penn State. And especially for the kids.

The few seniors who joined him on the field today hadn't enjoyed the same Happy Valley experience as their predecessors. There'd been too much losing. Too much turmoil. Paterno felt guilty about that.

Now, he and his players believed, things were about to change.

"We now have the confidence that we can win big-time football games," Posluszny would say. "We're going to be a team that contends for the Big Ten title."

Paterno knew this was going to be a competitive year in the Big Ten.

Michigan, Ohio State, Purdue, Wisconsin, Minnesota, Iowa. The Nittany Lions would play all but Michigan this year and any of them could be the team to beat. But like his squad, all of them were flawed—though certainly to a lesser degree. There wasn't a super team. In fact, the Big Ten was probably only the fourth best conference in the nation this year—after the SEC, Big Twelve, and Pac Ten. So who was to say Penn State couldn't make some noise?

Akron was from the tough little Mid-American Conference. MAC schools, eager for the media exposure and the approximately $425,000 a trip to State College earned them, had recently become annual early-season fodder for Penn State. The pressure for victories in State College was eliminating big-time interconference matchups. Since the addition of the Nittany Lions in 1993, each Big Ten team played eight of the ten others. In the remaining three or four games,

Paterno didn't need severe nonconference tests at home. So former opening-game opponents like Texas, Southern Cal, and Georgia Tech had been replaced by Toledo, Central Florida, Temple, and Akron. The Beaver Stadium crowds would be enormous regardless of the opponent, so why take a chance on losing? This would be Penn State's twenty-first game against a MAC team. The Lions had won nineteen.

In 1999, before the current struggles dawned, Penn State had beaten Akron, 70–24, in its opener. But the following season, another MAC team, Toledo, upset the Nittany Lions, 24–6, in their Beaver Stadium debut. While this Akron team appeared to be physically overmatched, no one anymore could safely predict a Penn State victory.

Akron had gone 7–5 the previous season. They were small and shallow on both lines, but they did return senior quarterback Charlie Frye. Frye had thrown for 3,549 yards and 22 touchdowns last season, practically double the combined 2003 totals of Mills and Robinson. And since Brookhart had installed the West Coast offense, Frye figured to put the ball in the air even more this year.

At 3:37 P.M., Robbie Gould kicked off. Akron couldn't move the ball and quickly punted to Penn State, who had sent Robinson back in yet another role, punt returner. The Nittany Lions' offense answered a lot of lingering questions merely by taking the field. Even though Tony Hunt had trouble with some preseason conditioning tests and had had difficulties in the classroom, he had beaten out Austin Scott for the starting tailback's spot. Mills was the quarterback, and Robinson was lined up as a flanker.

The two QBs connected immediately, Robinson picking up 2 yards to the 23 on a short first-down pass. Then, on second down, Hunt took a handoff and, after a spectacular full-body spin, scurried 77 yards for the season's first touchdown.

If the excited response of 98,866 fans—nearly 9,000 below capacity on this Labor Day Weekend—could have been translated, it would have spoken of a reawakened hope. Akron's subsequent field goal did little to extinguish the enthusiasm, particularly because Penn State struck again quickly, with a 5-yard touchdown run by Mills for a 14–3 lead.

As Paterno had hinted, Penn State frequently utilized Mills and

Robinson simultaneously, alternating them at quarterback and, less often, flanker. And just before the end of the first quarter, they produced a moment that would have been unthinkable during most of Paterno's career.

On the first play after safety, Mike Guman recovered an Akron fumble at the Zips' 18, Mills flanked right. On the snap, he deked his defender once and rumbled toward the right corner of the end zone. Just as he reached the back, a perfectly placed pass from Robinson settled into his arms.

Few in the stadium—outside of the Paterno watchers in the press box—noticed that the touchdown play had been preceded by a heated sideline discussion between Paterno and new offensive coordinator Galen Hall. It appeared the head coach had won.

Scott, who ripped off several long runs on the next drive, ran a yard for a second-quarter touchdown and soon afterward Terrance Phillips leaped in traffic and brought down a 17-yard TD pass from Mills that, after Gould's missed extra point, left the score 34–3.

That last drive was more evidence of Paterno's revamped, freewheeling attack. It included a reverse, a deep throw, and a draw that Robinson ran out of the shotgun formation the coach had eschewed for decades. With under a minute left in the half, Mills would return the favor for Robinson, hitting the versatile junior on a 10-yard touchdown pass that made it 41–3.

The outcome had long since been decided when Scott's 5-yard run extended Penn State's advantage to 48–3 in the third quarter. Akron finally scored against Penn State's backups with under five minutes left in the game.

In the final meaningless minutes, the mood in the stadium was boisterous and confident. Students began peppering Akrons's indecipherable mascot, Zippy, with chants of "Zippy sucks! Zippy sucks!" Someone in the student section held up a sign that read, JOEPA FOR PREZ. For the fans, the easy victory was a sign that this might be a pleasant fall in Happy Valley. It certainly would temporarily quell the speculation about Paterno. But for the coach, who had been on the right side of many Beaver Stadium shellackings, the win proved little.

Afterward, it was difficult to tell if he was just being his typically cautious self, or whether somewhere in that spectacular display he had sensed the trouble that lay ahead.

"I can't get excited about one win," he told the press gathered afterward. "I don't know whether we are good, bad, or average. We'll see. We've got to get better. We're certainly not good enough to handle some of the teams we've got on the schedule. The quality of our team isn't good enough right now for us to figure that we're good enough. So I think we've just got to keep practicing hard and working hard and see what happens."

The quarterbacks' play had been efficient and, given that each had thrown and caught a TD pass, wildly entertaining. Mills, in fact, became the first player in the Paterno era to score touchdowns on a pass, a run, and a catch in the same game. He had completed nine of eleven passes for 108 yards and two touchdowns.

Robinson completed three of four passes for 42 yards and a touchdown, caught three more passes for 35 yards and a touchdown, and ran the ball four times for 19 yards.

"He and Zack Mills have got to carry this football team," Paterno said again after the game. "I hope we can keep those two kids healthy. I mean, that's the biggest concern I have. . . . Our potential to be a really good football team will depend on whether those two kids can stay healthy."

Hunt had rushed for 137 yards and a touchdown, averaging an astounding 17.1 yards a carry. His fellow sophomore tailback Scott picked up 116 yards on eleven rushes. It was the first game in eleven years since Ki-Jana Carter and Mike Archie had done it in 1993 that two Nittany Lions backs had run for 100 yards each.

Most significantly from Paterno's perspective, the receivers had been better than adequate. In addition to Robinson's three catches, Gerald Smith caught four balls for 48 yards. Nine other Penn State receivers had one catch each.

"I think they caught everything and they ran good, precise routes," Paterno said. "I thought the timing of our passing game was good. At times, Akron rushed us with a couple tough stunts to handle. I think they did better and hopefully will continue to get better."

Defensively, Tom Bradley's unit, with Guman and Wake the only senior starters, had been aggressively dominant and much more consistent than at any time in the 2003 season. They had allowed Frye the short stuff—he completed twenty-nine of thirty-six throws—but for only 223 yards and no touchdowns. They also sacked him twice and junior cornerback Anwar Phillips had intercepted two of his passes.

Three junior defensive linemen, Tamba Hali, Ed Johnson, and Scott Paxson, looked bigger, stronger, and smarter. It was apparent that, as Paterno had mandated, each had spent considerably more time with John Thomas, the strength and conditioning coach.

"All of those kids played last year and all of them have more years ahead of them. I think they will get better as they go along. They are stronger. Kids come into college and there are a lot of ways to get them stronger," Paterno said without mentioning steroids. "We have avoided some ways that some other places have done and it takes us a little longer maybe to get them where they want to be. . . . I think our down guys are pretty good. They have a lot of potential ahead of them."

As for the new staff, everything worked so well in the blowout that there had been few occasions for disagreements, the most notable exception coming when Hall and Paterno had jawed at each other prior to Mills's TD catch. His son Jay had been up in the coach's box while Hall stayed on the sideline.

More jarring for Paterno than any coaching malfunction may have been the absence of Fran Ganter, his assistant for the previous thirty seasons. Ganter watched the game from Penn State's radio booth, no doubt amused that the offense had been souped up in ways that Paterno would not have allowed him to try.

"A couple of times I looked around [and thought], where was he?" Paterno said of Ganter. "I am delighted with the way that Galen Hall and the staff handled the game. I thought they did an awfully good job. A lot of the things that we did, Fran probably would have fought me to try to get them done a couple of years ago. I miss Fran."

But perhaps the most significant aspect of the rout took place in the fourth quarter when Paterno inserted freshman Anthony Morelli at quarterback. With Mills, Robinson, and senior third-stringer Chris Ganter, the ex-coach's son, ahead of him, it had been widely assumed that Morelli would redshirt his freshman season. That's what Paterno had almost always done in the past.

Sportswriters peppered the coach with questions about his decision to play Morelli at the tail end of a lopsided game. Their puzzlement was understandable. Their access to the coach having been extremely limited during the long off-season, they had not yet recognized this transformed Paterno.

The Joe Paterno of 1982 might never have wasted a year of eligibility so cavalierly. The Joe Paterno of 2004 didn't hesitate.

"Morelli is a very good prospect, and playing Zack and Robinson the way we're playing them I think we had to have someone [ready in reserve]," Paterno explained. "I like Chris Ganter. But I think Morelli has a little something special. A little stronger arm than Chris and I think he just needs to play so that if we got in some kind of jam he'd be ready. If our wideouts continue to come along and get better, then probably the move to play Morelli may not have been the smart thing. Right now Robinson and Mills have to be on the field. If something happened to Zack, I'm not sure what route I'd go. . . . We think we have some things we can do with two quarterbacks in there, one being Robinson, of course. And I'm not sure we want to give up on some of that stuff if something happened to Zack."

Overall, Paterno was pleased. He had been tough with this team. But he also had tried to pump them up, to lift them out of the doldrums into which his program had descended. Last season they frequently had been as lethargic as the Beaver Stadium crowds that watched them. Today, both displayed a passion that pleased him.

At just after 7:30 P.M., after several hours spent pacing beneath a late-summer sun, after dealing with all the red-hot pressures that surrounded him and his program, after answering dozens of questions from still-skeptical reporters, Paterno looked fresh. His blue oxford shirt remained crisp and perspiration free. He was, *Reading Eagle* reporter Rich Scarcella remarked that evening, remarkably vigorous looking for a man of his age, especially one who had just spent an afternoon in the furnace of big-time college football.

It would soon serve as a striking contrast to the beaten-down, slumped Paterno who would emerge on future Saturdays.

CHAPTER 6

THE EPISODE that transformed Joe Paterno into the most widely respected college football coach of the second half of the twentieth century began with a sideline meeting and six words that, for him, shimmered like the armor of an avenging knight:

"A summer house on Cape Cod."

Even as Paterno led his 10–1 Penn State team onto the Tulane Stadium field before the start of the Sugar Bowl on the final day of 1972, he couldn't get those six words out of his mind.

It had been like that ever since Billy Sullivan, the smooth-talking owner of the New England Patriots, had approached him six weeks earlier.

On that day, November 18, 1972, Penn State had just won its ninth consecutive game, 45–26, at Boston College. In the chilled twilight at Chestnut Hill's Alumni Stadium, Sullivan asked Paterno if he'd have any interest in coaching his NFL team the following season.

With the victory at BC, Paterno's teams had won 49 of 54 games since the start of the 1968 season. That kind of success naturally attracted attention from the NFL. The Philadelphia Eagles, New York Jets, and Pittsburgh Steelers had all approached him at various times. The Steelers had made the most ardent attempt in 1969. Paterno eventually turned Pittsburgh down, in part because his wife, a small-town Pennsylvanian, had been reluctant to move, especially to become an

NFL coach's wife. Sue Paterno had been to one NFL game in her life— in Pittsburgh, as it turned out—and what stayed in her memory were the loudmouths and the rowdy drunks.

Sullivan was a public-relations man and had long wanted to put a professional football team in his hometown, which had been without one since the Redskins abandoned Boston for Washington in 1936. The NFL, then a struggling league and wary of overexpansion, had continually rebuffed him. So in 1959, he put up $25,000 and become a charter member of the American Football League.

Thirteen years later, with the AFL and NFL having recently merged, and his team's surname now "New England," his Patriots still had not won a title. Following a 6–8 season in 1971, Patriots GM Upton Bell had wanted to fire coach John Mazur and replace him with Paterno. Sullivan wasn't yet ready to pull the trigger on Mazur. But a year later, in the midst of an even worse 3–11 season, the owner had no other choice. Mazur was fired and Phil Bengston, his top assistant, finished the '72 season as interim head coach. By that time Bell would be gone, too, but not before finally selling Sullivan on Paterno's merits.

A week after the owner and the Penn State coach talked briefly at Boston College, on the night before the Nittany Lions would defeat Pitt in their final regular-season game, Paterno was at home, in his bedroom slippers, when the phone rang.

"Joe," said Sullivan, "what if you not only coach my team but own a piece of it as well?"

Immediately, in the forty-six-year-old coach's head, the thought bobbed to the surface like some long-submerged dream.

A summer house on Cape Cod.

The prospect of owning a vacation home somewhere along that sixty-five-mile-long, hook-shaped sliver of sand where New England Brahmins had summered forever held a powerful allure. Paterno had been scarred by Yankee snobbery as an undergraduate at Brown. All those smooth, spoiled, rich sons of New England wealth and tradition had looked down their patrician noses at him, with his Italian name, his dark features, his working-class background, and Brooklyn accent.

"There's no question," he recalled. "As a swarthy kid from Brooklyn, I was different. They just assumed I wasn't as smart as them."

A half century later, Paterno could still recall a Brown fraternity party he had gone to as a freshman. He had walked into the frat house that night not really knowing what to expect. He had seen plenty of movies about college life, and while their plots were hopelessly juvenile, the films portrayed a certain atmosphere that he found appealing: thick books being cradled in thick arms; letter sweaters; a pipe-in-teeth intellectual confidence; casual sophistication. So he showed up for cocktails in a new white sweater, one that his mother had given him. Not that he had much of a wardrobe from which to choose. Paterno had just gotten out of the army. He had little money. His tuition was being paid for by a Brooklyn-born Brown alumnus who published comic books. "I still see and feel that room, those people," he said.

"I walked into a calm sea of blue blazers, sharkskin suits, and Harris Tweeds," he later wrote. "I knew I had blown something when all those cool-eyed faces turned toward me and my sweater, slowly, so as not to tip and spill their stemmed glasses that seemed to hold nothing but clear water, except for an olive in each. I heard somebody whisper, 'How did that dago get invited?' My clothes scratched at my skin and a chill surged down my insides."

Paterno would go on to become the star quarterback at Brown. At Penn State, he would be praised by *The New York Times* and *Sports Illustrated*, and even by President Nixon for his coaching abilities. And all the time he remembered his old classmates, most of whom were by then entrenched in old Boston law firms or Wall Street investment banks.

That's why Sullivan had tempted him so. It wasn't just the salary he knew he could demand. Or the piece of the team he'd been promised. It was all that being wealthy in New England implied. Paterno had grown up living in rented homes. Now he could own not just a home, but the Cape Cod retreat that "every rich Yankee kid I'd met at Brown assumed was coming to him, the same as inheriting his dad's club membership."

Not long afterward, Paterno and Sullivan met at the Plaza Hotel in New York City, halfway between their respective homes. The numbers Sullivan mentioned floored the coach, who had started at Penn State twenty-two years earlier as a $3,600-a-year assistant and was now earning $30,000 a season. Now he was offered a four-year deal, with a starting salary of $200,000 that would increase $25,000 in each year, up to $275,000 in the fourth. He'd get a $200,000 home, two cars, and, eventually, a three- to five-percent share of the franchise. The package's total worth, excluding the ownership portion, was a staggering $1.4 million.

In addition, Paterno was enamored of the cultural life that Boston offered and believed the city would be a stimulating place to raise a family. He told Sullivan he'd talk it over with his wife and that he'd give him a decision soon after his fifth-ranked Nittany Lions faced No. 2 Oklahoma in the December 31 Sugar Bowl.

"But I really wanted it," he would say later.

The coach kept mum about the proposal as he readied his team for the scary Sooners, a 13 1/2-point favorite. But someone on the Patriots' board of directors objected to the size of the salary offer Sullivan had made and leaked the story to the press. By the time Penn State arrived in New Orleans on the day after Christmas, there were whispers. *The Boston Globe* even sent a young reporter, Bob Ryan, just to trail Paterno.

That week Penn State alumni stayed near the French Quarter in the Royal Sonesta Hotel, where the coach and Sullivan would hold one of their private meetings. Nittany Lions fans who had spotted the two men began buzzing about Paterno's talk with the white-haired stranger. The rumors reached back to State College. Robert Patterson, the university's vice president for finance and operations, was dispatched to New Orleans. His mission was to keep Paterno at Penn State by getting him to agree to a long-term contract.

"I had come to Penn State in 1967 and during that time football had been so successful that it became clear it was going to be an integral part of the university and its growth," Patterson recalled. "And Joe Paterno was a key part of that. We had heard these rumors about the Patriots and we decided that the time had come to get him a contract."

Paterno, having been at Penn State since 1950, by then had been granted tenure and a full professorship in the College of Liberal Arts. But like many football coaches in that era, he continued to work year to year without a formal contract.

"I'd get paid and in July, if everyone else at the university got raises, I got a raise," he remembered. "I operated like everybody else. I never had a contract."

Paterno recalled a 1968 conversation on the subject with Bear Bryant during a ceremony at which the Penn State coach was being honored as Coach of the Year. Paterno mentioned to the legendary Alabama coach that while he had no contract, he did have tenure. Bryant looked at him like he had two heads.

"Your contract should be for five years and you ought to be able to roll it over," Bryant advised. "You ought to have a car and you ought to have a country club. You ought to have two hundred tickets—season tickets."

Bryant told the younger coach that Penn State was going to benefit enormously if he built a nationally prominent program. And Paterno's compensation package ought to reflect that.

After the Royal Sonesta meeting with Sullivan, Paterno was on the verge of accepting the job. The night before the Sugar Bowl, he asked his brother to walk with him in the French Quarter. He told George of the Patriots' offer and asked him to come along as an assistant.

"It looked as if he was seriously considering the job," said George Paterno.

Between those considerations and the ongoing discussions with Penn State's Patterson, Paterno was seriously distracted that week. His team played that way too.

Not much went right for Penn State in the Sugar Bowl. Star running back John Cappelletti came down with a stomach flu that morning and couldn't play. The Nittany Lions managed just 49 yards and 11 first downs against Chuck Fairbanks's defense. If they hadn't recovered five Oklahoma fumbles, the final score would have been a lot worse than 14–0.

The Patriots rumor ripped wide open when Paterno and Sullivan were spotted standing "a few steps apart" at the post–Sugar Bowl party. Bob Ryan's January 2 *Globe* story revealed that the two were continuing to negotiate. The holdup appeared to be a disagreement over the size of the coach's stake in the club.

The delay remained the heart of the story for days. With the NFL draft less than a month away, the pressure on Paterno to decide intensified in Boston. Several sports columnists there speculated about other possible reasons for the holdup. In 1975, after twenty-five years at the university, Paterno would become eligible for a half-salary pension, not an insignificant enticement for a college coach in that era. Others believed Paterno wanted to succeed the retiring Weeb Ewbanks with his hometown Jets. He also had a connection with Ewbanks, who had been a Rip Engle assistant when Paterno played at Brown.

The public was not aware that Paterno also had a half a dozen meetings with Patterson in the interim. Had the coach taken Bryant's advice to heart? Was he leveraging the NFL team's interest in his dicussions with Penn State?

"No," Paterno said, "I didn't use the Patriots to get more money. Obviously, I was pleased that they wanted to give me a contract, but in the end it was a very, very difficult decision for me."

It may have been the case, but Bucko Kilroy, the onetime Patriots GM, recalled that a few years later Paterno, through a Philadelphia sportswriter, let it be known that he might again be interested in the New England job. "I went down to a Holiday Inn in New Jersey and met with him," said Kilroy. "Nothing came of it but he later told me he got a good contract out of it."

Meanwhile, the reaction to the news about his possible departure had State College frantic.

Residents had come to relish the attention Paterno's program brought to their town. More than nineteen thousand postcards were sent to the coach, pleading with him to remain at Penn State. That month's edition of the local magazine *Town & Gown* had Paterno's picture on its cover, alongside the words "Joe: Don't Go Pro!" The news dominated the *Centre Daily Times* (hardly surprising, since it was competing for space with developments such as was chronicled beneath this spellbinding headline "None Hurt in Sunday Accidents").

But Paterno knew fans could be fickle. Even in State College, they'd get over his departure as soon as Penn State won its next game.

According to his hometown paper, a petition urging the coach to stay circulated among Penn State fans on a bus headed for the Sugar Bowl. Everyone on board signed. On the way back, following the Lions' shutout loss, a similar petition made the rounds. This time only five passengers put their names on it.

On Friday, January 5, New York sportswriter Dick Young reported that Paterno had accepted Sullivan's offer. The source, it later turned out, had been Sullivan himself. Paterno had phoned the owner the day before and accepted the job in principle. Sullivan agreed to send his private jet to State College that Friday, and he and Paterno were going to make it official at the Plaza.

But Paterno's vacillations intensified. One minute he wanted to go and the next he couldn't imagine leaving Penn State.

Curiously, the trip to New York City wasn't the only flight he had scheduled for that Friday morning. He had made alternate plans to fly to Pittsburgh with Patterson. They would visit with Chuck Queenan, a lawyer there who had represented Steelers quarterback Terry Bradshaw. If need be, they'd finalize his first contract with Penn State.

The night before, Thursday, January 4, Sue Paterno called their closest friends, Penn State sports information director Jim Tarman and his wife, Louise, and invited them to their house. Paterno told Tarman that he was probably going to take the NFL job and asked Tarman to come to Boston with him. "Pro ball was a dog-eat-dog business for money and you needed extremely loyal assistants, people who could protect your backside," said George Paterno.

While the Tarmans pondered the move, the two couples celebrated the Paternos' apparent good fortune with champagne toasts.

But, more so than her husband, Sue Paterno remained uncomfortable with the thought of relocating. That helped explain Paterno's continued indecision. What would the move do to his young family? He thought back to his days studying Virgil's *Aeneid*, a book that had shaped the attitudes he carried into adulthood. "When you choose wrong, as Aeneas found out," Paterno said, "life comes down on you with some terrible whacks."

The Paternos stayed up late talking. At about 3:00 A.M., his doubts seemingly resolved, perhaps by the champagne, he telephoned Patterson and told the Penn State administrator he had decided to accept the Patriots' offer.

"After I got that call, I got in touch with the pilots who were going to fly the university jet and told them we wouldn't be going to Pittsburgh the next morning," said Patterson, retired now and an affiliate professor of transportation at Penn State's Smeal College of Business.

The coach went to bed, joking to his wife in an effort to reassure her. "This will be the first time you've ever slept with a millionaire," he said. She didn't laugh.

Paterno tossed and turned in bed as he continued his mental grapplings. State College was so comfortable. He loved coaching and molding young kids. They were so hungry to learn about football and life. It wouldn't be like that in professional football. A bad season or two and he might be wishing he had never left.

"I knew damn well what it was," Paterno later wrote of the temptations pushing him toward the NFL. "The money. The house on Cape Cod. Hobnobbing with the hottest shots in a big-time town, being their hero, not having to worry, for once, about the example I have to set in a small college town, being watched by my kids. It was the only chance at a million dollars I'd ever have."

Early on the morning of January 5, he awakened his wife and told her they weren't going anywhere. Paterno reached Sullivan before the owner had departed for New York, thanked him, and turned him down. "God bless you, Joe," the owner responded. Sullivan, ironically, wound up hiring the winning coach in the Sugar Bowl, Oklahoma's Fairbanks. (Fairbanks would go 37–34 in nearly five seasons in New England. But days after his 11–4 Patriots clinched the franchise's first division title in 1978, reports surfaced that he had accepted the head-coaching job at the University of Colorado and he was fired.)

After talking with Sullivan, Paterno telephoned Tarman and Patterson.

"I guess it was about seven-thirty when he called and said he'd be staying at Penn State," recalled Patterson. "Now the flight to Pittsburgh was back on. So I called the pilots and told them to be ready shortly. They said they couldn't go now because after I had canceled the flight, they went out and got drunk. They said they needed twelve hours before they could fly again. I told them, I didn't care how they did it but I wanted that goddamned plane ready to leave in an hour."

They flew to Pittsburgh and met with Queenan.

"They showed me the contract and said, 'What do you think about this?' " Paterno recalled. "I said, 'Where do I sign?' They asked me if I didn't want my own lawyer to look at it. I said, 'No, I trust Bob Patterson.' "

While Paterno's salary has always been something of a state secret, administrators now hint that the deal he signed that day earned him about $100,000 a year. Whatever the details, and they were never made public, Paterno decided he also needed more life insurance. Patterson contacted a Pittsburgh doctor and set up a quick physical.

"Joe had been up most of the night and I didn't think it would be the best time for him to be taking a physical examination," said Patterson. "But he went ahead with it anyway and, fortunately, passed."

When Tarman learned neither he nor Paterno would be going to Boston, he set up a news conference for 10:00 A.M. Saturday in Rec Hall to deal with all the questions the university had been getting about its football coach, especially in the wake of Young's story.

Most of the sportswriters who attended were by then aware of that story and assumed the news conference had been convened as a farewell for Paterno. They were genuinely surprised when the coach, wearing a glen-plaid sport coat and seated next to President John Oswald, revealed he was staying. He told reporters that unless there were some "drastic change" at the school, he planned to remain there the rest of his career.

"I thought about the Sugar Bowl game," he told them, "and I didn't want to go out a loser."

That raised an obvious question and someone asked it.

"Joe, does that mean you'd have taken the job if you'd beaten Oklahoma?"

"That," said Paterno, "is an iffy question."

As far as anyone knew, no coach had ever been offered a $1 million contract, let alone turned it down. That fact alone made Paterno an instant national celebrity. No matter which side of the era's political divide you resided on, his decision had an unmistakable appeal.

Those who were dismayed by all the striking societal changes of the 1960s and early 1970s saw it as a reaffirmation of basic values. Here was a man who cared more for educating young people at a small-town college than making a fortune in the big city. On the other side of the political spectrum, Paterno's action was viewed in an antiestablishment light. He had turned his back on material gain, thumbed his nose at the powerful institution of the NFL.

It also gave Paterno a platform upon which he could expound on the theories he was developing about college sports. He would use it very quickly to criticize recruiting excesses, academic abuses, freshmen eligibility, the overemphasis on football, commercialization, polls, and the lack of a season-ending play-off. Writers began to characterize him as a Don Quixote figure, tilting at the sport's windmills. George Paterno used that analogy, too, when he wrote of how his older brother's rejection of the NFL had empowered him. He now possessed a moral authority that most other coaches lacked. In his late brother's words, the Penn State coach came out of the episode with "heavy artillery and a million Sanchos."

Most of those Sancho Panzas were sportswriters, who began to lather praise on the coach. In their adoring eyes, his very public display of conviction, in combination with his Grand Experiment and the run of outstanding Penn State teams, made Paterno the ideal of what a college coach should be.

National newspapers and magazines commissioned stories on this coach who had made such a startling commitment. *Sports Illustrated*'s William Johnson wrote that Paterno "did not believe that money is the root of all the fruits of life. . . . In these days when feet of clay and souls of brass seem to be the identifying marks of so many leaders, the mere fact that Joe Paterno expresses himself with an unforked tongue is apparently enough to warrant standing ovations and hero worship."

Interest in Penn State football increased in the immediate aftermath, prompting the school to make plans to enlarge Beaver Stadium again. Marketing surveys of the Nittany Lions' fan base in 2004 revealed that many of those allegiances were formed just after Paterno turned down the Patriots.

The construction of the Paterno legend was moving ahead at full throttle. And like any legend, he was credited with qualities he didn't possess. Paterno's harder-edged complexities and shortcomings—his impatience, his biting tongue, his manipulative nature—rarely came through in the aggrandizing portraits. All that most Americans could see was his nobility. He seemed single-handedly to be defending loyalty, simplicity, and virtue against the disturbing forces that were just beginning to shake sports and the wider world.

While he welcomed the attention—and the unmistakable help it gave him in recruiting and fund raising—there was a part of him that was uncomfortable. When *Sports Illustrated*'s Johnson asked him if he considered himself a "folk hero," he cringed.

"I get letters from people who seem to think that if only Joe Paterno can spend twenty minutes with a kid, then his troubles will be all over," he responded. "Nuts. People want to give me too much credit. I'm a football coach who has won a few games—remember?"

Still, grateful Pennsylvanians planned banquets to honor the coach. Requests for speaking engagements and interviews flowed into his office. Penn State even asked him to deliver its commencement address that June. Like Paterno himself, that speech was humorous, philosophical, didactic, and at times eloquent.

"W. H. Auden said it beautifully," Paterno noted in that June 16, 1973, address, "when he wrote on the death of Sigmund Freud: 'Every day there dies among us those who were doing us some good and knew it was never enough but hoped to improve a little by living.' Live your life so that by some little thing you will improve your life just by living. But be realistic enough as you continue your adventure in life to understand that regardless of how strong you are and how smart you are, you will at times become discouraged."

While Paterno was being anointed a sporting saint, it might have been left to his little hometown paper to remind his worshipful fans that not everyone had the same vision of the man.

"[He] has critics," noted a January 9, 1973, editorial in the *Centre*

Daily Times that otherwise hailed Paterno's decision to stay. "Those jealous; those who disagree with his philosophies; those who can't believe he's sincere in his outspoken stands; those who can't tolerate or understand his brutal frankness."

Paterno never did get that house on Cape Cod, although he did, years later, purchase a summer home along the New Jersey Shore. But the national reverence he came to command helped him overcome some of the bitterness he had felt about Brown. Over the years, as his prominence grew, old college classmates began to contact him or bring their children and grandchildren to visit with him in State College. The coach suddenly became an active and involved alumnus.

In 1997, Brown graduate Roger D. Williams pledged $1 million to establish a football coaching chair in Paterno's name. Two years later the coach showed up at an "off-year minireunion" to receive the William Rogers Award, recognizing "an outstanding alumna or alumnus whose service to society in general is representative of the words of the Brown Charter: living a life 'of usefulness and reputation.' "

He was among 297 who attended the Class of 1950's fiftieth reunion in the summer of 2000. Everyone knew who he was by then. There were cocktails and dinner on Friday.

On Saturday, there was a forum on leadership. Its principle speaker, dressed in a blue blazer instead of a white sweater this time, was Joseph V. Paterno of Brooklyn, still swarthy after all those years.

CHAPTER 7

THROUGH THE WIDE WINDOWS of Suite 1217 in the Sheraton Newton, downtown Boston's nighttime skyline glistened like a sequined gown. Inside the room that had been set aside for Joe Paterno's weekly media cocktail reception, several sportswriters were clustered near a wide-screen TV tuned to ESPN's Friday night college football game, Florida State versus Miami. Bowls filled with salty snacks sat untouched atop tables. Little blue flames lapped at the bottom of silver trays brimming with meatballs and chicken tenders. The small towers of plates and napkins flanking the food had not yet been disturbed.

Away in a far corner, as alone and unnoticed as a wallflower, stood a portable bar. A bored young bartender absentmindedly rolled an empty glass in his hand as Jeff Nelson, Penn State's sports-information director, approached. Without pausing—apparently without even thinking—Nelson reached out to adjust a bottle of Jack Daniel's, its black-and-white seal unbroken, its fetching amber contents untouched.

It was 9:30 P.M. on September 10. Penn State's traveling party had arrived at the hotel, which sat atop a Mass Pike overpass, a half hour earlier. The Nittany Lions would be playing Boston College the next night at eight, in a nationally televised game in nearby Chestnut Hill.

Every Friday night in football season, home or away, Paterno and the sportswriters who regularly covered his team—three or four in the early years, dozens now—assembled informally for drinks, snacks, and off-the-record conversation. The receptions had been a significant ritual for as long as Paterno had coached at Penn State. When Paterno first got the head-coaching job, he and Jim Tarman, the future Penn State AD who was then the sports-information director, had traveled around the East with a suitcase full of liquor, selling Penn State football. The format worked. The happily lubricated newsmen wrote glowingly of the bright young coach and his Grand Experiment.

Soon the traveling shows morphed into the Friday-night affairs. The first of those were held at Tarman's State College home, where Paterno and several writers would drink and talk for hours. Eventually, they moved to Paterno's house, then graduated to the Toftrees Hotel and Resort and later the Nittany Lion Inn. On the road, they always took place at the team hotel.

Nelson, a slight, bespectacled and extremely efficient forty-three-year-old who had been at the university for eleven years, was familiar with the road routine. Arriving at their destination on Friday night, the coach, his assistants, and players would collect their room keys and gather in a ballroom or conference room for a quick meeting. Then, usually before 10:00, Paterno would head for the reception.

The Jack Daniel's was for the coach. A glass or two of the Tennessee sippin' whiskey whittled away some of his harder edges. It also loosened his tongue. No subject was off limits during these informal sessions. He'd discuss with the writers freshmen redshirts, Republican politics, the literature of ancient Rome.

Occasionally, Paterno, who could be unusually glib even without whiskey, got burned by the format. In the late 1970s, when asked, not for the first or last time, if he were interested in entering politics, the coach said, "What, and leave college coaching to the [Barry] Switzers and [Jackie] Sherrills?"

The remark, disparaging the prominent Oklahoma and Pittsburgh coaches for suspect academic and ethical practices in their programs, turned up in *The New York Times* and elsewhere. Though the response actually served to further set him apart from the run-of-the-mill renegades in college coaching, it upset and embarrassed Paterno enough that he briefly boycotted the Friday-night receptions.

Typically, though, both sides benefited. The sportswriters got some valuable insights, saw and heard another side of the coach. And Paterno clearly enjoyed the give-and-take. He liked the Jack Daniel's too. For decades, one of the bags that Tarman and his successors brought on road trips contained a bottle of the coach's preferred sour-mash whiskey.

On this night, a few of the early arriving writers in 1217 nibbled on peanuts or popcorn. They wandered over to the bar, ordering beer, water, or diet soda. No one dared ask for a Jack Daniel's.

Several of them had come from a dinner hosted by Boston College in a Legal Sea Foods restaurant at a nearby mall. The conversation there had focused on Paterno and his future. Boston writers remarked on how impressed they had been with the seventy-seven-year-old Paterno's recall during their teleconference with the coach earlier in the week.

Whenever the suite's door opened, they all turned their heads, thinking it might be the coach. Paterno, who rarely missed one of the receptions, had been absent the week before, but that was only because of a conflict with the season-opening Beaver Stadium pep rally. The writers, who hadn't had an off-the-record crack at him in more than nine months, were eager to talk.

Maybe he'd clear up some of the lingering uncertainty about his future. That seemed to be the only Penn State topic their editors were interested in these days anyway. Despite their surface cynicism, as much a necessity of their trade as tape recorders and laptops, these dozen or so sportswriters relished the intimate sessions—for personal and professional reasons. The privilege of one-on-one conversations with a coaching legend lent them and their jobs a little cachet. And because Paterno increasingly limited access, they were essential for keeping informed. On the record, Paterno answered questions for only about fifteen minutes after games and thirty minutes during Tuesday teleconferences, one question for each reporter. That was it. You couldn't even try to catch him at the locker-room door after games without being shooed away by the sports-information staff.

Asked about Paterno's ever-more-restrictive rules and his diminishing availability, a Penn State marketing official hinted that the coach had lost trust. He compared the media to "attack dogs" and said "it only takes a few [bites] to make the fence go up."

Most of Penn State's beat writers fell into two categories: young and ambitious, or old and crusty. With very few exceptions, they were—and always had been—white men. Penn State was, for many of them, their only connection to big-time sports. The rest of the year most of them covered high school games for papers in small- and mid-size towns like Lewistown, Carlisle, or York. They derived a large measure of pride from their association with Penn State, from writing articles their readers craved about the Nittany Lions' exploits, from having a drink with Paterno on football Friday nights. A few years on the beat and some began to feel they had a stake in Penn State football.

But with all the recent losses, their jobs had become more unpleasant. Paterno frequently was disagreeable and difficult, making himself and his players unavailable, increasingly snapping at their questions. Asked earlier in the week to explain his decision to start Robinson as a wideout against Akron, he said simply, "I thought it would help the team."

Readers and editors badgered the writers constantly, wanting to know what was going to happen to the coach. Would he stay even after another disastrous season? Were Penn State administrators pondering ways to push him aside? Were powerful alumni calling for his head? What the hell was going on?

As the relaxed writers continued to grouse and graze, they traded a variety of speculations, some half-baked, some plausible. The opening-week's victory over Akron had done little to quiet the buzz about Paterno.

Did you hear, said one, that the coach's four-year contract extension had been a reward for his agreeing to replace Ganter and take some authority away from Jay?

Another had been told that if this season turned sour, administrators were prepared to urge Paterno's wife to try to persuade her husband to step down.

"Big Penn State donors" among his readership informed another writer that Paterno planned to bow out at season's end if the Nittany Lions were at all successful.

At 9:55, the coach still had not shown up and the writers began checking their watches.

"Is he coming tonight?" asked Jerry Kellar, an ex–offensive lineman at Temple and now a *Wilkes-Barre Times Leader* columnist.

"Sue's on this trip with him," said Nelson. "But as far as I know he's coming."

By 10:30, the room was more crowded. A few writers who had been to dinner in downtown Boston arrived, and were surprised to learn that the coach had not. For a while, the Florida State–Miami game was interesting enough to distract their attention from his absence.

"If he's not here by now, he's probably not coming," Nelson finally offered during a commercial.

That led to more questions. Why would he not show up two weeks in a row? Was he ticked off by all the criticism he and his trouble-prone players had taken in the media the previous season, all the calls for him to resign? Or was this a further indication that he wasn't going to be bound by the old routines anymore?

"Maybe Sue won't let him come," said one writer.

Finally, at around 11:00, one by one, the sportswriters began to depart.

Nelson scurried around the room, collecting empty glasses, brushing popcorn crumbs off the sofa. The bartender, his still idle hands folded behind his back, remained at his post.

The bottle of Jack Daniel's remained untouched.

Earlier that day, gray and bald heads had populated every window of the King Coal tour bus that sped north on Route 84, along the stretch of Connecticut River that runs between Hartford and Springfield. They were Nittany Lions fans on a weekend trip, en route to the next night's game. Most were retirees who had come from used-up towns in Pennsylvania's anthracite coal region, places like Shamokin, Mount Carmel, and Ashland.

Paterno, for generations, had mined the rich vein of scholastic talent found in the state's gritty blue-collar towns. In particular, the close-knit communities in northeast Pennsylvania's coal country and those in the hills and valleys surrounding Pittsburgh had yielded him a mother lode of talent. The sons of hard-nosed coal miners, and rail and steel-workers, were as tough as their names implied—Mike Munchak (Scranton), Jack Ham (Johnstown), Ted Kwalick (McKees Rocks), Denny Onkotz (Northampton). But when the industries that employed their parents began to disappear or relocate, the jobs vanished. The population aged. The small-town high schools consolidated. The state's economy stagnated.

Homestead, an old steel town southeast of Pittsburgh, was a good example. In 1950, the town had twenty thousand residents and its huge steel mill employed fourteen thousand workers. The mill closed in 1982. In 2004, Homestead's population was about four thousand, many of them elderly.

Only the retirement haven of Florida had a greater percentage of elderly residents than weary Pennsylvania. That demographic shift, triggered by a changing economy, had begun to affect Paterno's pro-gram. There simply weren't as many quality players in the state. And those there were were nearly as likely to go to a Big Ten rival or a Florida school as to Penn State.

On Saturday night, Boston College would dress twelve Pennsyl-vanians.

"It's not the hotbed it used to be," Paterno explained. "You take the Johnstown area. . . . When I came here, there would be six or seven players that we would like to have. There might be three or four Notre Dame or Pitt or Michigan or Ohio State would want. There won't be two or three there anymore. What happened was a lot of the little coal towns joined together as one school. Where you used to have five schools with maybe sixty kids each out for football—three hundred kids—now you might have one joint school with fifty kids out."

In 2004, you could, in fact, argue that Paterno had much in com-mon with his adopted home state. Each had a glorious past, a depress-ing present, and an uncertain future. A rapidly changing world seemed intent on making both irrelevant.

Penn State did not reveal any statistical data about its fan base. But if the weekly Beaver Stadium crowds provided an accurate reading, it, too, was graying rapidly. "If you were thirty or forty when that bond occurred [with Penn State football in the late 1960s and early 1970s], you're seventy-plus," marketer Guido D'Elia noted. "We have a very high attrition rate we have to deal with." Those on the tour bus certainly were Paterno's contemporaries. They continued to appreciate the man who had brought so much glory to their sons, their hometowns, their state. As such, they were less inclined to criticize the coach than the school's students, or the more casual Penn State fans in Philadelphia and Pittsburgh.

They longed to be impressed and the previous week's victory over Akron had encouraged them as much as the bookies. Las Vegas had upgraded the Nittany Lions into a two-point favorite over Boston College, even though they had not won a nonconference road game since beating Miami in 1999.

Many of the old-timers on the bus had been at Beaver Stadium the week before. That big victory had felt reassuringly familiar—particularly the explosive offense. Two 100-yard-plus tailbacks brought back memories of Lydell Mitchell and Franco Harris. Tony Hunt's 77-yard TD gallop on the season's second play recalled Curt Warner. And not one but two quarterbacks had great days—Mills and Robinson running, catching, and throwing for touchdowns.

That couldn't possibly have been a mirage, could it?

Paterno had pinpointed the last Boston College game as the beginning of the end for his 2003 Penn State team. He had mentioned it so often in the spring and summer and now during this week of preparation that his players had begun to talk about exacting some revenge.

A year ago, after an opening-game victory over Temple, Penn State hosted BC, the two Eastern teams' first meeting since 1992. The Eagles exploded for three first-quarter touchdowns in a physically dominating 27–14 victory. What would become the worst season in Paterno's career was off and crawling.

"They laughed at us last year, basically," Michael Robinson said. "[With a 21–0 lead] the game started to seem like it was a joke to them. They really handed it to us. I'm not going to say they relaxed, but they were like the game was over. We all remember. We've got to go up there and play Penn State football and see what happens."

Sophomore linebacker Tim Shaw said, "[This week's game] is a little bit of a payback."

Paterno and his assistants had used the game as motivation. When players erred in practice, he told them they obviously didn't recall the butt-whipping BC had administered a year ago. It may have been as thorough a physical and psychological beating, he reminded them, as any Penn State team had endured in their lifetimes.

"There is no question, as I look back on last year's game with Boston College, that we didn't measure up physically in a tough football game," Paterno told reporters that week. "We have . . . to get that out of our craw."

All that strong talk struck BC coach Tom O'Brien as a little odd. Hadn't Penn State lost nine times in '03? What about the other eight defeats? Were they somehow more acceptable? It wasn't like his Eagles had been pathetic. Their 8–5 season concluded with a victory over Colorado State in the San Francisco Bowl, making them the only school in the nation to have won bowl games in each of the last four years.

"It sounds like they blamed their loss against us for their whole year last year," said O'Brien. "Reading all the stuff, it seems like Boston College is the whole reason they went three-and-nine."

The desire to make a statement against BC may also have served to divert the players from two deaths that hit the Penn State football family. That week sophomore cornerback Darian Hardy's father had died of cancer. And the fourteen-year-old nephew of tight end Isaac Smolko was killed in a bicycle accident in Alabama.

In the past two years, Paterno and his team had seemed to suffer a near nonstop run of death. He had lost his brother, George, who had been the color analyst on Penn State radio broadcasts for years, to a heart attack in 2002; that same year, Ganter's wife, Karen, fifty-three, had died of a sudden brain aneurysm, falling dead in her kitchen as she and her husband talked; Kevin Dare, the brother of cornerback Eric and a fellow Penn State student, had died in a pole-vaulting accident during track practice; and just a few months earlier, Kevin Baugh had been murdered.

Time on the football field became their respite from tragedy. And another victory would heal them further.

The Eagles had opened this season with a 19–11 road victory, but because it came against a Ball State team that went 4–8 in 2003, no one was quite sure what it signified. As Paterno prepared for the game, the matchup that most concerned him was BC's athletic defensive line against his still-inconsistent offensive front. Boston College had registered five sacks in its opener, led by the large and talented Mathias Kiwanuka's two. Junior tackle Andrew Richardson would be matched up with Kiwanuka.

"I think Andrew will do a good job," Paterno predicted. "I thought he did a good job last week and I think he will get better. He and Levi Brown are a little bit in the same category as some of the defensive linemen were last year. A lot of them were young, new, and had to play themselves into being a little bit better. I think Andrew will get better. He has a tough job this week. Obviously, we're going to try to help him in the schemes we're going to use. We're not going to hang him out there and say, 'Hey, if you don't get it done, we don't get it done.' We're going to, obviously, change up on things. . . . He's a smart kid and a good athlete. He's a tough kid. Playing against somebody as good as this kid is will make him even better eventually."

In private, though, Paterno and his staff looked for ways to get the more elusive Robinson more snaps at quarterback, something they hoped might counter BC's anticipated pass-rush. Robinson had had four carries, four passes, and three receptions against Akron. Penn State had to get the ball more often to its only game-breaker.

"If you get the ball in his hands, he can run over you, run around you, you can throw it to him short and you can throw it to him downfield," said Paterno. "You can put him in the backfield and he can be a tailback. You can put him in at quarterback and take Mills and put him outside. Michael Robinson gives you a lot of options."

Penn State got some good news when they learned that freshman BC tailback L. V. Whitworth, who had accumulated 129 yards on twenty-one carries versus Ball State, would miss the game with a knee injury. But quarterback Paul Peterson, a twenty-four-year-old ex–Mormon mission-ary who had transferred from BYU, worried Paterno with his poise, his mobility, and his ability to throw on the run.

After what he termed "a good week of practice," Paterno and his team flew to Boston Friday night. Trips there were always bittersweet for him. He remembered the good times he'd had in that city as a post-war student at Brown, "chasing the girls," or going to Fenway Park to watch Ted Williams hit.

But it also brought to mind what might have been. He could have owned a piece of the New England Patriots—perhaps as much five percent—had he accepted Billy Sullivan's coaching offer in 1972. The Patriots were now valued at $756 million by *Forbes*. Five percent of that would be more than $37.5 million.

Paterno's past was peppered with Boston connections. After high school, the future coach nearly had gone to Jesuit-run Boston College. "I went to a Jesuit high school. My dad wanted me to go to a Catholic college and the Jesuits all wanted me to go to Boston College, Ford-ham, or maybe Georgetown," he said. "I decided that I just didn't want to go up there." He had also been accepted into Boston University's law school and had planned to attend until Engle offered him the job as a Penn State assistant in 1950.

Asked during the summer when he had last thought about possibly abandoning coaching for the law, Paterno laughed. "Last year," he said.

The Penn State traveling party had arrived at the Sheraton Newton at 9:00 P.M. Friday. Paterno believed strongly in the power of a good night's sleep. That's why he insisted his teams stay in Newton, in a lo-cale separated from—and nearly devoid of—any of Boston's charm, history, culture, or nightlife.

The players disembarking from the two buses were dressed in suits or sport coats and wearing ties. Paterno and several of the assis-tants and administrators who made the trip had on the familiar blue blazers. Seven true freshmen—quarterback Morelli, defensive tackle Robinson, linebacker Connor, offensive tackle Harrison, receiver Mark Rubin, kicker Patrick Humes, and tight end Jordan Lyons—had made the trip. Their number was further evidence that Paterno's desperation had caused him to rethink his core philosophies, though the coach adamantly continued to insist that was not the case.

"I don't know where you get that business about I was always reluctant to play freshmen. I always get a kick out of that," he said at one point. "If they are good enough, you play them. I have always felt that way. . . . I have never been reluctant to play the best kids we have."

He was, however, reluctant to play those who missed or were late to meetings. And the previous Monday, Austin Scott, already brooding about losing his starting tailback spot to Tony Hunt, showed up late for a running-backs meeting and was absent for a full-squad meeting. His behavior was especially curious because, following the Akron game, Scott had apologized to the team for failing to show up for some preseason meetings. Paterno made him practice with the scout squad and told him he wouldn't line up at tailback against Boston College.

"Yeah, I'm upset with Austin, he missed a meeting," said Paterno when a newspaper later revealed the real reason for the tailback's benching against BC.

Scott would blame the incidents on a faulty alarm clock. "I have a backup plan," he later explained. "I bought an extra alarm clock, call people, tell them to call me at certain times just in case my alarm clocks don't go off. There's no reason to miss anything in the future."

Whenever he was asked about Penn State's recent decline, Paterno would bristle. The bad records, he frequently implied, were the results of bad breaks. He never failed to point out that as recently as 2002 his Lions were only a few questionable officiating calls from a Bowl Championship Series berth.

There was some justification in his complaint. If instant replay had been around to overturn a series of costly and apparently erroneous late calls that went against them in losses to Ohio State, Iowa, and Michigan— the latter two in overtime—the Lions might well have ended that regular season 12–0. Stung as badly as Paterno was by the controversy his reaction to those calls created, the Big Ten had decided to become the first major conference to utilize instant replay for its 2004 schedule.

Had it been in effect for the game against Boston College, which attracted a sellout crowd of 44,500 to Alumni Stadium, Paterno might not have had to sprint up the sideline to scream at an official early in the first quarter.

The Nittany Lions appeared to have stopped BC's initial drive. But Hardy, recently returned from his father's funeral, was whistled for running into punter Johnny Ayers. Despite the fact that replays appeared to show Hardy tipping the kick, Boston College had a gift first down on its 46.

To some extent, Paterno's increasingly aggressive sideline behavior had become illustrative of the state of his program. Except for those moments when he paused to watch a play unfold, he could no longer stand still during games. He moved constantly within a 50- or 60-yard range, walking out his anxieties, his curiosity, and, with ever-increasing frequency, his frustrations. It's as if he had become a human version of the explosives-rigged bus in the film *Speed*. Stopping would be a catastrophe.

He didn't wear a headset but frequently went charging after assistants who did to demand some change or ask what had gone wrong on a busted play. When the offensive or defensive teams gathered around their coaches, Paterno would come bursting into their midst like a bouncer hurrying to break up a fight. And, after good plays and bad, he wore his emotions on his sleeve. To a lesser degree, he had been behaving that way for decades. But in the amosphere of defeat that had shrouded his program in recent years, his sideline habits appeared more desperate, more edgy, more pathetic.

The roughing-the-kicker flag infuriated Paterno. He rushed toward the Big Ten referee working the game, gesturing frantically as he spat out his displeasure.

"He said the umpire didn't think it was tipped," Paterno explained of the conversation. "Everybody else . . . I think the other officials thought it was tipped. I don't know, you'd have to ask them. We thought it was tipped, obviously."

He continued to fume right through Boston College's next three plays, which produced a minus-2 yards and led to another Ayers punt—and another roughing-the-kicker penalty. This one, though, on linebacker Posluszny, was clearly a violation.

With a third chance, BC capitalized, a bootlegging Peterson hitting tight end David Kashetta on a 6-yard scoring pass that gave the Eagles a 7–0 lead.

At that point, Paterno went back into his positive-reinforcement mode, clapping as he paced, seeking out players for reassuring taps on their butts and backs.

Early in the second quarter, a Mills interception triggered what would become a series of turnovers. Junior defensive back Calvin Lowry recovered an A. J. Brooks fumble. But three plays later, senior fullback Paul Jefferson lost the ball after a pass reception. Shortly afterward, Peterson hit Grant Adams on a 26-yard TD pass. BC led 14–0 and Paterno looked glum again.

Against much better competition this week, Penn State's offense appeared overmatched. Its receivers looked slow, rarely got any separation, and dropped passes. So desperate was Paterno for a wideout that he began utilizing—and calling plays for—Brendan Perretta, a five-foot-seven walk-on redshirt freshman.

As for the offensive line, it couldn't get any push against the BC front. As a result, Mills, who would play exclusively at QB this night, was under constant pressure and Hunt looked like a different back than he had against Akron.

If that weren't distressing enough for all those Penn State fans occupying a corner of renovated Alumni Stadium, as well as those watching on ABC, there was a reoccurrence of the sideline-coaching indecision that had been so troubling in recent seasons.

"I'm glad I'm on the field and not on the sideline with all the chaos," Mills had said earlier. "It's pretty comical sometimes."

Down by two touchdowns, facing a fourth-and-1 at the BC 48 with just over a minute left in the first half, Penn State appeared to have little choice but to go for it. And that was the initial indication from the sideline. But suddenly, with the clock running, Paterno and his coaches began a heated discussion. With fifty seconds left, and the play clock winding down, the Lions signaled for a time-out.

Somehow, the initial decision was reversed and Paterno sent the punt team out. Boston College got the ball back and held on until halftime.

"What does that say about the state of Penn State football," *Boston Herald* columnist Michael Gee noted to colleagues in the press box, "when the coaches feel like they can't even make one yard when they have to?"

The indecision, the confusion, the wasted seconds, the lack of faith, all suggested a crisis in confidence along the Penn State sideline.

"I didn't want to punt it right away and give them a couple chances—you don't know what can happen. A punt can be blocked," Paterno would explain after the game. "I did debate going for it but then I figured if we don't make it, in two plays it's a field goal and then we're three [scores] down. I knew we were getting the ball in the second half and I thought we could get a couple of scores."

But if they were initially thinking about keeping the ball, why did they let the clock run down?

"If we were going to give it to them, I wanted to give it to them with as little time as I could," Paterno said.

Then why the time-out?

"I wanted to make sure that we were all on the same page. To make sure that the kids knew not to get careless where it could be blocked or could be returned, because they're a good return team."

Rather than scream at the ineffective offense, Paterno and Hall tried to stay positive at halftime.

"Coach Hall brings a little bit more laid-back attitude toward us," said Robinson. "He told us that when things don't go our way, we can't panic."

The relaxed approach appeared to work. Mills—wearing a T-shirt honoring the memory of high school teammate Billy Gaines, who had died in an alcohol-related fall the previous June—completed all five passes on Penn State's first second-half drive. The last was a 13-yard touchdown to fifth-year senior wideout Ryan Scott that cut BC's lead in half, 14–7.

It was the first career reception for Scott, a native of Renton, Washington, who lacked a wideout's speed. He had been one of those fifth-year seniors Paterno urged to leave after 2003. Instead, he pleaded for a last chance, had a superb spring and Blue-White Game, and now was contributing.

"He said, 'Coach, I think I'm better than you think I am,' " Paterno recalled.

Scott's catch animated the Penn State sideline and all those Nittany Lions fans who, in the absence of a huge parking lot on BC's cramped campus, had spent the afternoon grilling on tiny patches of the college green.

But the joy didn't last long. Boston College responded with a 74-yard scoring drive on its first possession of the half, Peterson capping it with his third touchdown pass, a 2-yarder to tight end Mark Palmer. It was 21–7. And 14 points looked like an awfully large deficit for this Penn State offense.

Indeed, neither team would score again. Mills's interceptions would end three of the Lions' next four drives. That gave him a Penn State–record-tying four in the game—one fewer than he threw in all of '03. Overall, Penn State turned the ball over five times that night.

"He was under a lot of pressure," Paterno said of his quarterback. "Really, they did a good job with that. They were putting a lot of pressure on him with only four guys coming. So you know it wasn't like he had some people that he could go to. . . . And obviously, when we were down and somebody had to make a play, he might have forced the ball a couple times, but that was just because he was trying to make a play."

As Paterno had feared, Peterson's elusiveness was a sizable advantage. He ran seven times for 27 yards and completed twenty-three of thirty-one passes for 199 yards and three touchdowns. The injured Whitworth's backup, Andre Callender, finished with 114 yards on twenty-seven carries. For Penn State, meanwhile, Hunt collected 52 yards on fourteen carries as the Lions could manage only 73 yards on the ground. A wide-open Phillips had mishandled a pass at the BC 5, one of several more drops by wide receivers. And despite all the talk about increasing Robinson's workload, the junior was involved in only nine plays—four carries for 35 yards and five receptions for another 54. The final score was 21–7.

Asked if he were comfortable with his star playing such a limited role, Paterno was vague. "They did a good job on some things. I think we'll make some adjustments. I wouldn't want to say we're going to do exactly what we've done, but I think we'll make some adjustments."

Following the Lions' sixth consecutive road loss, Paterno looked old and tired as, just before midnight, he walked into the postgame news conference. One writer described his demeanor as a mix of "puzzlement, discouragement, and dejection." Even the coach's surroundings here were funereal. In the Skating Lobby of Kelly Rink, which adjoined the stadium, black drapes had been fixed to the podium table and the wall behind for his news conference.

Paterno cradled his head in his right hand and answered questions in a tone dripping with disappointment.

"They just played better than we did," he began. "They played hard. They played very well. Now I'll have to look at the tapes. We obviously didn't block them very well. They didn't do anything fancy. They beat us. . . . I tried to tell people, you know, we weren't home free because we beat Akron. That's not to take anything away from Akron. I think I said that to everybody else. But BC played very well. We did not play well. I thought we were ready to play well.

"We turned the ball over, what, four, five times? You can't win games with five turnovers. What'd we get? One? And they get five. You can't win. . . . I don't have all the answers right now. I've got to go home and look at tape and look at people, see if maybe we've got to change some people."

At this point Paterno hid Austin Scott's punishment from the media, insisting that the tailback hadn't played because "right now [Hunt] is a little better."

The coach was called immediately on what seemed to be a disingenuous response. Even if that were the case, why in the fourth quarter had he used senior Mike Gasparato, the No. 3 tailback on the depth chart, instead of Scott?

"Hunt took himself out and we were throwing the football, and Mike's a little better at pass protection [than Scott]," he said.

Though it was only one loss, Paterno's mood indicated that, in this feeble Lions effort, he may have been able to glimpse more.

CHAPTER 8

IT FINALLY GOT TO PATERNO at the end of the 1973 season. The pollsters might be willing to continue to overlook his team, but he would not.

So after Penn State beat LSU, 16–9, in the Orange Bowl, he had an annoucement for the reporters who gathered outside his locker room that night.

"This was the best team I've ever coached," he told them. "We have as much right to claim the top place as anyone else. We're undefeated. . . . I have my own poll, the Paterno poll. I took the vote a few minutes ago and the vote was unanimous: Penn State is number one."

Then, when he got home to State College, the coach ordered rings for his team. Before graduation that spring, he presented them to his players. It was a gesture that displayed the coach's generosity as well as his frustration.

"I still wear mine," said Tom Shuman, that 1973 team's quarterback. "It doesn't say we were national champions but it's got my name on it, our record, a replica of the Orange Bowl trophy. It was a nice gesture, and to be honest with you, it was kind of fitting since all of us felt like we were as good as any team in the country that year."

Paterno's 1973 Nittany Lions won all twelve of their games. They won them by an average of 26 points. They averaged 40 points in eleven regular-season victories and yielded under 11. They rushed for a phenomenal 2,994 yards. They had the Heisman Trophy winner. They had ten players selected in the next NFL draft. They had seven defensive players who would be drafted.

And they finished fifth in the polls.

In that season's final Associated Press rankings, Penn State ended up behind, in order, Notre Dame, Ohio State, Oklahoma, and Alabama. Alabama, upset by Notre Dame in the Sugar Bowl, topped United Press International's list, which was calculated before the bowl games and also had Penn State fifth.

His third perfect season had been accomplished with a conservative, straightforward style that would be linked to Paterno forever, even after his wide-open 1994 team averaged 47 points a game. The Nittany Lions ran the ball four times as often as they threw it—643 rushing attempts to 161 passes. Shuman was a competent replacement for John Hufnagel, but the rush-heavy offense would limit him to just 83 completions on the season.

"I was the question mark that season," said Shuman.

Defensively, Penn State was loaded again with smart and aggressive players like Ed O'Neil, Mike Hartenstine, and Randy Crowder. The unit was so deep, in fact, that O'Neil's backup was Greg Buttle, a future all-American and NFL star.

By the end of that season, Paterno was wondering what he had to do to win a national title. His teams had won 62 of their last 68 games. They'd finished in the top ten of the Associated Press polls every year but one (1970, when the 7–3 Lions were 18th). They'd been perfect three times in six years, produced all-Americans and NFL all-stars. And yet there appeared to be a sizable portion of the college-football world that continued to classify Penn State football as inferior.

Part of it, of course, was a perception problem. For all its success, Penn State was still something of an interloper. Paterno and his program had not yet gained admission into the elite group of college-football powers that included Alabama, Ohio State, Texas, USC, Notre Dame, and Nebraska. Since 1960, those six schools had won every national title.

It was Paterno's misfortune that his unbeaten seasons had coincided with perfect years by three of them—Ohio State in 1968, Texas in 1969, and Notre Dame in 1973. At that stage of their coach's career, the Nittany Lions weren't ever going to win a beauty contest with those schools.

"The sportswriters at the time, for whatever reason, just didn't want to give Penn State much credit," said Shuman.

Then there was the issue of its schedule, dominated as it was by eastern competition. Except for Penn State, no eastern team had finished in the top ten since 1963. Army, Navy, Pitt, and Syracuse were in a downward spiral from their glory days. In 1973, the Lions played Stanford, Iowa, and North Carolina State, but also Maryland, Syracuse, West Virginia, Pitt, Ohio U, and all three service academies.

Most of the sportswriters and coaches who voted in the national polls rarely saw Penn State. They could judge them only by the level of their competition. And, in most of their minds, there was no way eastern schools and the service academies matched up with teams from the Big Ten, the Pac Ten, the Big Eight, or the Southeastern and Southwest Conferences.

"We all felt like we could've beaten Notre Dame that year," said O'Neil, who, along with his teammates, had watched the Irish's victory in the Sugar Bowl, played on December 31 that year, the night before the Lions beat LSU in the Orange Bowl. "But we never got a chance. What could we do?"

What Penn State could do was upgrade the schedule. And as a result of his 1973 disappointment, Paterno decided to do just that. There would be home-and-home dates with Ohio State in 1975–76 and with Miami in 1976–77. Before the decade was over, Penn State would play SWC teams like Texas A & M, SMU, and TCU, and Big Eight foes like Nebraska and Missouri. And eastern football, thanks to Pitt's recruitment of Tony Dorsett, a player Paterno didn't land because he wouldn't guarantee him that he'd start as a freshman, soon took a big step forward.

As frustrating as 1973 was, the year did provide Penn State with an enormous amount of positive publicity—and victory in at least one national poll.

Tailback John Cappelletti became the school's first and only Heisman Trophy winner. Even though voters in the Southwest had Cappelletti fifth on their collective ballots, his election proved Penn State could win a nationwide vote.

As impressive as Cappelletti's 1973 numbers were (1,522 yards, 17 touchdowns), it wasn't a banner year for Heisman candidates. His vote total was more than double that of runner-up John Hicks, an offensive lineman from Ohio State, and the third-place finisher, running back Roosevelt Leaks of Texas. Kansas QB David Jaynes was fourth. (The best-known name among the top ten that year was Ohio State's sophomore running back Archie Griffin, who would capture the Heisman the next two seasons.)

In the long run, though, what may have helped Penn State's program as much as the Heisman was Cappelletti's acceptance of it.

A tough but tender-hearted running back from suburban Philadelphia, he received the award on December 13, 1973, at a banquet in the New York Hilton. His touching speech not only moved the nation and precipitated both a book and a television movie, it also added to Paterno's growing mystique.

Cappelletti's speech made the front page of every sports section in America and was featured on the three networks' weekend newscasts. That was the nation's first up-close glimpse of a Penn State player, and it only confirmed the positive image of Paterno that had arisen two years earlier when he rejected the Patriots' lucrative offer.

The night of the award presentation, Paterno was sitting just to the right of Cappelletti when the tailback tearfully dedicated the trophy to his younger brother, Joey, who was dying from leukemia. Speaking from a text he had composed with his older brother, Marty, a Temple journalism graduate, and which had been reviewed by *Philadelphia Inquirer* columnist Bill Lyon, Cappelletti began his memorable talk by thanking his parents and his coach at Monsignor Bonner High School. Then he turned to Paterno, telling the large audience of his family's first encounter with the coach.

"When he came in the door, he looked over, and on the couch was my brother, Joseph, lying there," said Cappelletti. "He was very ill at the time, more so than usual . . . and coach Paterno was more concerned and talked more about what he could do for my brother than what he could do to get me at Penn State. . . .

"I think everyone here knows mostly about his coaching accomplishments at Penn State. His record is a great one, probably the greatest in the country. . . . [But] he's more concerned with young people after they get out of school than when they are in school—what he can do for them to make better lives for them. . . . I don't think there is a more dedicated man anywhere concerned with young people and a better teacher of life on and off the field."

After mentioning his Penn State teammates and backfield coach Bob Phillips, Cappelletti commenced the paragraph that would cement his place in both Heisman lore and popular culture.

"The youngest member of my family, Joseph, is very ill," he began, sobs halting his words, tears rolling from his eyes as he tried not to look at the table where his family, including Joey, sat. "He has leukemia. If I can dedicate this trophy to him tonight and give him a couple of days of happiness, this is worth everything. I think a lot of people think that I go through a lot on Saturdays and during the week as most athletes do, and you get your bumps and bruises and it is a terrific battle out there on the field. Only, for me, it is on Saturdays and it's only in the fall. For Joseph, it is all year round, and it is a battle that is unending with him, and he puts up with much more than I'll ever put up with, and I think that this trophy is more his than mine because he has been a great inspiration to me."

The nation first had learned about eleven-year-old Joey Cappelletti and his illness a few months earlier. At that time, the Penn State tailback had promised his ailing brother four touchdowns in the game closest to his birthday, against West Virginia on October 27. He had scored three times before Paterno, always reluctant to pile it on an opponent, pulled his star in the second half of what would be a 62–14 rout. Teammates who knew of Cappelletti's pledge informed the coach. Paterno reinserted him. Cappelletti soon had his fourth touchdown and Joey his birthday gift.

When the Heisman winner's speech was complete, sobs were audible in the Hilton ballroom. Vice President Gerald Ford, who during his stumbling talk had called the Heisman winner "Joe Cappelletti" and his coach "my good friend John Fraterno," was crying. O'Neil, his hard-nosed teammate and closest friend, said he "couldn't find the strength in my legs to stand up" for the ovation that followed. Paterno, for one of the rare times in public, removed his glasses and dabbed at his eyes.

Finally, Bishop Fulton Sheen, the charismatic Catholic prelate whose TV show had been a nationwide phenomenon in the 1950s, rose to deliver a blessing.

"Maybe for the first time in your lives you have heard a speech from the heart and not from the lips," he said. "Part of John's triumph was made by Joseph's sorrow. You don't need a blessing. God has already blessed you in John Cappelletti."

Less than three years later, with his big brother at his bedside, Joey Cappelletti died.

Later on the night of the banquet, at a Penn State reception in a Hilton penthouse, Paterno and Patriots owner Billy Sullivan met again.

"Do you see now why I couldn't leave?" Paterno asked him.

"Yes," said Sullivan, "I think I do."

No one would have wanted it that way, of course, but when the book *Something for Joey* appeared and later was transformed into the highest-rated TV movie of 1977, Paterno's reputation expanded again.

Suddenly, this coach who already was reputed to be the embodiment of all that was good about college sports was a central figure in a story that ranked with *Brian's Song* and *Pride of the Yankees* among the most memorably inspirational sports films ever.

The Cappelletti episode became part of the growing Paterno mythology, along with his Grand Experiment, his principled stands against football corruption, his attachment to Penn State, and, of course, his simple values, perhaps best exemplified by the uniforms his players wore.

In fact, perhaps more than any single element of his career, it was Penn State's plain blue-and-white uniforms that came to define Paterno in the decades that would follow.

Oddly enough for a school that has become renowned for its ultraconservative attire, Penn State's original colors—as selected by a three-student panel in 1887—were pink and black. The first cheer for a Penn State football team went:

Yah! Yah! (Pause) Yah! Yah! Yah!
Wish. Wack. Pink. Black.
P-S-C.

But perspiration, repeated washings, and sun exposure quickly faded the pink to white. Soon blue and white replaced pink and black, and in 1890, the school's new colors were officially born.

Penn State's uniforms were colorless even before Paterno took over. Photos from the 1948 Cotton Bowl reveal that the Nittany Lions wore all-white in their 13–13 tie with Doak Walker's SMU Mustangs. There were brief glimpses of flair afterward—striped pants and socks were worn occasionally into the 1970s. And in at least one 1950s photo, Lenny Moore is wearing a white jersey with two blue stripes wrapping around the sleeves.

Paterno's belief in the power of a simple, unchanging trademark dated back to October of 1943, when his Brooklyn Prep coach, Earl "Zev" Graham, a former Fordham all-American, took him to Yankee Stadium for a World Series game between the Yankees and the St. Louis Cardinals. A Dodgers fan by birth and inclination, Paterno was nonetheless drawn to the image of professionalism projected by the Yankees, a tailored uniformity that included pressed pinstripes and polished shoes. The impression that winning and appearance were somehow linked was born that day.

"[Coach Graham] said, 'Now watch how the Yankees walk.' And sure enough, DiMaggio and those guys walked with a little swagger," Paterno recalled. "He said, 'Look at their shoes.' I said they were nice—I didn't know what he was talking about. The Cardinals come out. He said, 'Now take a look at the Cardinals' shoes.' Every Yankee had polished shoes. They were all polished. The Cardinals had scuffed-up shoes, some of them didn't have the same length in their pants, the whole bit. He said, 'The Yankees are different.' You know, they had the pinstripes and the whole bit. And I think that's something that we try to do."

Paterno's continued insistence on unadorned uniforms was the coach's way of establishing both an espirit de corps and a unique identity for his program. Football is a team game. Players who understood that and were willing to submit their individuality to it were, he believed, more likely to be successful and unified.

"Whatever you do, you do trying to create a tradition," he would say. "We talk to people about the fact that we're conservative and we like team people. We're not looking for flashy people. I think people every once in a while need symbols to reinforce those sentiments."

Paterno's fashion sense turned out to be as shrewd as his football instincts. By dressing his teams in anonymity, he managed, just as he had hoped, to both pull them together and grant them a unique image. When players complained, he quoted Napoleon, who had said that part of what made a distinctive leader was a distinctive appearance.

During an era when America was conspicuously shedding the conformity of the 1950s in dress and most everything else, the Nittany Lions' uniforms were seen as drab eyesores.

"My friends used to tell me that when Penn State wore its plain white uniforms, they used to try to adjust their TVs because it seemed like there was too much snow on the screen," said Shuman.

As other schools experimented with wild helmet insignias and every possible color combination short of pink and black, Penn State stuck to its blue-white blandness: plain pants; black shoes; short white socks; nameless blue jerseys with white numbers, or, on the road, the opposite; and white helmets that, once the numbers were removed in the late 1970s, were adorned only with a thin blue strip down the middle.

"A lot of people ask me about the lousy-looking uniforms that we have," Paterno said. "But . . . you see us on TV and you say, 'Hey, Penn State is playing.' And your wife says, 'How do you know it's Penn State?' And you say, 'Look at the lousy uniforms.' "

More recently, however, as a retro craze has overtaken sports fashion, those uniforms have become hip again, and a point of pride for Penn State players and supporters—even if they do now include a

Nike swoosh, a tiny reminder of the tide of commercialism that has washed over even Paterno's program.

"I've had guys who played on that team tell me that before the 1986 Orange Bowl, Penn State players voted not to wear the little bowl insignia on their uniforms," said Shuman. "They said that even that little orange was too flashy."

While complaints about the uniforms—once common in the locker room—have virtually vanished in recent seasons, Paterno still fights with players about their off-the-field attire. No hats indoors. No facial hair. No earrings. Coats and ties on the road. He occasionally has relented, as on his edict that players wear socks to class even in warm weather.

"Why? Well, you're sitting in the front row, the professor looks down, the girl next to you and the guy next to you have lousy-looking, dirty feet, and you've got socks on," he said in explaining why he had instituted the ban in the first place. "[It might make] the difference between a B and a C, so don't be stupid."

The rule against hats is such a pet peeve with Paterno that he has had a sign placed in the locker room—"Nobody in this room comes in with a hat." Paterno likes to tell the story of his pregame meeting with Alabama's Bear Bryant before their 1979 Sugar Bowl confrontation. Bryant was not wearing his trademark houndstooth hat. The Penn State coach asked him why.

"He said, 'I don't wear a hat indoors.' Can you imagine that?" Paterno said. "We're playing in the Superdome and he said, 'If I wore a hat, my mother would get upset.' They're all symbols. In and of themselves they mean nothing. If I tell a kid I don't want his earring on, it doesn't mean a thing [other than you're] a Penn State football player. You're something . . . different. I want you to be different."

That 1979 Superdome conversation with Bryant came before a game that would keep the Nittany Lions from a fourth unbeaten season and the national championship Paterno coveted. After years of griping about a lack of respect in the polls, Paterno finally had a chance to win a title on the field.

In 1978, Penn State was 11–0 and No. 1 going into the Sugar Bowl. But Alabama prevailed, 14–7, twice stopping Penn State on fourth-quarter goal-line plunges. Those two up-the-middle running plays provoked criticism about Paterno's conservative nature that would linger for the next quarter century. The close defeat, he later said, was the most gut-wrenching of his career. It precipitated an off-season of deep reflection. "I just got outcoached," he said. "I didn't prepare well enough."

With a little more than seven minutes left in that New Year's Day game, Alabama led, 14–7. But Matt Millen forced a fumble and Joe Lally fell on the ball at the Crimson Tide 19. Penn State had a second-and-goal at the six when quarterback Chuck Fusina hit Scott Fitzkee near the goal line. But as the receiver turned toward the end zone, he was struck hard and stopped two feet short.

It was third-and-goal. Paterno called for bruising fullback Matt Suhey, the son of the couple with whom he had lived nearly thirty years earlier, to take it up the middle. Suhey had been the team's leading rusher, and this time his power dive brought to mind a powerful magnet. As he hit the line, the entire Alabama team was sucked toward him like so many iron filings. Paterno thought—still believes—Suhey got in. The officials disagreed. The ball would be marked six inches short of the end zone.

Now there was one play remaining. Paterno assumed that Bryant would have his defense ready to stop another Suhey plunge or a quarterback sneak by Fusina. He called a time-out and summoned Fusina to the sideline. According to his 1989 autobiography, *Paterno: By the Book*, as the quarterback approached, he decided he wanted him to fake a run and pass to the tight end.

"A couple of my soundest assistant coaches insisted I play the percentages—just crash through the couple feet for the touchdown," he wrote. ". . . That moment was one of the few in my life when I backed off from a strong instinct and let myself worry about what people might say if the decision was wrong."

Instead, he told Fusina to give the ball to tailback Mike Guman and have him run behind all-American tackle Keith Dorney.

"It was the only play to go with," he rationalized immediately after the game. "If you've got less than a foot to go, you've got to figure you can take the ball and go up over the pile."

Before the referee could spot the ball, Fusina asked him how far the Nittany Lions had to go. "About a foot," he was told. Alabama defensive end Marty Lyons, hearing the conversation, shouted, "You'd better pass for it!"

Guman took the handoff and left his feet. Lineman Don McNeal hit him low and linebacker Barry Krauss high, the latter striking with such force that he cracked his red helmet right along its seam. In the muscle-bound geology of football, the force of all that impact raised a red-and-white peak in the center of the pile.

But the play's result was clear this time. Guman had not scored. Alabama took over. Paterno's national-title hopes had been snuffed out again.

"Alabama just beat us at the line of scrimmage," said Paterno. "We should have been able to bang it in from there."

By then, Paterno had earned a reputation as a persistent critic of college football's excesses. It was widely believed that the teams in Alabama's SEC were among the worst perpetrators. Some said the SEC stood for "Surely Everybody Cheats." Many of that conference's coaches took exception to Paterno's moralizing. And according to his brother, that resentment contributed to the Alabama defeat.

"It was rumored every coach in the conference was offering information to Bear Bryant about how to beat Penn State," George Paterno wrote. "It was the South, coached by the kingfish of the 'good old boys,' against the extremely confident, annoying, skinny 'Wop' leader from the East."

The loss to Bear Bryant severely stung Paterno's ego. He second-guessed himself for months, taking out his frustration on his staff and players.

"I couldn't tolerate all that self-blame," he wrote.

CHAPTER 9

THOUGH THE PENN STATE PROGRAM had little firsthand knowledge of the phenomenon, a 3–9 season can transform the attitudes of malleable young players. The football careers of most of these Nittany Lions had been filled with winning—games, championships, accolades, and personal awards. When that suddenly and unexpectedly stopped, characters were tested. Some players sulked. Some blamed coaches or teammates. Some retreated into themselves, while others pushed harder.

Paterno understood that until the winning resumed, they all were extremely vulnerable. So heading into a new season with the 2004 Nittany Lions he had constantly sought to prop them up with positive reinforcement. Every forward step they took became a signpost on their journey back to prominence. The haircuts, extra work in the weight room, the willingness of seniors to step forward, the encouraging rout of Akron, all were, in their minds, displays of a renewed spirit and a football rebirth.

"A three-and-nine season is miserable for everybody," said sophomore offensive tackle Levi Brown. "Nobody wants to go through that. So you try to get some of it, like the constant losing, out of your head. . . . We're trying to capitalize on every little good thing we do."

The best therapy would be early-season victories. Paterno had told his players there was no reason they couldn't start 3–0, a perfect springboard into the killer Big Ten schedule that began at No. 20 Wisconsin on September 25.

Now, after the loss to BC, hopes had to be revised, confidence bolstered. The size of the psychic wound Boston College inflicted on Penn State hinted at just how fragile Paterno's once rock-solid program had become.

"That was a game everybody was real emotional about. We wanted to win," said senior wideout Ryan Scott in its somber aftermath.

Fearing this first setback might trigger another season-long retreat, Paterno and the seniors immediately moved to counter that possibility. Before flying back to State College late that Saturday night, the coach, surprisingly upbeat in the locker room despite his downcast performance with the media, told his players to keep their heads up.

"You played hard," he said. "But there are an awful lot of areas where you need to improve. You've got ten games left. You can win them all. But you can also lose them all. It's up to you."

"At practice Monday," he said, with a glance at Austin Scott, "I expect you all to work hard."

When Monday came, no one was surprised when some of the seniors—Mills, Wake, and Gerald Smith—called a players-only meeting, a preemptive strike against any negative residue. Its theme was clear: The loss to Boston College didn't mean they were headed for a repeat of 2003.

"[They] looked everyone in the face," said defensive tackle Scott Paxson, "and said whatever happened last year isn't going to happen this year."

"I don't want to go back to last year," Mills told them.

"We're not the same team as last year," Robinson said.

Smith might have been the most emotional of the speakers. In the spring, he had been one of those eager to rectify the locker-room problems that helped sink the previous season.

"There was a lack of leadership last year," he would say. "The upperclassmen this year really wanted to step up and set a foot down and try to establish a positive foundation for the team. We're young, fairly young, and that's one thing we wanted to do."

Now, with his teammates all around, and with his career-best five catches against BC lending him a pulpit, the wide receiver from Ellicott City, Maryland, reemphasized what Paterno had told them Saturday night.

"[Gerald said] we can go two ways," Mills recalled. "We can let this loss get at us and affect us the whole season. Or we can get better."

That first practice for the Central Florida game lasted about fifty minutes. It was routine—mostly meetings and film study. Paterno and his aides discussed a couple of minor position moves. The man who once wanted to move Hall of Fame QB Jim Kelly to linebacker had tried senior defensive end Jason Robinson at tight end against Boston College. Junior receiver Gio Vendemia also had been moved, to cornerback.

According to Paterno, his players had been "alert" during the workout. That encouraged him. He had wondered how he was going to handle them, both after the BC game and throughout the following week. That was a coach's perpetual dilemma: Good cop or bad cop? Praise them or bury them? Last year he would have angrily lit into them.

"That's one of the biggest things you get to do in college coaching or any coaching—whether it's high school, college, or pro—depending on how your kids play, the depth of their concern about having gotten licked, and that kind of thing," he would explain. "If you have a couple of flippant kids and some kids just walking around after the game like it really wasn't that important, obviously, you take a different attitude. . . . There are a lot of things that go into it and sometimes you make a decision that you regret. I wish that there was a formula that told you, 'This is exactly the way you do it every week.' I think that for this football team I want to encourage them because they have worked hard and are concerned about getting on with it."

After fifty-four years, he had developed pretty good instincts. And this time, unlike the wake of the '03 loss to BC when he thought his team had given up, he sensed a different attitude. There was no need to panic. Paterno believed this team had played "good, tough, and hard" in the loss.

Paterno liked that about them. It would have been easy for his players to doubt their coach, to buy into the notion that he was over the hill and incapable of substantive change. Instead, they had made a commitment to listen to him, to practice and play hard for him, to follow his rules. Consequently, the staff decided to remain upbeat at what they saw as a critical juncture.

"They're trying [to be positive]," center E. Z. Smith said. "They get intense when they have to be. And if they need to get intense with us, we understand that it's the nature of the game. But for the most part they are very positive."

His players had been waiting for Paterno's response. The coach's surprisingly buoyant demeanor was another indication that he was going about things differently this season. The Nittany Lions, with nine games left, including their entire conference schedule, welcomed his positive attitude.

"He told us we still have a chance to do some big things this season," Michael Robinson said. "People are talking about salvaging the season. It's a loss in the second game. What are we salvaging? The season has barely started."

A daylong rain, the nasty remains of Hurricane Ivan, pounded Penn State's campus on Friday, September 17. Before it ended early the following morning, up to eight inches had fallen on central Pennsylvania, triggering the area's worst floods in thirty-two years.

That Friday night, outside the Nittany Lion Inn, a seventy-three-year-old campus hotel, a continual flow of cars splashed up the circular driveway. Their doors opened outside the lobby entrance. Umbrellas bloomed and guests emerged beneath them. Though operated by the university, the inn, like the athletic department and the school's dining facilities, was classified as an "auxiliary enterprise." It had its own budget and generated its own revenue. Big contributors, powerful alumni, former Penn State players, all preferred the blue-blazered ambience of the Nittany Lion Inn on football weekends. That afternoon, a board of trustees meeting had taken place at the inn and many of its thirty-two members were staying around for the following day's game. The guests typically packed its bar, "Whiskers," on Friday nights, before and after the booster banquets that also were held there.

Paterno's teams' achievements over the last several decades had made it impossible for the average fan to book a room there on football weekends. But in the final weekends of the miserable 2003 season some had been available. It was one more sad reminder of the delicate condition of Penn State football. But on this rainy night, the two-story hotel was full and bustling. In a basement banquet room set up for Paterno's media cocktail reception, a handful of reporters talked and drank as they waited for their host.

Once again, the coach failed to show up. What had initially been seen as an aberration now had the appearance of a trend. The sportswriters increasingly were baffled.

Wilkes-Barre's Kellar believed Paterno might have been annoyed when the *Centre Daily Times* reported that week that the reason Austin Scott had not played against Boston College was that he had missed a meeting. Jenny Vrentas, a junior engineering major who was one of three *Daily Collegian* writers on the school paper's football beat, suggested Penn State's players and coaches may have been upset by her criticism during the week of defensive back Anwar Phillips. Phillips's fellow defensive back, Alan Zemaitis, had exposed that displeasure during a teleconference a few days earlier.

Or, perhaps, they were all too paranoid. Maybe the old coach simply didn't want to get drenched in the storm. That seemed unlikely. Paterno didn't casually cast traditions aside, particularly ones that he had fathered.

"No," said David Jones, a veteran Penn State writer for the *Harrisburg Patriot-News* and a longtime thorn in Paterno's side. "He's at war."

Meanwhile, the persistent storm was causing problems for that week's opponent, Central Florida. At Orlando's airport, the possibility that the team's flight to State College might have to be diverted elsewhere meant UCF's chartered jet had to take on extra fuel. Considerable weight had to be shed before the plane could depart. The cheerleaders, athletic department official Art Zeleznik, and faculty athletics representative Bill Callarman were removed and booked on a commercial flight through Portsmouth, New Hampshire.

As it turned out, their jet was redirected, to Harrisburg. Players and coaches boarded buses there for the two-hour trip to State College along Route 322, which would soon be closed because of flooding. They wouldn't arrive at their hotel until late Friday night. At 2:30 A.M., the eastbound lanes of I-80, the main east–west access to State College, also would be shut down, guaranteeing even more congestion in the traffic that poured in and out of town on a football Saturday.

Paterno, as was his weekly habit, praised Central Florida in the days leading up to the game, even though that school's football program appeared to be the antithesis of all he had built in Happy Valley.

The Golden Knights had little or no tradition. They wore garish gold uniforms, relied on speed and spontaneity, had serious academic problems, and a small and fickle fan base. And in George O'Leary, the former Georgia Tech coach, they also had their third coach in eleven months.

The forty-one-year-old college in booming Orlando hadn't fielded a football team until 1979, when Paterno was in his thirtieth season at Penn State. Then came a slow march up the ladder, propelled by the promise of TV riches, from Division III to Division II in 1982, to Division I-AA in 1990, and finally to the big-time Division I-A level in 1996.

As the level of competition increased, so had the size of the university. Its student body had grown from thirteen thousand in 1980 to more than forty-four thousand in 2004, making it second in size only to the University of Florida in its home state.

"We've become the school of choice for the average Florida student," said ex–football coach Mike Kruczek.

But not yet for the average Florida football fan. The Knights, surrounded by all the Orlando area's entertainment options, drew an average of only 21,920 fans to its games at the 73,000-seat Gator Bowl in 2003. Still, given its enticing location, Florida's bottomless high-school talent pool, and an apparent willingness to accept academic risks among its matriculating players, Central Florida, which was set to join Conference USA in 2005 after three seasons in the MAC, possessed enormous potential.

"I really believe Central Florida is a sleeping giant," O'Leary had said when he took the job the previous December.

While Miami, Florida, and Florida State enjoyed a sizable advantage in reputation and recruiting, Central Florida hoped to close the gap with the hiring of O'Leary and the recent construction of a $7 million, football-only training facility on campus.

Finding players wasn't its problem. There are enough Division I prospects coming out of Florida each year—250 to 275 by most estimates—that UCF could do quite well with the table scraps. Forty-nine of the sixty-three players O'Leary brought to State College were Floridians, many of them drawn there by a schedule that included attractive interconference opponents like Wisconsin and Penn State.

Paterno, on the other hand, hoped to get something out of the matchup too. In part because his coaching staff remained so static, he had never established strong connections in populous southern and western states like Florida, California, and Texas, where many of the best and speediest prospects were being developed.

His philosophy had always been that by recruiting in distant locales, he might be ignoring talent in Pennsylvania, New Jersey, and Maryland. That had worked for decades, until the nexus of football talent, along with jobs and population, shifted south and west in the 1980s and 1990s. Penn State's roster for the Central Florida game, for example, included only one Floridian, John Wilson, a backup offensive tackle; one Californian, fourth-string backup QB Mike Hart; and no Texans. Among its Big Ten rivals, Minnesota had eight Floridians, Ohio State five. Purdue had fourteen Texans, Wisconsin eight. Michigan had ten Californians.

O'Leary had replaced interim coach Alan Gooch, who had filled in after Kruczek was fired early in the Knights' disappointing 3–9 '03 season. Kruczek's final year in Orlando had been marred by eight player suspensions—including cornerback Omar Laurence, who was accused of possessing not one but two guns on campus. At that season's end, sixteen of the team's sixty-two players were on academic suspension. The school's graduation rate for athletes, according to AD Steve Orsini, was just thirty-three percent.

UCF took more criticism when it hired O'Leary. His base salary of

$700,000 was nearly four times more than Kruczek had earned. And he had been forced to resign at Notre Dame when, just days after accepting the pretigious job in 2001, it was revealed that he had lied about academic credentials on a résumé.

"Nobody is perfect," Paterno said of O'Leary. "George made a mistake on a résumé. I would hope that we don't excommunicate him. The days of the Inquisition, I was hoping, were over."

On the field, things weren't going much better. UCF had been moving in reverse ever since it went 9–2 in 1998 behind future NFL all-Pro quarterback Daunte Culpepper. The Golden Knights went 16–19 in the three succeeding seasons and had opened the 2004 season with two lopsided losses against nationally ranked opponents—34–6 at Wisconsin and 45–20 to West Virginia at home.

This was the kind of game Paterno always hated to play. A victory, even one as decisive as the win over Akron, wouldn't signify much of anything. A loss would be disastrous.

If the latter happened, he knew that his team—with games against Wisconsin, Minnesota, Purdue, and Iowa in the next four weeks—could be so devastated that it might not win again this season.

Central Florida was going to want to run the ball, especially if, as Paterno expected, the Beaver Stadium turf was wet and slippery. O'Leary hadn't yet decided from among three first-year quarterbacks. The Knights' offense, such as it was, consisted largely of senior tailback Alex Haynes, who had run for 193 yards in the two losses.

Still, Central Florida was quick and dangerous. An early score or two might inflame Penn State's self-doubt. In the Nittany Lions' 2002 home opener, UCF had nearly ruined the one good season Penn State had experienced in the previous four, just missing a noteworthy upset before succumbing, 27–24.

"I think Central Florida has played a couple of tough opponents," said Paterno. "Wisconsin is really a good football team. I don't know what people are ranking them. I know West Virginia is ranked right up there and West Virginia has some awfully good skill people and very, very clever people. Central Florida can do a lot of things. They have a couple of wideouts that played against us that hurt us. They have a running back who is a really good running back. They are a football team that is kind of just feeling its way. . . . When you look at them, they scare you because of the fact that they do have tremendous potential. They really do. There isn't anyplace they don't have speed. They have an awful lot of speed."

Like Akron, Central Florida was a midlevel Division I-A school willing to play big-name foes on the road for a big payout guarantee. They had turned up as a semiregular on Penn State's schedule, in part because Alabama, beset with NCAA problems, had begged out of its scheduled games with the Nittany Lions in 2004 and 2005, and because of Central Florida's connections with their athletic department.

Central Florida AD Orsini was from Hummelstown, Pennsylvania. He had been recruited by Paterno. His brother, Mike, played defensive back for the Nittany Lions between 1971 and 1973. His father, Tony, had been a senior running back when Paterno arrived in State College.

"Tony was a tailback in 1950," said Paterno. "He was a good, tough kid, with not a lot of speed—like most Italians—and couldn't run very well, except away from the cops. That was our only claim to fame for speed when I was in Brooklyn. Tony was a great guy. Then when young Mike came along, Tony's son, we recruited him. . . . We debated on whether we wanted [Steve] and we waited too long and then Notre Dame came in and made him an offer and we were late with it."

The tail end of the ugly hurricane weather blew past State College just before game time, leaving a sunny, windy Saturday afternoon with temperatures in the mid-sixties.

There were wide-open gaps in the parking lots and patches of empty seats inside Beaver Stadium when the 12:10 P.M. game began, an indication of the access problems motorists were experiencing. In addition, many fans, convinced that an easy Lions victory was inevitable, stayed away when they saw the early-morning weather.

The mood among those in the announced crowd of 101,715—the total who had bought tickets—was confident. Even as far as Penn State had fallen, they couldn't conceive of the Lions losing to 0–2 Central Florida. In the press box, forty-five minutes before kickoff, a sportswriter for the *Altoona Mirror* began banging out his game-story's lead:

"Penn State dominated Central Florida yesterday," it began, "bouncing back from last week's disappointing loss to Boston College."

He never did have to rewrite. Penn State clearly "dominated" the smaller Knights, 37–13. But despite the score, it wasn't the kind of victory that forecast great achievements in the Big Ten.

Paterno was transparently angry several times on the sideline. He barked at Mills after the quarterback floated up an ill-advised pass while being hit. He snapped at Scott when the running back returned to the bench following a fumble. He stomped his feet when Terrance Phillips dropped a pass. And when McQueary chastised Phillips for short-arming a pass, Paterno got in his two cents' worth of screaming too.

But it was the turnovers that really irked the coach. Paterno's teams traditionally avoided them. The coach harped constantly at every practice on holding on to the ball and avoiding penalties. "Those are things I'm really serious about," he would say. Years after graduating, players claimed his high-pitched complaints about fumbles or holding infractions continued to echo inside their heads.

Against Central Florida, Penn State turned the ball over six times—the most by any Paterno team since a 42–21 loss at Alabama in 1982. Mills, with a pair of fumbled snaps and four interceptions, had a hand in all of them. In two weeks, he had thrown eight interceptions and lost two fumbles, single-handedly accounting for ten of Penn State's eleven turnovers.

"We're getting close to being able to compete," said Paterno. "But if we have six turnovers [at Wisconsin], it won't matter if we take a bunch of six-hundred-pound gorillas."

On a positive note, Paterno had finally managed to get Robinson fully involved, utilizing the kind of versatile attack he and Hall had envisioned in the spring. The junior had a career-best seven receptions for 93 yards, nine carries for 53 yards, and completed his only pass.

In fact, Robinson was involved on six of Penn State's first eight plays. The junior took the first two snaps at quarterback, with Mills flanked wide, and ran for 12 yards. Robinson was a tailback on the third play, took the handoff, and picked up 5 more yards. On the fifth play, Robinson was back under center and this time he hit Mills on a 39-yard pass play. After a Tony Hunt carry, Robinson, at tailback again, gained 5 yards and, at wideout on the following snap, caught a 3-yard pass to the UCF 13.

"I thought maybe we hadn't used him enough against BC," said Paterno. "So we decided we were going to get him involved real early."

That drive eventually stalled when Mills and center Smith fouled up the exchange and UCF recovered on its own 15.

"Every day the quarterbacks and centers come out ten minutes ahead of everybody else just to work on the snaps," said an exasperated Paterno. "I don't know. The one on the goal line I think just popped right out. We should never have that. We should never, ever, have a fumble on the exchange. There's some things we may overlook, some things we may not do as diligently as some other things. But we should never, ever, have a fumbled exchange. To have two in one game is very disturbing."

UCF led briefly after the first of two Matt Prater field goals late in the opening quarter. But three TD runs by Hunt in a span of 5:44 of the second and third quarters, one by backup Gasparato (he would aggravate a leg injury on the run and it would turn out to be the final carry of his career), a 1-yard Mills-to-tight-end John Bronson scoring pass, a safety, and a Robbie Gould field goal gave the Lions the win.

Hunt had his second 100-yard game, collecting 127 on sixteen carries. Austin Scott's exile ended when he entered early in the second quarter. He rushed six times and gained 47 yards.

Mills completed nineteen of the twenty-three passes that weren't intercepted, for 229 yards. Paterno again inserted Morelli late, the freshman completing both of his throws for 9 yards.

The wideouts, except for Robinson and, to a lesser degree, Smith (three catches for 58 yards), struggled again, dropping several balls.

On defense, the young squad appeared to be gaining confidence. With freshman Connor getting considerable time at Wake's outside-linebacker spot, Penn State limited Haynes to 59 yards on the ground. Connor also intercepted a second-quarter pass.

"Dan has been practicing well," said Paterno, "and I didn't think

Derek had been playing as well as I would have liked. So it was like, well, let's give Dan a shot. And when Dan got in there, he played well."

Overall, Penn State surrendered only 60 yards on the ground to UCF and another 121 on passes. The Golden Knights could manage only 3 points off the six turnovers. Connor, linebacker Posluszny, and defensive back Lowry were particularly effective in what was the best performance in more than a year by Tom Bradley's defense.

"We're getting better," Tim Shaw said of the linebackers. "The D line is getting better. . . . I see improvement every day."

Once again after the game the coach told the press that a home rout of an overmatched opponent had shown him little. The next two games, he said, on the road at Wisconsin and Minnesota, would at last provide some answers about the 2004 Nittany Lions.

"Before this game started, we were focused on UCF," said Jefferson, "but we talked about how we're going into the Big Ten. . . . I think we all feel we've got a legitimate chance to do some damage in the Big Ten."

Next Saturday, before a crazed crowd at Camp Randall Stadium in Madison, there would be plenty of damage.

CHAPTER 10

AT NOON ON SEPTEMBER 17, the day before the Central Florida game, Penn State's board of trustees had conducted its bimonthly public meeting in the Nittany Lion Inn's boardroom. Throughout the summer, Paterno's detractors had held out hope that the thirty-two-member body might, during its two football-season meetings in September and November, deal in some way with the festering doubts surrounding the coach. The trustees seldom tackled athletic issues. But football and Paterno, given the fame and fortune that combination had generated for the university, were certainly on their minds that day. Five of them, in fact, had once played for Paterno—Jesse Arnelle, Dave Joyner, Steve Garban, Paul Suhey, and Lester Rowell. And there were indications from Penn State insiders that a few of those ex-players had spent the summer and fall trying unsuccessfully to persuade their old coach to devise some kind of exit strategy.

Instead, with most of its official business having been conducted at a closed-door gathering the previous day, the board concluded an agenda of perfunctory duties in a mere twenty-five minutes. The trustees agreed to submit to the state legislature a $71.8 million budget request for 2005–06, a figure that would restore the roughly $17 million the fiscally strapped legislators had trimmed in recent years.

While the connection was, of course, never mentioned by the board, the university's budget was closely linked to Paterno's fate.

Once-prosperous Pennsylvania, facing the same kind of financial crisis as other aging industrial states, had been unable to support the level of growth Penn State's alumni and administrators insisted was necessary. According to a 2000–01 study by New York's State Education Department, Pennsylvania, on a per-student basis, spent fewer tax dollars on appropriations to public institutions than any other state. In 2003, the state cut more than $10 million from student-aid programs.

Fewer state dollars meant a growing reliance on contributions. And since Paterno was Penn State's unchallenged money-raising champion—not to mention a significant donor himself—any examination of his job status had to be handled with great care and caution. Realistically, they couldn't replace the golden goose until they found a new source for twenty-four-karat eggs.

That's why chairwoman Cynthia Baldwin would say only that while the trustees were "behind Joe," his future was not a board issue. She had been happy to defer all questions about the coach to President Graham Spanier and AD Curley.

"It's the way it should be," one anonymous trustee told *The Philadelphia Inquirer*. "We don't want to do things the way they do at some other schools, where board members splinter off into groups and become divisive over a football coach. The president has asked our feelings about Joe on an individual basis, but that's so he doesn't operate in a vacuum."

Spanier had been so besieged that he had begun responding to queries on the subject only via e-mail. "All of us who are sports fans prefer to win," he wrote in one, "but it is important to maintain perspective."

The four-year contract extension, which the coach had signed in May and which they had approved, took some of the immediate focus off the trustees. Privately, though, several remained deeply concerned.

"Just because Joe got the contract extension should not be taken as a sign that we are happy about the state of affairs with the football program," one trustee told the *Harrisburg Patriot-News*.

Most of the day's remaining business was mundane, the passage of resolutions like the one that officially changed the name of the Pesticide Research Lab to the Chemical Ecology Lab.

When the meeting officially adjourned at 12:25 P.M., the name

Paterno had been mentioned just once, when it was noted that the coach's wife, Sue, had been cited as one of eight 2004 recipients of Penn State's Distinguished Alumni Award.

As far as it related to the dark forces infecting Penn State football, the sloppy victory over 0–3 Central Florida accomplished very little.

It didn't revive the enthusiasm of fans who knew the turnover-prone Lions' next five opponents were formidable Big Ten teams with a combined record of 13–1. "People aren't excited about Penn State football," senior Brian Tuchalski told the *Los Angeles Times*, which sent a reporter to State College that week to chronicle the unusual angst. "Instead of going to the games, they would rather drink all day and watch it on TV."

It didn't convince anyone, not even Nittany Lions players, that the program's long-lost swagger and reputation had been restored. "People don't respect Penn State, they don't fear Penn State like they used to," safety Calvin Lowry said that week. "When you step on the field, there's not that fear in people's hearts like there used to be."

It didn't quiet the discontent with Paterno. "Joe, fucking retire before they have to fire you for ruining the program you helped build," the creator of the blog *BottleofBlog.com* pleaded in a posting that week.

And it certainly didn't do anything for the harried coach's mood. The post-victory criticism, especially that directed at Mills, irked him. During his Tuesday afternoon teleconference, he frequently was feisty and curt.

The sportswriters, all but a few of whom participated by telephone, were permitted just one question in the weekly electronic news conferences. They had to make sure it was framed in a way that (A) wouldn't irritate Paterno, (B) wouldn't sound like a criticism of a player or assistant coach, and (C) would produce an answer sufficiently detailed to give them an interesting story.

"I've been finding lately that I spend more time composing my one question than I do writing my story," Wilkes-Barre's Kellar said. "It's crazy."

Paterno knew exactly what the writers needed. And usually he gave it to them—long and thoughtful answers that avoided clichés and often challenged the accepted wisdom. He was equally adept, though, at veering away from subjects he didn't want to discuss. But increasingly in recent years, particularly in the aftermath of player arrests, he had been angered by some of their more probing questions, questions he believed were either intrusive, judgmental, or designed to stir controversy.

Ray Parillo of *The Philadelphia Inquirer* began that week's session by asking what appeared to be a perfectly logical question about Mills, the quarterback who had thrown eight interceptions in the last two games:

"Joe, are you confident that Zack Mills can put the problems that he has had the last couple of games behind him?"

"Yes."

After a considerable pause and a few unrelated questions came another attempt:

"Last year you made a point to tell people who were critical of Zack Mills that he was doing a lot better job without a lot of support than people perceived. What would your assessment be of how he has played so far?"

"I think Zack is fine."

Finally, on a third polite effort to elicit a usable response about Mills, Paterno ruled the subject off-limits before the question was even complete.

"Let's get off of Zack," he said. "Zack is playing good, solid football. Last week I told you that he had some things that didn't go his way. I am not going to get into that. I could get in here and start pointing fingers at the center-quarterback exchange and the whole bit. I think they are doing fine. They are fine. Zack is fine."

The week between Central Florida and Wisconsin made it clear that this was a different Penn State universe than the one Paterno had presided over for more than a half century. Five or six years ago, the start of Big Ten play would have been cause for optimism and blue-and-white fervor. Now it was an occasion to worry, to assess just how long and difficult the Lions' journey back to respectability might be.

"I think it's going to take a couple of sustained seasons, honestly," said Michael Robinson of winning back opponents' respect. "You have one [winning] season and teams think it's a fluke. You have two and they think you're lucky. . . . Every time you go out to play one of them, show them they are playing Penn State. We're still a good football team run by good coaches and a good administration."

That was not an easy argument to make at that point. Penn State hadn't won a Big Ten opener since 1999. It hadn't won a single Big Ten road game in its last seven. Their last victory in each case had come against Indiana. The Hoosiers, who traditionally had been the conference's doormat, now had company.

"You can just tell how [opposing] players talk during the week of the game," Lowry said. "When they had the great teams here at Penn State, people wouldn't do that stuff. They'd keep their mouths closed and play. People come with the mind-set 'We're going to beat Penn State' now. They don't care about our history. People don't fear us. That's what we need to get back."

Paterno had been short with reporters when they asked him how he thought the rest of the Big Ten looked at Penn State's program on the eve of the conference's opening weekend.

"I haven't got the slightest idea," he said.

Well, would he at least concede that heading into a road matchup with Wisconsin, a 10-point favorite, the perennially lofty expectations for his program had been diminished?

"I don't think our expectations are anything different than they have been since I've been here fifty-five or some years ago. Our expectations are to go out and play as hard and as well as we can and hopefully win a couple of games. . . . Your memory," he told the questioner, "can play games with you."

The Penn State–Wisconsin game was being televised at 4:45 P.M. by ESPN, which considered the matchup attractive enough to serve as a lead-in for *Hustle*, the all-sports network's new telemovie about Pete Rose.

Just about the time that Paterno and his players were arriving in buses at Camp Randall Stadium, Chris Hort, the coach's son-in-law, was taking advantage of a football-free Saturday back in Pennsylvania. On this first autumn weekend, the leaves in the surrounding hills were beginning to brighten. The sun was shining and the borough's shady streets were clear of the football traffic that clogged them on Saturday afternoons whenever Penn State played at home.

That afternoon Hort, the thirty-seven-year-old husband of the coach's thirty-nine-year-old daughter, Mary Kay, and the father of three of his grandchildren, wanted some exercise. He put on his protective helmet, grabbed his bicycle, and pedaled off from his home in Port Matilda toward State College ten miles away.

Sometime around 3:00 P.M., he was riding down Park Road near Beaver Stadium in what police would later describe as "the shadow of the north end zone." A female pedestrian noticed him pedaling toward her. She briefly turned her head. When she looked back, Hort was lying motionless on the ground. There were no cars in sight.

Doctors and nurses en route to their afternoon shift at nearby Mount Nittany Medical Center stopped to assist until police and emergency medical personnel arrived. Hort had suffered a serious head injury in the mysterious fall, even though he was wearing the helmet, which showed minor damage in the rear.

"It's possible that he hit his head on exposed metal like a drain of some sort, but we do not know yet," said State College Police Sgt. C. D. Fishel.

Hort was rushed to the nearby medical center, where doctors quickly summoned a life-flight helicopter to transport him to the intensive-care unit at Altoona General Hospital, thirty-five miles away.

Word traveled quickly to Madison. During the first quarter, Sue Paterno learned of her son-in-law's accident. Accompanied by Curley and her friend Kay Kustanbauter, the executive director of the Nittany Lion Club, the coach's wife departed the stadium on a university jet and flew home. Back in State College, a second university jet was dispatched to Madison to carry home the coach, who still knew nothing of the incident.

Throughout the 615–mile flight to State College, all Sue Paterno could think of was how eerily reminiscent her feelings were. On an afternoon almost thirty years earlier, October 14, 1977, her oldest son,

eleven-year-old David, had fallen off a trampoline at school and frac-
tured his skull. That time it was Joe Paterno who took the initial call.
Knowing his wife was driving to Syracuse with friends for the next
day's game, he contacted state police, who pulled over the women's
vehicle and gave his wife the news.

David was unconscious when doctors in State College sent him to
Geisinger Medical Center in Danville. Paterno, praying fervently, accompanied the boy on the sixty-five-mile ambulance trip. "It was," he
later said, "the longest ride of my life."

For just the second and last time (his father's death in 1955 being
the other), Paterno missed a Penn State game. By Tuesday of the next
week, the boy and his father had recovered.

Now, on top of all the losses, the criticism, and the recent spate of
team-related deaths, came this troubling news.

Maybe, Sue Paterno thought, fate really had conspired against her
husband. Perhaps he had, after a half century of fairy-tale success, exhausted all his good fortune.

What else could possibly go wrong?

Had she been listening to the Penn State game, she'd have gotten
her answer in a hurry.

Three hours after his son-in-law's life-threatening accident, Paterno
still knew nothing of the mishap. What he did know, as he looked at
the motionless, prostrate body of Michael Robinson, was that in less
than one quarter of football he had lost his two best offensive players,
his top two quarterbacks.

Standing near the middle of Wisconsin's football field, Paterno
watched as Robinson was hoisted into an ambulance. Less than thirty
minutes earlier, Mills had been helped off the field to the locker room.

It was the one thing Paterno had feared most. He knew that even
with Mills and Robinson, his offense was subpar. Without them, well,
he couldn't envision too many ways the Nittany Lions could reach the
end zone.

Mills had been hurt on the game's opening play when Robinson,
who had been lined up as a wideout, ran down his left-sideline bomb

and made a spectacular twisting catch. The 49-yard play advanced the ball to Wisconsin's 32 and appeared to signal the awakening of a moribund offense.

But while everyone was watching the ball, Mills took a hard shot from Wisconsin defensive end Erasmus James. James, a six-four, 263-pound senior, was so fast and agile that NFL scouts already were describing him as "can't miss" and "a pass-rushing terror."

Mills tried to stay in the game, but on Penn State's second play, he was intercepted—incredibly his ninth in less than three games, his eighth in less than five quarters. The hit had partially separated the senior quarterback's left shoulder, which would later require a cortisone shot in the locker room. He had hurt the right one earlier in his career and still had not regained his arm strength. When he awkwardly jogged to the sideline and revealed his latest injury, Mills was removed and Robinson was informed that he'd be at quarterback the rest of the way.

Wisconsin was ready for him. Their quick defensive front shut off his scrambling lanes. And his absence as a wide receiver meant the Badgers could stick eight defenders close to the line and force Robinson to throw. With the first quarter nearly complete, he had run five times for −3 yards, and completed just one of three passes.

Wisconsin, having converted yet another Nittany Lions turnover—a Tony Hunt fumble at Penn State's 44—into a touchdown on a 5-yard John Stocco run, led 7–0 when, with 1:55 left in the period, and facing a first-and-10 at his own 18, Robinson dropped back.

Penn State's offensive line had had little luck trying to to slow Wisconsin's pass-rush. On this play, the defensive linemen came at the quarterback from all angles. Robinson evaded the first wave and spun to the right. As he did, a diving James, who had overpowered Andrew Richardson, met him in a teeth-rattling collision. The defender's helmet slammed into Robinson just as the QB was being hit by Jason Jefferson. The Nittany Lion crumpled instantly from the high-speed assault. The ball fell softly from his hands, like a drop of blood from a wound, though officials would rule it was not a fumble. Robinson was still on the grass as a crowd began to gather above him. Players on both teams surrounded the fallen quarterback, who by then also had drawn the serious attention of the two team doctors. Paterno hovered over Robinson, and along the Penn State sideline, several teammates prayed or held hands.

Back home in Richmond, Virginia, the player's mother, Rita Ross, screamed and scampered nervously around her house, praying out loud that her son would move. After several torturous minutes, he still had not done so. A Madison Fire Department ambulance, No. 63, rolled out onto the field and a stabilizing board was unloaded.

"Seeing that happen to Michael Robinson, that brought a lot of memories back," said Tom Bradley, Penn State's defensive coordinator. "Anytime they take out that board, you get a sickness in your stomach."

The board had come out four years earlier, on September 23, 2000, at Ohio Stadium. That day Penn State freshman Adam Taliaferro severely injured his spine when his head had collided with an Ohio State player's knee on a kickoff.

Joe Paterno, remembering David's ordeal, had cried like a baby when he told his team of Taliaferro's paralysis. Sue said she had rarely seen her husband so shaken. At least once a week for the next several months Paterno visited Taliaferro at the Philadelphia hospital where he was rehabilitating. He would be paralyzed for eleven months before regaining most of his motor skills.

Finally, strapped to the board, Robinson, his hands folded across his lap, his feet pointed outward, his neck encased in a brace, was loaded onto the vehicle and driven to the university's hospital.

"I remember dropping back," Robinson recalled. "I looked at Terrance Phillips, and I came off the second receiver . . . then all I remember is Dr. [Wayne] Sebastianelli trying to wake me up."

That happened in the ambulance, en route to the University of Wisconsin Hospital. Once the player was conscious, Sebastianelli kept prodding the left side of his body.

"Feel that?"

"Do I feel what?" Robinson responded.

It would be more than an hour before Robinson regained complete feeling.

Lost in the concern over his condition was the whispered suggestion that James's helmet-to-helmet hit on Robinson should have been penalized. Asked about that a few days later, Paterno was reluctant to get involved in another officiating dispute.

"Don't get me into that, OK?" he said. " I think all of you saw the game on television and, if not, probably had a chance to look it over. I think you can make your own decision on that."

But Robinson's mother had no doubts. She told *Sports Illustrated* she hoped someone would injure James, a reaction that prompted the Wisconsin all-American to suggest that "what she should wish for is a better offensive tackle to protect her son."

After Robinson left the field, Paterno immediately told Galen Hall to eliminate most of the plays they had drawn up that week. Then, surprisingly, he turned not to Morelli, who he had said two weeks ago was being primed for just such an occurrence, but to third-string QB Chris Ganter. Paterno told the son of his longtime assistant to keep it simple. Ganter, a fourth-year junior, was brave but ineffective in the longest exposure of his career.

"I really thought about playing Morelli a couple of times," Paterno would say. "In fact, Jay Paterno and I talked about that in the second half. Neither he nor Chris Ganter got a lot of reps during the week. It's tough to get three quarterbacks ready. We really had to change a lot of things we'd planned to do. We weren't comfortable that Anthony would be familiar with a lot of the things because we hadn't been practicing them a lot during the week."

Just about the only noteworthy development for an offense that managed just one field goal was the debut of Mark Rubin. The possession receiver from Amherst, New York, had a pair of catches for 21 yards. More significantly, he became the fifth true freshman Paterno had played this fall.

Defensively, the Nittany Lions again played well enough to win. They shut down the Badgers' passing game but couldn't contain their running game in the second half. What was somewhat embarrassing was that the bulk of the damage was done by a 270-pound fullback who rarely carried the ball and who had been fasting for twenty-four hours. Matt Bernstein became Barry Alvarez's top option after in-game injuries to Jamil Walker and Booker Stanley. Wisconsin already was without top back Anthony Davis, who sat out the game with an eye injury.

Bernstein had attended Yom Kippur services with his family Friday and, in approximate observance of the holiday's mandate to fast from sundown to sundown, didn't eat between 4:45 P.M. the previous day and just after kickoff, when he had turkey and orange slices. Fortunately for the Badgers, the relatively late kickoff had permitted him to play.

He carried the ball twenty-seven times for 129 yards, most of it in the second half as Wisconsin mercifully killed the clock against the depleted Lions in a 16–3 victory that left the Badgers with a 4–0 record.

Penn State was 2–2, 0–1 in a conference in which they now had lost nineteen of their previous thirty-three games.

Paterno was smiling as he shook hands after the game with Wisconsin's Barry Alvarez near midfield. He had recently been told that while Robinson had suffered a concussion and some early paralysis, he was now groggy and sore but able to move freely. The quarterback would spend the night in the Wisconsin hospital.

As Paterno walked off the field, Art Baldwin, the husband of Board of Trustees chair Cynthia Baldwin, approached. The two men huddled and Baldwin informed the coach about Hort. Paterno's face turned ashen. As he returned to the locker room, his thoughts turned back to David and Taliaferro, and overwhelmed with emotion, he cried.

With Baldwin, Spanier, and Jay Paterno accompanying him, the coach left the stadium without talking with the waiting media. He was driven, with a police escort, to Dane County Airport. There, as his team huddled in prayer for Robinson and Hort in their locker room, they boarded the jet and returned to State College.

Bradley addressed the puzzled media, who soon would be informed of Paterno's departure and Hort's injury.

"Coach was leaving, and I said, 'Coach, we'll get everybody home, go ahead,' " Bradley said. "He's a family guy from top to bottom; that's number one with him. If you saw the tears in his eyes, you'd know that's a sad occurrence. I feel for him right now. Our prayers are with him and Mary Kay and her family. It's going to be a tough situation. It doesn't sound good right now."

"It's pretty crazy all the stuff's that been going on," Mills said afterward, his arm in a sling. "It's one thing after another."

CHAPTER 11

THOUGH AUTUMN HAD officially arrived earlier that week, the afternoon and evening of September 25, 1982, were pleasant enough for shirtsleeves in Happy Valley. As the sun set, an artificial glow illuminated the sky over packed Beaver Stadium. For the first time in the team's ninety-five-year history, Penn State was playing a home game beneath lights. The temporary lighting—it would be another four years before permanent illumination was installed—was a concession to TV, which would broadcast the game between Joe Paterno's eighth-ranked Nittany Lions and Tom Osborne's second-ranked Nebraska Cornhuskers to a nationwide audience that afternoon.

It was late in that game's fourth quarter, with Nebraska in front, 24–21, when Mike McCloskey broke toward the sideline on a simple out-pattern. With each hurried stride Penn State's tight end took, the rumbling murmur of more than eighty-five thousand voices rose in pitch. He turned his head and body in time to see quarterback Todd Blackledge's second-down pass twisting toward him through the haze. By then, a Nebraska linebacker was coming too.

From above, the geometry of the pass play seemed miscalculated. While McCloskey was headed for a corner of the field just shy of the south end zone, the ball appeared to have been thrown a little too quickly and looked as if it would fly, untouched, out of bounds.

The tight end recognized this and, with the instinctive calculations of a veteran, adjusted. He increased his stride, extended his arms, and began to lunge toward the sideline. His hands reached the ball, but as he tried to pull it into his body, it squirmed in his arms like a restless baby. Suddenly, his attention shifted toward the fast-approaching white line. McCloskey threw down his right foot, dropping it like an anchor near the stripe. Then he lowered the other.

That second foot landed out of bounds. But what about the first? All that was required for a legal catch in college football was that a receiver have one foot in bounds. When his right foot scraped along the grass, it had been perilously near the sideline stripe. And even if it had come down in bounds, did McCloskey have possession of the ball at the time?

Nearby, an official's arms jerked forward as he prepared to make a call. The frenzied crowd took a deep collective breath.

Two thirds of Penn State's 1982 season remained. But that play, that call, would end up being its most significant moment. Had the ruling gone the other way—as television replays showed it probably should have—Joe Paterno might still be looking for a first national championship.

"A quirky wind," Paterno later said of the play, "had gusted in our favor."

There was something quirky indeed about that 1982 team. It just didn't mesh with the popular image of Penn State football. Paterno's philosophy, as everyone knew by then, emphasized the game's practical arts—defense and running the ball. But that year, in his seventeenth season as head coach and nearing his fifty-sixth birthday, he had made an adjustment many thought they'd never see.

"We are going to try and make big plays happen," Paterno predicted before the season.

It was easier said than done. Senior Curt Warner was a superb and threatening tailback. The West Virginia native had run for 1,044 yards as a junior in 1981. He needed to be a focus of the offense. But Paterno also had a strong-armed quarterback in Blackledge, and two gifted wide receivers, Kenny Jackson and Gregg Garrity. That kind of a passing talent could gobble up big chunks of yards faster than Warner. So even as the tailback was being touted as a preseason Heisman Trophy candidate, Paterno was altering his offense to incorporate more passes.

Actually, in the '82 season, Warner would carry the ball more times (198 to 171) and rush for just three fewer total yards than he had in '81. But he also caught 24 passes and was overshadowed by Blackledge in an attack that clearly tilted toward the pass.

"Some of the dreams that I had kind of went down the drain," Warner would say later of that season. "But I think I became a tougher football player. By the end of the season I was as tough a football player as there was in the country."

As a result, this Paterno team would become, for Penn State, a statistical anomaly. Its defense wouldn't even finish in the top fifty nationally. And the offense, for a first time ever under Paterno, would gain more yards through the air than on the ground.

Blackledge, at six-three, 227 pounds, was the first protypical NFL QB Paterno had coached. That season he would throw 46 more passes than any Penn State QB ever had—292 in all, a school-record 22 of them for touchdowns. His season total of 2,218 yards would be just three shy of Chuck Fusina's five-year-old Penn State record.

Paterno had recognized this team's potential when he first began to assemble it. The Sugar Bowl loss to Alabama in 1979 had ratcheted up his already potent craving for a national title. And even though he had lost eleven starters from the 10–2 1981 team, he began campaigning early.

"If this isn't the best team I've had here," said Paterno, in an uncharacteristic burst of braggadocio before the season opener, "it's certainly as good as any."

Following home victories over perennial eastern doormats Temple, Maryland, and Rutgers, Penn State was 3–0 and ranked eighth nationally when a far more formidable opponent came to Beaver Stadium.

Nebraska was No. 2 in the polls and it was hard to make a case that any team in the country had more talent. Osborne's Cornhuskers possessed a devastating offense, with running backs Roger Craig and Mike Rozier, wide receiver Irving Fryar, quarterback Turner Gill, and offensive linemen Dave Rimington and Dean Steinkuhler. A week earlier, in routing New Mexico State, 68–0, they had amassed a mind-boggling 883 yards in total offense, a respectable three-game total for many teams.

This game, which had attracted a record crowd to Penn State's stadium, was exactly the kind of attention-grabbing, poll-impacting, intersectional matchup Paterno had envisioned when he moved to upgrade his schedule a decade earlier. Reluctantly, he had come to the realization that the rest of the nation didn't care how many times, or by how many points, his teams beat Maryland, Rutgers, West Virginia, and Army. He understood now that the pollsters, in making their subjective decisions, factored in the reputations of the losers as much as the performance of the winners.

"I don't think our fans were all that thrilled anymore about watching us win some lopsided game against an eastern team," Paterno would later recall. "The competition in the East then just wasn't what it once was."

So Paterno had signed a deal with Nebraska for a series of four games from 1979 through 1982. The Cornhuskers had won the first two, but a year earlier, in Lincoln, the Lions had prevailed, 30–24.

That schedule, both more appealing and more difficult, would turn out to be a crucial element in the Nittany Lions' 1982 season. If the victory over Nebraska had instead been a win over a more traditional opponent like Army or Navy, Penn State almost certainly would not have been in a position to play for a national championship on New Year's Day. After they beat Nebraska, the Nittany Lions immediately shot up five spots in the polls to No. 3, helping dull the effect of what would be their only loss that season, 42–21, a week later at Alabama.

In the Nebraska game, Penn State's defense, led by end Walker Lee Ashley and safety Mark Robinson, both of whom would enjoy long NFL careers, limited the Cornhuskers' running game to 61 yards in the first two quarters. On offense, utilizing Warner's legs and Blackledge's arm in equal proportions, the Lions would build a 21–7 lead in the third quarter.

But Nebraska, aided by missed field goals and a touchdown overturned by a penalty, rallied. The Cornhuskers' comeback was capped when Gill dived in from the 1-yard line to finish off an 80-yard, fourth-quarter drive. It put them ahead, 24–21, with just 1:18 left.

Out of time-outs, Penn State began the ensuing drive on its own 35. In the past, having relied so lopsidedly on the run, Paterno's teams would have found it nearly impossible to traverse 65 yards in just over a minute without benefit of a single time-out. This team was different. Its pass-oriented offense gave it more resiliency. Five times in 1982 these Nittany Lions would come from behind to triumph.

After huddling with Paterno on the sideline, Blackledge calmly marched his team down the field. On a fourth-and-11 at Nebraska's 34, he hit Jackson for exactly 11 yards. Then, after scampering for six yards on first down, the quarterback dashed out of bounds at the 17 with just thirteen seconds remaining.

The next play was the pass to McCloskey.

Standing at the 50-yard line, Paterno waited intently for the ruling. "I couldn't see anything from where I was," he said. "But I knew he was close to being out of bounds."

As the official ran toward the spot where McCloskey had crossed the sideline, he balled his hands into fists, folded his arms close to his body, and thrust his elbows downward to signify a legal catch. With nine seconds remaining, Penn State had a first down at the two.

Nebraska players pleaded with the officials, insisting a mistake had been made. Across the field, Cornhuskers assistants, though not Osborne, screamed their displeasure.

Recalling his Sugar Bowl frustration in 1979, Paterno now called for another pass play. Blackledge took the snap, looked left, and then swiveled his head back to the right. Backup tight end Kirk Bowman, a former guard who had earned his nickname of "Stonehands," was open—so open that he was flailing his arms, desperately hoping to catch the quarterback's eyes. Finally, Blackledge saw him. And though his throw was low, Bowman bent down to catch it for the go-ahead score.

"The thing I remember most," said Paterno, "was Kirk Bowman making the catch in the end zone, because I think that was maybe the first or second catch he had ever made in his life at Penn State as a tight end. It wasn't an easy catch either. Todd Blackledge didn't put that ball on the money."

Penn State students, most of whom were occupying the grandstand areas surrounding the end zone where the Lions scored, literally jumped for joy. Replays of the moment on CBS show the entire crowd hopping up and down in delirious unison. As the game ended, fans stormed the field and, with a frightening intensity, ripped down the goalpost closest to where McCloskey had made his catch. Later, only slightly less frantic, they paraded it past the Nittany Lion statue and Old Main.

Players from Nebraska, which would go on to finish at 12–1 and No. 3 in the country, remain convinced that one call cost them another national title. McCloskey, they still insist, was out of bounds. From some angles, slow-motion replays confirm their belief.

Penn State's players are split. "You look at the film," McCloskey said, "and you make up your own mind. . . . I was dragging my foot along the ground. It's difficult to tell."

But Paterno admitted in his 1989 autobiography that after seeing the televised replays, he was convinced that, "without question," McCloskey was out of bounds.

Shortly afterward, Nebraska students took to wearing T-shirts that portrayed Beaver Stadium's field as a familiar, rectangular grid—except for the slight bump protruding from the 2-yard line.

Paterno got another coaching lesson from Bear Bryant the next week, in the 42–21 loss at Alabama. Afterward, he challenged his team.

"You've got six games left," he told them in the locker room, "let's see what you're made of."

Penn State responded as he had hoped, rolling over the next four opponents—Syracuse, West Virginia, Boston College, and North Carolina State—by a combined score of 158–24. On November 13, when they traveled to No. 13 Notre Dame, the Nittany Lions were No. 5 in the nation.

The trip to Notre Dame was yet another illustration of Penn State's scheduling revolution. A year earlier, the Nittany Lions' schedule—with Nebraska, Miami, Alabama, Notre Dame, and Pitt—had been rated the nation's toughest. This year's included all of those teams but Miami.

The game against the Irish would be the second in a twelve-game contract the two independent powerhouses had signed in the late 1970s. It would be Paterno's first trip to the place Knute Rockne transformed into a college football's golden-domed Camelot. Growing up Catholic in Brooklyn, he was well aware of Notre Dame's mystique and the school's potent hold on generations of fans who had never even visited South Bend. Since coming to Penn State, he had lost a lot of recruits because of it. But as much as he admired the school's proud football heritage and its commitment to academic excellence, he occasionally was irritated by the arrogance he believed surrounded the Irish program.

He experienced it quickly that weekend. Reporters who met Penn State's plane at the South Bend Regional Airport on Friday night asked the coach how it felt to be making a first visit to such hallowed ground, as if the Nittany Lions were football bumpkins making their debut in the big-time spotlight.

"We'd played a lot of big games in a lot of big places by then," Paterno would recall, "and I'm thinking, *Who do these people think they are?*"

During their hotel meeting that night, the coach couldn't bite his tongue any longer. He delivered one of his rare fire-and-brimstone talks, reminding his players that Penn State possessed a mystique of its own.

"You're going to hear all about Notre Dame tradition," he told them, "and you know what? It doesn't mean a thing unless Knute Rockne leaps out of the ground and tackles you. . . . When you put those black shoes on tomorrow, and you put on that jersey without your name on the back, and you put that plain helmet on, that's tradition. *Penn State* tradition!"

The next afternoon, Penn State came from behind to defeat Notre Dame, 24–14. And in the season finale two weeks later, against Dan Marino's fifth-ranked Pitt, the Nittany Lions held on for a 19–10 victory.

They were 10–1, ranked second, and headed for a Sugar Bowl matchup with Heisman winner Herschel Walker and No. 1 Georgia, which had beaten Georgia Tech, 38–18, in its final game. Since Penn State already had beaten No. 3 Nebraska, and since No. 4 SMU had a tie and, much like Penn State in the past, difficulty in gaining respect from poll voters because of a weak schedule, the Sugar Bowl would provide a clear-cut showdown for the national championship—only the sixth time since the Associated Press poll began in 1936 that No. 1 and No. 2 would meet in the postseason.

A year earlier, in a New Year's Day Fiesta Bowl victory over Southern Cal, Penn State had controlled that year's Heisman Trophy–winning tailback. Marcus Allen could manage only 85 yards on thirty carries in the Lions' 26–10 triumph.

For that game, Paterno and Sandusky had devised something they called a "Magic Defense," for its now-you-see-it-now-you-don't qualities. Fronts switched from five, to six, to seven, even to eight men. Sometimes there were two down linemen, sometimes five or six. Linebackers came from everywhere.

The constant movement and change was an effort to confuse blockers, or at least to keep them guessing. More recently, the "Magic" had mesmerized Nebraska's Mike Rozier, holding him to 86 yards—52 below his average—in that November victory. But Walker, sprinter-quick at six-foot-two and 230 pounds, presented an even sterner challenge.

"You hit him low," said Sandusky, "and he moves his feet. You hit him high and he'll knock you over with a forearm. It takes more than one man to get him."

The practices between the November 26 finale with Pitt and the New Year's Day game in New Orleans's Superdome were brutally wearying. After years of complaining about polls, Paterno had failed in his first attempt to win a national title on that same Superdome turf four years earlier. Now he was determined not to let this opportunity at redemption slip away.

He assigned freshmen Eufard Cooper and Steve Smith to take on the role of Walker in the workouts. Smith, in particular, provided an excellent imitation of the Georgia star. But soon he was so beat up that he begged for a stand-in.

"Poor Steve Smith," recalled linebacker Scott Radecic. "We nailed him and nailed him until he said, 'I'm tired of being Herschel Walker,' and wanted to quit."

Paterno threw himself into the preparations as never before. Players said they had never seen their coach so determined. By game day, he was stressed, anxious, and edgy. A friend who had been granted locker-room access before the game asked the coach how he expected Georgia's Vince Dooley to utilize Walker early in the Sugar Bowl.

"If we knew that," snapped Paterno, "we wouldn't be sitting here fidgeting."

If Paterno was nervous, it wasn't contagious. His players came out poised and ready. With Blackledge hitting McCloskey and Garrity for long gains on the initial drive, the offense marched quickly down the field. Warner scurried the final two yards into the end zone.

The "Magic" was baffling Walker. Late in the first half, Penn State held a 20–3 advantage. But Georgia rebounded quickly. A Bulldogs touchdown with five seconds remaining in the half and another on the third quarter's opening drive made it a 20–17 game.

Georgia had the momentum on its side as the fourth quarter began. Warner, who would outgain Walker, collecting 117 yards and two touchdowns to 103 yards and one score for the Heisman winner, was bothered by leg cramps, and Penn State's offense had been unimpressive in the second half. Looking to shake things up, Paterno sent in a play, "643," on a first-and-10 at Georgia's 47.

Blackledge faked a handoff to Warner, who darted toward the center of Georgia's defense. That feint froze the linebackers and at least one of the safeties. Meanwhile, on the flanks, four Penn State receivers, covered by only three defensive backs, sprinted downfield. Garrity broke clear down the left sideline and Blackledge heaved the ball toward him.

But the quarterback was anxious and his pass soared farther than intended. Garrity accelerated—as best he could anyway—lunged for it, and caught the ball as, still off his feet and fully extended, he sailed into the end zone. A photo of the moment, some say the most memorable in Paterno's long career, would appear on the cover of the next *Sports Illustrated*.

Penn State's 27–17 lead wouldn't last long, though. Kevin Baugh, who had broken two spectacular punt returns earlier, fumbled one midway through the final quarter and Georgia turned it into a score that, after the Bulldogs failed on a two-point try, made it a 27–23 game.

Then came one of the most important decisions Paterno would ever make. On a third-and-3 at Penn State's 32, with ninety-seven seconds remaining, his conservative instincts, as well as his assistant coaches, were urging him to call for a safe running play. Even if it failed, they could punt the ball deep into Georgia territory.

But the Bulldogs' offense was in a rhythm now and he did not want to give them another chance. From where he stood pondering the decision on the Superdome sideline, he could see the end zone where Alabama had stifled his dream and his power-running game exactly four years earlier.

Blackledge wanted to throw it, pleading with his coach that he could complete a short pass. He figured Georgia, as it had done on second down, would be defending against the run. He told Paterno that if that were the case, he'd check off and throw it to Garrity.

"My gut believed him. . . . I was not the same person I was [in 1979]," Paterno later wrote in his autobiography. "[In 1979] I wasn't big enough, strong enough, grown enough to face the ridicule if we had thrown the ball and the pass had been intercepted. The scare of it faced me down, and I lost. This time I didn't care about the ridicule. I cared about the first down, the risk. . . . I knew this time that I was not afraid to lose."

He told Blackledge to throw it.

The six-yard quick-out to Garrity was completed.

Penn State ran the ball three more times, eating up the seconds, before, with only six left, Ralph Giacomarro had to punt it away. When the Georgia return man was tackled, the clock ran out.

• • •

It was all a blur after that.

Paterno had just realized the compelling ambition of his professional life, winning a national championship, and yet somehow the moment was shrouded in an otherworldy haze. Part of that was because his glasses had been knocked off when celebrating players hoisted him onto their shoulders. Someone must have retrieved them because a photo of that victory ride shows Paterno wearing the tinted trifocals.

The picture also showed that when the moment he had worked a lifetime to achieve arrived, Paterno was in shirtsleeves, his collar unbuttoned, his tie loosened. The returned glasses, sensitive to light, were nearly completely opaque, obscuring whatever his eyes might have revealed. He was being jostled atop the moving pack of players like a tenderfoot on a mechanical bull. A wide smile was emerging on the coach's face even though he appeared to be doing his best to prevent it. And above his head, smoky Superdome lights shone like jewels in a crown.

That night Penn State hosted a party at the team hotel and Paterno stayed until 2:00 A.M. Then he excused himself and went to bed, where he would remain awake most of the night savoring the victory and all that had preceded it.

The next day, thousands of fans and state politicians in central Pennsylvania greeted the Nittany Lions at Harrisburg Airport. Paterno and the players then attended a rally at the university's Harrisburg campus before boarding buses for the long ride to State College. All along Route 322, people from the small towns that abutted the two-lane road lined up to share in this moment with the national champions.

"Through county after county," Paterno would write of the scene, "for country mile after country mile, U.S. Highway 322 was lined with people, people, people, cars, cars, cars, honking horns, horns, horns, no end of them, waiting through that winter night just to wave, to shout a greeting, to clap their hands for an all-too-brief moment as their champions passed by."

The crowds were even thicker in State College, where the buses unloaded their passengers at a packed and frantic campus rally. The following day, in the snow, there was a parade through town and another gathering on the broad lawn in front of Old Main. Paterno spoke at every stop.

He was enjoying the moment. No one had worked harder or, as *Sports Illustrated* noted that week, "was more deserving" of a national title. But he was also looking ahead, calculating what he and Penn State would need to win another championship in a changing collegiate sports world.

"Where would he go from here?" brother George later wrote. "For the Don Quixote of football, the impossible dream came true. What quest was he planning for the future?"

The answer came quickly. As coach of the national champions, Paterno had a bully pulpit. He planned to use it to transform the entire university. And the weapon he knew would be necessary in changing the school's academic culture and maintaining its football dynasty was money.

In a speech to Penn State's trustees just a few weeks after the Sugar Bowl triumph, he pointed out what the administrators were then only just beginning to understand: The national title provided the school with an unprecedented opportunity. Sports had grown so powerful, and garnered so much media attention and recognition, that they could be used to drive a school's growth. Penn State was suddenly on the radar of students, professors, and administrators from across the nation. It was up to the university to create the kind of environment that would lure them to State College.

Paterno lambasted the staid intellectual life at Penn State, labeling it "reactionary." He urged that professors with new and controversial ideas be imported. He wanted to see a better library, better classroom technology, a more challenging curriculum, and more scholarship money. As *Sports Illustrated*'s Rick Reilly noted of Paterno's speech, "It may go down as the only time in history that a coach yearned for a school its football team could be proud of."

Though Paterno clearly was speaking from a sense of idealism, there was a practical side to his message too. The better the academics and the facilities became, he knew, the easier it would be for him to sell Penn State to recruits and big-money contributors.

Penn State desperately needed to build its endowment. In 1978, according to a *Chronicle of Higher Education* study, its endowment of $11.3 million ranked 103rd among U.S. universities. A changing economy that stagnated Rust Belt states like Pennsylvania had led Harrisburg to slow the growth of its subsidies to the school. Athletics was soon going to feel the pinch unless it could begin collecting more cash from a suddenly energized alumni base.

The converted trustees immediately announced a $200 million fund raising drive with Paterno as its vice chairman. The coach and his wife began making generous contributions themselves. Those donations continued to grow until, in 1998, the Paternos would donate $3.5 million to endow faculty positions and scholarships and to help with two building projects, including a library addition that now bears their name. By 2000, *Philanthropy* magazine estimated the Paternos had donated well over $4 million to the university.

"I'm a little bit like Andrew Carnegie," Paterno said. "If you die with money, your life was a failure. . . . I really, honestly believe that we have an obligation to help people who haven't been as fortunate as we have been."

The football coach also became a formidable and enthusiastic fund-raiser for the university, flying all over the country in Penn State's jets to clinch the deal with a big donor or to solicit contributions at a banquet.

Spanier recalled a joint visit they had made to a major contributor. The president was going to detail the project for which they sought the funds and Paterno was going to close the deal, asking for a $3 million gift. When his turn came, the persuasive coach asked instead for $5 million. And got it.

"My heart skipped a beat," Spanier said.

What awed alum, after all, could turn down a personal request from the coach of a national championship football team?

"He understands the power of his presence," said AD Tim Curley.

"And he's always been willing to use it for the good of the university as a whole."

It worked. Penn State and its football team soon became as well known for the loyalty of its alumni, the high graduation rate among athletes, and an overall emphasis on education as for its victories.

According to the most recent NCAA Graduation Rates Report, eighty-eight percent of the Penn State football players who enrolled in 1995–96 graduated. The Division I-A average was a mere fifty-two percent. And among African-Americans, Penn State football's graduation rate of eighty-two percent was nearly double the forty-two percent national average.

Don Ferrell, Penn State football's academic adviser for decades before his recent retirement, said Paterno's reputation was the residue of the reality the coach has created around his program. While he might ask from time to time that a certain number of academic exceptions be admitted, he demands those players devote themselves to classwork.

"I always told Joe when kids were having trouble, and he always backed me," Ferrell said. "When kids weren't performing academically, he'd look at me and say, 'Did they flunk?' I'd say, 'Yeah,' and he'd take care of them. I never had to go out on a limb and do something against my character or integrity."

Paterno, better than any other coach, has managed to walk the narrow line between football and academic performance. By 2004, when Penn State victories were rare, graduations were not.

"I told the squad the other day," he would say after that season, " 'You know, I look at you, every one of you guys is going to graduate unless you transfer.' I feel good about that. I also said, 'Goddammit, I wish you'd win a couple more games.' "

CHAPTER 12

THE SEASON'S FIRST MONTH was complete and if Paterno's new approach had made a difference, the change wasn't visible.

In the days leading up to the Minnesota game, the coach's age and troubles had become even more solidly entrenched as punch lines on sports-radio shows and Web sites around the country. Much of the irreverent snickering came from fans of other college powerhouses, some of whom had chafed over the years whenever Paterno leveled criticism at their coaches or programs for ethical or academic lapses.

Those visiting Oklahoma's *Soonerfans.com* that week were treated to a clever photo exhibit starring Penn State's coach. Some enterprising critic superimposed onto a variety of other images a photo of Paterno leading his team out of the Beaver Stadium tunnel. In the original, the wild look in the old coach's eyes suggests a frothy breakdown. His arms are raised at arthritic angles above his surprisingly gray head. And his mouth is wide open in the midst of what appears to be a terrifying scream.

That frightening waist-up image of Paterno was then overlaid onto other bodies in photographs that depicted him running with the bulls in Pamplona, finishing a Special Olympics race ahead of smiling competitors, drumming with a heavy-metal band, screaming at a family of ducks as they cross a busy highway, or angrily confronting *Seinfeld*'s Soup Nazi.

Thus inspired, another Oklahoma supporter altered the Wheaties box that contained Paterno's profile. In his new version, *Wheaties* had been replaced by *Geritol* and the caption beneath the coach's likeness read "Joe Paterno: Old Man."

Meanwhile, on a Notre Dame fans Web site, *NDNation.com*, a recent discussion about the coach led someone to post a David Letterman–like list—Top Ten Undisclosed Terms of Joe Paterno's Contract Extension. They included: "No. 7: Paterno bowed to pressure to modernize his offense; agreed to install the single wing. . . . No. 4: Instead of a cooler of Gatorade, victorious players may only douse coach with a cup of warm soup. . . . and No. 1: Penn State agreed to move its campus to Naples, Florida."

Paterno claimed he didn't hear the jokes or the criticism, and that even if he had, it wouldn't bother him. These attacks on a legend did, however, offend some of his colleagues.

"If they can criticize Joe Paterno like that, the rest of us have no chance," said Glen Mason, whose Minnesota team would face Paterno's that Saturday night. "It bothers me. I only say that because we are so hypocritical at the collegiate level. I've always said I'm not a pro coach, I'm a college coach. I'm held responsible for a lot of other things than just winning games, like graduation rates, grade point averages, the conduct of my players. Those things are really important in the job description, but if you don't win enough games, they're going to say you are a bad coach."

Mason, a New Jersey native who first got to know the Penn State coach when he was an Ohio State assistant, admired Paterno so much that he began wearing a tie on the sideline in silent tribute. In defending this idol, Mason recalled a 1997 game he coached at State College. The No. 1–ranked Nittany Lions won, 16–15, thanks to a missed call late in the fourth quarter. When the two men met at midfield for the postgame handshake, Paterno asked if Mason would permit him to visit the Gophers' locker room so that he could apologize for the officials' mistake.

"I could only imagine my reaction in that situation," Mason said. "I'd be so excited that we didn't lose and were still number one, with national-championship hopes still alive. . . . The first thing he says to me is, 'You got robbed; the worst call I've ever seen in coaching. It's a shame your team didn't win. Your kids outplayed mine. Your coaches out-coached us.' I couldn't believe it. The guy never ceases to amaze me."

The week of the Minnesota game, Paterno again had impressed—or irritated—his coaching colleagues by speaking out against a proposal most of them were forced to support. It came when he was asked for an opinion on the likely addition of a twelfth game for Division I foot-ball programs, something money-hungry programs everywhere had been pushing.

"We always brag on the kid who's an engineer or the kid who graduates in four years and so forth," he began. "But we don't take a good look at the majority of our squads who are kids who really need exposure to a college life. If I were a kid today and someone said to me, 'You're good enough to play big-time college football,' I'm not sure I'd do it. You've got to be at weight training. You work all winter. You work all summer. And now we're going to give them a twelfth game? And we're only giving them the twelfth game so we can take care of the other sports. . . . I'm for the football player. Twelve games in a league like the Big Ten, I think that's tough. It's not necessary and it's not fair to the football kids."

Still, his aging voice continued to be drowned out. By the jokes. By the criticism. By the losses. In his mind, there was only one remedy: victories. They weren't going to come easily. "This stretch of games that we are going through is probably the toughest stretch in all of the years I've been here," he said. He admitted that he needed to keep reinforcing his team with one of his favorite bits of philosophy.

"If you're knocked down," he told them over and over, "you can't lose your guts. You need to play with supreme confidence or you'll lose again, and then losing becomes a habit."

An air of desperation had begun to circulate through the Penn State locker room like a spirit-sapping disease. It would grow in strength over the next several weeks, infusing every game with an enormous importance. Time and patience always seemed to be in short supply.

"I'm sick of losing," junior cornerback Alan Zemaitis said. "I'm

THE LION IN AUTUMN • 163

just so starving to win. I want to get back to the days when we had [tailback Larry Johnson] and those guys. I was just a young buck. We weren't going out there thinking we were going to lose back then."

As he heard the latest bad news, Paterno thought that sooner or later life was going to have to be penalized for piling on.

On that previous Saturday afternoon at Mount Nittany Medical Center, as his team was losing in Madison and his badly injured son-in-law was being examined in the emergency room a few floors below, another of Paterno's friends and former players died. Bob Mitinger, an all-American defensive end at Penn State in 1961, a prominent State College lawyer, an influential Nittany Lions supporter, succumbed to cancer at sixty-four.

"We've had a tough year," Paterno said. "Bob was one of the toughest, fiercest competitors that we have ever had at Penn State. He was a real strong person in the community. I can still see him when I was an assistant coach. . . . There are a lot of good people who have gone through this program and Bob was one of them, one of the better ones."

Off the field, life seemed to be imitating the Lions' experiences on it: bad news heaped atop bad news. There was nothing the coach could do but try to turn these ceaseless tragedies into motivation. If nothing else, he hoped, maybe they would bring his players closer together. He had lectured them on that very topic the previous spring.

"Take a look around, because the best friends you are ever going to have in your life are sitting around you," Paterno had told his team. "Thirty years from now you guys will be friends. Football is important and we want to do well, but we want to respect each other and hang in there together regardless of what happens."

Meanwhile, as the coach held his weekly Tuesday news conference, Hort remained in critical conditon at the Altoona hospital.

"I would rather not get into my situation personally," he said to the reporters, declining to provide any details. "We are going through some tough things and I don't want to get into that. . . . I appreciate everybody's concern. . . . There are young kids involved in this, so I would appreciate if there were not a lot written about it. We are trying to protect them."

Athletic department employees, careful not to violate the coach's wishes or breach the university's secretive policies, indicated privately that Hort remained in a coma. It now appeared, they said, that the coach's son-in-law would survive but that he might suffer some minor paralysis. No one knew what had caused the accident.

For a floundering 2–2 team in the teeth of its Big Ten schedule, the injuries to Hort and the two quarterbacks generated more distraction and doubt. Paterno's fabled focus had been so diffused that he had considered canceling Monday's workout. His players and assistants persuaded him to change his mind. According to tight end Isaac Smolko, after the loss at Wisconsin none of his teammates "thought it would be a good idea to take a day off. We need to get better."

Paterno worked them for about an hour on Monday. Then he delivered yet another message of hope. Sometimes he felt like he'd been encouraging them almost nonstop since the spring.

"I'm proud of how you handled it," Paterno said of their performance in Madison. "Nobody got down. Nobody gave up."

As for the rest of the practice week, the sessions on Tuesday, Wednesday, and Thursday were of normal length and intensity. Many fans didn't realize how little time college players had to prepare together on the field. And when they traveled to their weekend destination, Fridays were pretty much wasted too. "We do a little more on Friday than we used to, but not much," he explained. "We don't even put helmets on. We wear shorts and walk through substitution procedures and things like that." Paterno found that the most beneficial thing he could do on those travel days was to make time for a long, head-clearing walk.

Even with his team in desperate need of help, he rarely sought to alter his practice routines. They had served him well, with very few significant changes, for a long, long time.

"You have to be careful," he said. "Sometimes things just don't go your way. If you start changing just for the sake of changing, you end up going backwards. We just have to hang in there and get better. It is as simple as that."

Besides, for all the importance he placed on the workouts, he understood longer or tougher practices weren't the answer. His Nittany Lions, nearly every one of whom was fearful that 2004 might easily deteriorate into another 2003, weren't going to improve until they tasted success.

That would be more difficult now. Even if a banged-up Mills were able to play Saturday, the absence of Robinson left an enormous void. Defensive coordinators had very few reasons to respect this Penn State's offense. That week, for the first, but certainly not the last, time, Paterno played up his team's youth. Critics called it an excuse. To Paterno, it was simply a logical explanation for his team's inconsistency.

"This is the youngest football team I have ever coached, against the toughest schedule we have ever played," he said. "We are playing undefeated football teams—big, strong football teams that are good football teams and well coached," he said. "We are playing them with a lot of young kids. There are not a lot of guys that I think are comfortable [enough] yet to make the big plays. You would hope that after they get into a couple of games they'd start to do that."

The clamor was building. Early in the week, a few more national columnists had urged Paterno to step down. In various Internet chat rooms, his suggested successors included Mason, Iowa's Kirk Ferentz, Utah's Urban Meyer, the unemployed Steve Spurrier, Terry Bowden and Jackie Sherrill, New York Jets head coach Herman Edwards, New York Giants offensive coordinator John Hufnagle, and a couple of Pennsylvania high school coaches.

On Friday, Patrick Reusse of the *Minneapolis Star-Tribune* telephoned Penn State alums in the Twin Cities to gauge their feelings about the coach before he arrived in Minnesota. For the record, all of them said Paterno had earned the right to stay as long as he wanted. But Reusse's editor told him he had been hearing nothing but complaints from the Penn State grads who were in town for Saturday's game. When the sportswriter called some of them, they indeed voiced their displeasure with Paterno, but refused to be quoted.

"It was like they were afraid maurauding gangs would be dispatched to their homes," Reusse said.

In addition, Las Vegas oddsmakers had made Minnesota a 14 1/2-point favorite. No one associated with the Nittany Lions could remember a Paterno team ever being such a sizable underdog. Part of the reason the spread was that large, of course, was that Mills, his non-throwing left shoulder still extremely sore, remained questionable for Saturday. And Robinson would definitely be out.

Robinson had spent Saturday night in the Madison hospital before returning to State College on Sunday. Back in his dorm room, he got a call from Taliaferro. He told Robinson that he understood what he was going through.

"Thank God that you're able to go back on the field," Taliaferro said, "because I wish I could go back every day."

"It was an emotional conversation, but we got through it," Robinson recalled.

He continued to suffer from headaches throughout the week as doctors performed a series of complicated cognitive tests. "Some of the things they were asking me, I don't think I would have been able to get a lot of it right even if I didn't have a concussion."

The tests, the doctors told Paterno, revealed the quarterback's concussion had been so severe that he might be out three or four weeks. "Our medical people tend to be conservative," Paterno said. With a bye week coming up on October 16, the coach hoped his most versatile performer might be able to return October 23, for the homecoming game against Iowa.

If Mills couldn't play, Paterno said, Ganter would start, with Morelli backing him up. The coach instructed his son Jay and Hall to prepare a game plan that stressed a controlled attack—lots of runs and short passes. How they could make that work, when he knew Minnesota would be jamming the line of scrimmage, was something they'd worry about later.

He had few worries about Penn State's improving defense—even if Minnesota's 542.8 total yards and 332 rushing yards were, respectively, third and fourth in the nation. Tailback Laurence Maroney was averaging 131.5 yards a game for the eighteenth ranked, 4–0 Gophers. Running mate Marion Barber III was not far behind, at 128.5.

"Minnesota is the best team we will have played so far," said Paterno, "and that is not to take anything away from Wisconsin. This is a very, very explosive offensive football team that has had a lot of success. . . . They do a great job with the play-action pass off the running game so you can't gang up on the run."

Penn State flew into Minneapolis on Friday night. As they did, back at the Rathskeller bar in State College, suspended wideout Maurice Humphrey, who was not yet twenty-one, was caught with a fake ID. It was a violation of his parole. He eventually would be sentenced to nine months in jail. Then a student at Penn State–Altoona, he had hoped to reenroll at the main campus next fall. Now, any hopes that the gifted receiver and Paterno had of his return to the team in 2005 were dead.

Back in Minneapolis, the Nittany Lions held their night-before meeting in a ballroom at the downtown Crowne Plaza Hotel. It had to be delayed when assistant coach Larry Johnson and a dozen or so of his players got stuck in a hotel elevator for fifteen minutes.

A scaled-down media reception was held in a nondescript room a few floors below. The sportswriters were getting the message. Only a few people showed up this week. Paterno was not among them.

The declining attendance had caused sports-information director Jeff Nelson to greatly reduce the menu and bar fare. Chips and salsa. Pretzels. Beer and water.

And an untouched bottle of Jack Daniel's.

The Hubert H. Humphrey Metrodome in downtown Minneapolis was a strange place for a team used to performing in the sunny glow of Happy Valley. The multipurpose stadium was dark and soulless, its ambience as unappealing as the fried cheese curds sold by vendors just outside its gates.

In the hectic hours before that night's 7:00 P.M. CDT game, workers hustled around the domed facility painting lines on the field, frantically storing sections of unused bleachers, and hanging maroon-

and-gold banners that contained numbers the Gophers had retired and names from a distant past, like Bronko Nagurski and Paul Giel.

For a time it looked as if the Big Ten game might have to be delayed. At 2:30 P.M., a baseball game was still being played on the Dome's turf field. The Cleveland Indians and the American League Central champion Minnesota Twins were tied at 5–5 in the eleventh inning of a game that would determine next week's AL playoff matchups.

The baseball game had begun unusually early, at 11:10 A.M., to ensure that workers would have plenty of time to convert the field and stadium to their football configurations. But the conversion would take at least four hours and, when the game rolled into extra innings, Minnesota officials got nervous. Penn State–Minnesota was being televised regionally by ESPN so its starting time was inviolable.

Finally, baseball fans were informed by the public-address announcer that if the game were not concluded in the bottom of the eleventh, it would have to be suspended, then resumed and finished the following afternoon. When the home team failed to score, fans booed as they reluctantly departed. And the Twins, who had been lobbying hard for a baseball-only stadium and who still had a shot at gaining homefield advantage in their opening postseason series, felt like doing the same.

"Just stop the game, and do football now?" Ron Gardenhire, the Twins manager, sarcastically told reporters. "That's pretty sad."

The snafu added weight to recent pleadings by University of Minnesota officials for state help in financing a new campus stadium. The school, whose Metrodome lease expires in 2011, estimated it would cost $220 million to construct a 55,000-seat facility. One alumnus already had pledged $35 million.

"I can't say enough how much that (not having a facility on campus) has retarded our growth," said Mason.

When the Nittany Lions arrived at the stadium shortly after 5 P.M., they walked across the field to get a feel for the artificial surface. Some of them paused and bent over at the second-base cutout to scoop up handfuls of dirt, as if this nondescript stadium with trash-bag walls and a sometimes sagging roof were hallowed ground.

Robinson was with them, dressed in a suit. He changed into a blue Penn State sweatshirt for the game and stood along the sideline with his teammates, wearing a headset to eavesdrop on the night's play calling.

For the second straight year, Minnesota, which had won the toss but deferred, began the game with an onside kick. On this one, Minnesota would recover, just as it had the year before. The ball bounded close to the Lions' Donnie Johnson, who, inexplicably, appeared to back away. "The guy over there didn't even make an effort," Paterno said after the game.

The successful gimmick on the game's initial play was enough to doom the Nittany Lions, given their fragile mental states.

"For them to start the game like that," said linebacker Wake, whom Paterno would again replace with freshman Connor a short time later, "it was a blow to our optimism."

Minnesota turned the surprise into a field goal. The Gophers still led 3–0 late in the first quarter but were backed up on a third-and-11 at their own 13. On a draw, Moroney scampered 64 yards. Shortly afterward he scored on a 1-yard plunge and Minnesota had a 10–0 lead.

That was plenty of points against a Penn State offense that, if anything, looked even feebler than it had at Boston College and Wisconsin, even with Mills at the helm. Paterno had made some changes, substituting Scott Davis for the struggling Charles Rush on the offensive line and starting Rubin at wide receiver. At one point, Penn State played freshmen Rubin and Perretta at ends and freshman Matt Hahn at fullback.

Rubin's start was Paterno's latest effort to send a message to his veterans and to get something out of the position. What did it say when your quarterbacks were your best receivers? Mills's longest completion of this season was a 49-yarder to Robinson. Robinson's best was a 39-yarder to Mills.

"You can only play somebody that doesn't do the job for so long," Paterno said. "We have kids that have worked really hard to get good. Sometimes in practice they look like they are just on the verge of becoming the kind of people you can win [with] . . . make a catch, make a run, and the whole thing with it. Then they don't do it in the game. I think then you have to sit back and say, 'Hey, is there somebody else that can do it?' "

Even though Minnesota had allowed 394 yards a game, the Nittany Lions ran for a total of just 15 yards on fourteen first-half carries. Mills looked uncomfortable. The wideouts dropped passes—six by game's end. And the coaching staff again appeared indecisive.

With 1:08 left in the half, Penn State faced a fourth-and-5 at Minnesota's 34. On the Nittany Lions' sideline, an animated discussion ensued between Paterno and Hall. Should they go for it? Or try a field goal? When it was decided to attempt a 51-yard field goal, Penn State mistakenly sent out twelve players and was forced to call a time-out.

So instead of running down the clock before the kick, they gave Minnesota the ball with 1:03 remaining after Robbie Gould's miss. Thanks to the rapidly improving defense, it did not cost Penn State any points.

Then, for a third consecutive week, the Nittany Lions allowed their opponent to put together a long drive on its first second-half possession. The Gophers culminated an eleven-play, 78-yard march with a 19-yard Barber TD that extended their lead to 16–0.

Penn State finally scored, late in the period, on a 6-yard toss from Mills to Smolko. Then, for the second time in three weeks, Paterno made a bizarre strategic decision. Down 16–6, with an offense that hardly looked capable of multiple scoring drives, the coach declined to go for two points after the touchdown. Two two-point conversions and another TD could have tied the game. By kicking the extra point, the struggling Lions made sure that they'd have to score at least twice more to triumph.

"If it had been later, we would have gone [for two]," Paterno explained later. "I figured a touchdown and a field goal [were possible]. We were doing pretty well."

Observers wondered what game he'd been watching. Penn State would finish with 21 rushing yards, and much of its 250 yards passing came after the outcome had been determined. Despite their coach's stated optimism, the Nittany Lions, to the surprise of no one, did not score again. The 16–7 loss left them winless in the Big Ten and 2–3 on the season.

The Lions' frustration and shortcomings had been highlighted on a backbreaking fourth-quarter play. Penn State seemed ready to get the ball back in good field position when Minnesota lined up for another third-and-11 at its own 21. But Ernie Wheelwright, well covered by Zemaitis, made a great leaping, acrobatic sideline catch of a Bryan Cupito pass for a pivotal 33-yard gain.

Wheelwright was the kind of big, fast, sure-handed receiver Penn State lacked, and his athletic reception was the kind of clutch play Paterno had been craving, in vain, all season.

"That," he said afterward, "is what we need to start doing."

Soon Paterno, head down, hands in pockets, exited the field with his players, losers again. Walking down a Metrodome corridor, the only sound the beaten Lions made was the clap of their cleats on concrete. One by one, like monks on their way to prayer, they filed silently into a locker room that on NFL Sundays was occupied by the Minnesota Vikings.

The dim light of the Metrodome corridor seemed to sap Paterno's legendary vitality.

Leaning forward from the waist, rubbing a hand through hair that on this night suddenly appeared thinner and grayer than ever, he ambled toward a tiny table and a folding chair that workers had set up for his postgame interview.

"Ahhhh, that chair'll feel good," he mumbled to himself as he fell into it.

All he really wanted to do was rest. A digital clock on a wall opposite him read 10:33 P.M. Home was 832 miles away and it would be another six hours before he would get there. He was weary already.

He didn't want to answer the questions he knew were coming. What else could he possibly say? Everybody in the place could see the problem. His wideouts couldn't catch a cold. The defenses they faced could afford to concentrate solely on stopping the run. It was a formula guaranteed to leave single digits in the slot beneath PENN STATE on Big Ten scoreboards.

"How many times can I say it?" Paterno whispered when the questions began. "We dropped passes. How many more ways can I say it? If we catch the ball and we hold them to sixteen, who knows? Rubin had a shot at one. Phillips had that one in the first half. Same way last week. We went into the ball game with the idea that we probably had to throw the ball. They played us to stop the run. But we had great chances to throw the ball. We just didn't catch it."

Paterno answered a few more questions, shook hands with veteran Minnesota sportswriter Sid Hartman, one of the few remaining working journalists who had covered Paterno when he was a Penn State assistant, and, with a halfhearted reminder that "we're not as bad as some people think we are," hurried off to the locker room.

By the time he emerged a few minutes later, Mills was still answering questions.

"Guys, hurry it up!" the coach barked at the reporters. "We've got a plane to catch and we're not going to get home until two or three in the morning as it is."

It would be longer than that before Paterno could rest.

CHAPTER 13

A VAST AND MENACING CLOT of dark clouds, so dense that it instantly darkened the autumn-plaid Allegheny Mountain ridges surrounding State College, settled directly above Beaver Stadium late on the afternoon of October 9.

The storm soon brought wind and rain into the massive steel facility, animating many of the 108,183 fans gathered there for the Purdue–Penn State football game. Hoods were catapulted onto bare heads. See-through ponchos were extracted from bags. And wide-striped umbrellas, most of them Penn State blue and white, rose like toadstools on a damp forest floor. The rain and darkness had rolled in unexpectedly on what had been a sparkling fall day. For these loss-weary fans, its sudden appearance, from beyond the northwest corner of the stadium, was just one more unsettling omen.

Far below, at an unsheltered spot along the east sideline, Paterno momentarily paused from his pacing to sweep away the raindrops forming on his famously tinted glasses.

He had spent enormous physical and emotional capital preparing for the game. Throughout the week, he had appeared obsessed with instantly resurrecting the Nittany Lions' reputation and his own. A victory over undefeated Purdue and Kyle Orton, its Heisman Trophy–contending quarterback, would put the train back on track.

A week earlier, following the loss to Minnesota, Paterno had looked weary, glum, and old. But between then and his regular Tuesday meeting with the media, he underwent a remarkable recuperation. He had identified this game as one that could catapult Penn State back into the headlines, a transforming opportunity that, though he did not say as much, might be the start of his last great grab for glory.

Discussing the upcoming game with reporters, he had been feisty and unusually confident.

"We are a pretty good football team," Paterno said, ignoring all the contrary evidence. "We really are. We are not getting beaten. We are losing games because we are beating ourselves. . . . I think if [Michael] Robinson hadn't gotten hurt, we may have won the last two games."

All week he had pushed his players, his staff, and himself harder than he had in years. In intensely grueling workouts, he challenged them all, particularly the wide receivers whose continuing ineptitude had become an obstacle to recovery.

"When you win the battle, when you get wide open, and you don't catch the football when the quarterback puts it there, who's beating who?" Paterno said. "You know the old [saying], 'We've met the enemy and it's us.' That's basically what's happening. If we can't throw the football, we're not going to be able to run it."

Always a nagger, he prodded his assistants more that week and worked them overtime to devise a game plan that would stifle Orton and unearth some offense from a wounded attack. But he retained veto power over the game plan, which would be devised in tandem by new offensive coordinator Galen Hall and Jay, the quarterbacks coach. And after they submitted it to him, he pared it down considerably, as usual.

Paterno had responded this way after losses in the past, not that there had been many. Only one of his first thirty-four Penn State teams had finished below .500. Then, he knew he could outrecruit and outwork most of his rivals. And even though he liked to say he had no ego, he was damn sure he could outcoach them. But now there was a palpable sense of desperation in his preparations for Purdue.

By this point in the season it was obvious that something profound had changed in Happy Valley. Penn State's problems were deep, systemic. They went beyond the inexperience, the questionable calls, bad breaks, and tough opponents Paterno constantly referenced.

Penn State players, many of them without helmets, on offense during a circa-1900 game at the original Beaver Field; the grandstand in the background accommodated five hundred fans.

New Beaver Field, located near the heart of campus, was the Nittany Lions' home from 1909 through 1959; here it is packed for one of the final games there.

Paterno *(far right)* played quarterback at Brown for Rip Engle *(far left)*, and when the older man was hired as Penn State's head coach in 1950, he brought along his eventual replacement as an assistant; here, they work on a play with an unidentified Nittany Lions player.

Undersized linebacker Jack Ham was discovered by Paterno at a Virginia prep school; the native of Johnstown, Pennsylvania, went on to become a key member of Penn State's unbeaten 1969 team as well as an inductee into both the college and professional Halls of Fame.

Fullback Franco Harris *(left)* and tailback Lydell Mitchell epitomized the run-first offenses Paterno favored; with the top running-back tandem in Penn State history, the Nittany Lions went 28-4 in their three varsity seasons, 1969–71.

John Cappelletti, the only
Penn State player to have
won the Heisman Trophy,
poses with the award in 1973;
days later, at a New York City
banquet, Cappelletti would
tearfully dedicate the honor
to his cancer-stricken brother.

Jubilant players carry Paterno off the Superdome field on January 1, 1983; after
seventeen seasons as Penn State's head coach, Paterno finally won a national
championship that day with a 27–23 Sugar Bowl victory over Herschel Walker's
Georgia team.

An emotional Paterno addressing a Rec Hall crowd at the "Rally in the Valley" the night before the Purdue game; the coach saw the October 9 contest with the unbeaten Boilermakers as an opportunity to transform the 2004 season.

Penn State AD Tim Curley *(left)*, wearing the ubiquitous blue blazer, presents a check to ex-Lions backup defensive back Eric Dare; Dare's brother, Kevin, a Penn State pole-vaulter, was killed in 2002 while competing in the Big Ten championships.

College Avenue in State College; Penn State's isolated, picturesque central Pennsylvania hometown is an integral part of the mythology Paterno has established around his program.

Fireworks illuminate the nighttime sky over Beaver Stadium at the conclusion of "Football Eve," a rally held the night before the 2004 opener with Akron.

Paterno mentioned often that quarterbacks Zack Mills (*left*) and Michael Robinson were the keys to Penn State's 2004 offense.

Michael Robinson fires a pass against Ohio State; Paterno consistently called the versatile junior one of the nation's most talented players but never found him a permanent home in a struggling offense.

Linebacker Paul Posluszny (31) huddles with a group of defensive linemen; Posluszny was part of a defensive unit that never allowed more than twenty-one points in any game.

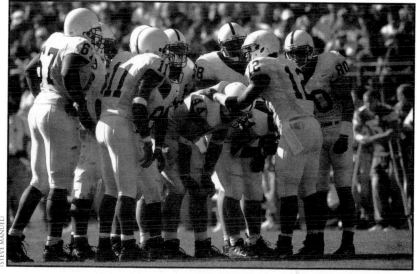

Robinson (12) calls a play in a Penn State huddle; quarterback injuries and a paucity of wide receivers made the 2004 Nittany Lions offense perhaps the worst in Paterno's long tenure.

Paterno glumly responds to questions after a 2004 loss; more than anything else, his postgame body language reflected the depressed state of his program.

(STEVE MANUEL)

(STEVE MANUEL)

Defensive backs Alan Zemaitis (21) and Paul Cronin (29) dive into a goal-line pileup against Indiana; Paterno and his son Jay both predicted that the late-game goal-line stand, which helped end a six-game losing streak, would prove to be a turnaround moment for Penn State football.

Though the public might not have noticed, he had, in response, changed quite a bit this season. But so far those changes had produced nothing but more losses and more criticism.

So Paterno cranked up the intensity for Purdue.

To coincide with the coach's increased level of devotion, Guido D'Elia, the athletic department's main marketer, had planned another Friday-night campus pep rally—a "Rally in the Valley"—and, for the next day's game, a "White Out," in which Penn State fans and students were urged to wear white shirts and jackets.

Just before the 9:00 P.M. rally at Rec Hall, the Nittany Lion Inn's first-floor bar, Whiskers, was packed with alumni. Most were middle-aged men and many wore navy-blue blazers. Some of these alums had their names inscribed on brass plaques that hung on a nearby corridor wall in the hotel. "The Laurel Circle" signified those who had contributed $1 million or more and it included the names "Joseph V. and Suzanne Paterno." Across the corridor were the plaques of "Mount Nittany Society" members (at least $100,000). Plenty of those contributions had been inspired, and even solicited, by Paterno.

Most of the drinkers had season tickets and had paid handsomely for that privilege. Like the rest of college football's superpowers, Penn State's best tickets were granted to those who had made sufficient donations. A few had made additional grants to athletics, enough to endow specific playing or coaching positions in much the same way that a chair in, say, the biology department would be endowed.

A scholarship for Penn State's starting quarterbacks was underwritten by a $250,000 donation from ex–PSU quarterback Kerry Collins. One elderly Pennsylvania couple contributed $500,000 to endow scholarships for both a football linebacker and a women's volleyball setter.

They all had invested heavily in Penn State football, and as much as they respected Paterno, they demanded a return. Clustered now in front of a behind-the-bar TV that was showing a college football game, these burly men talked—more loudly with each round—about old times, about their tailgating menus, and about tomorrow's matchup between the Lions and Purdue.

It was only when the subject turned to Paterno that their voices, perhaps in deference to the coach, descended into whispers. They didn't have answers. Only questions. Was he too old to adapt to the game's altered realities? Was the Big Ten too tough for a school that had feasted on weaker Eastern opposition through the coach's first quarter century? Were recruits turned off by the old coach's insistence on a colorless reserve rather than a bold swagger?

Their displeasure, freed now by the alcohol, was obvious. After twenty-nine defeats in fifty-three games since 2000, proud Penn State had become a Big Ten punching bag and they didn't like it.

They knew a coaching record such as Paterno had amassed in the last five years would have been unacceptable almost anywhere else. They also knew he was an exception, an anachronism. His splendid record over more than a half century had earned him a pass.

Firing Paterno, as some in the Whiskers crowd correctly noted, still remained an unimaginable option. And the coach was offering no indications that he planned to step down anytime soon.

So what could be done?

Gradually, without arriving at any possible solutions, the knot of alumni disassembled. A few decided to walk the short distance to Rec Hall for the pep rally.

At that moment, Paterno and his players were riding to the rally in a pair of large new touring buses. They had boarded them outside the Lasch Building, a five-year-old, $14 million, state-of-the-art football-support facility that was indicative of the power the sport had accumulated here. Paterno's spacious office, the size of a small restaurant, was inside. So were weight-training rooms, theaterlike film facilities, academic-support areas, and a plush players' lounge.

The nighttime journey across campus had turned into a procession as the team neared its destination, Rec Hall, the seventy-five-year-old brick gymnasium that once had been the home of Penn State basketball but now hosted its volleyball and gymnastic teams.

As a slow-moving university police car's spotlight illuminated the buses' way down Curtin Road, members of Penn State's Blue Band marched ahead, snapping out a martial cadence on snare drums. Students and fans stood along tree-lined pathways to holler encouragement or simply to wave at Paterno and the passing players. There was something almost melancholy about the crowd, as if they were trying to forget the unpleasant realities of 2004 by acting out their parts in a tradition-thick Penn State football experience.

The buses rolled to a stop outside Rec Hall, where the soft light seeping out of its windows beckoned on the chilly night. As always, the two captains, Mills and Wake, exited first. Paterno followed them down the steps. Inside, several thousand fans who had been primed by cheerleaders and Steve Jones, the radio voice of Nittany Lions football, exploded when they came into view.

Paterno immediately imbibed the enthusiasm. His arms instinctively launched into the air. The band's rendition of the fight song reverberated loudly throughout the building as he and the players, after bouncing two by two down the center aisle, climbed up onstage and took their seats.

Just prior to their arrival, Larry Johnson, a record-setting running back at Penn State, Class of 2002, and now a Kansas City Chief in the NFL, had addressed the crowd. Johnson had grown up in State College. His father, Larry senior, is a longtime Paterno assistant.

Ironically, it was the younger Johnson who had touched off much of the current controversy swirling around Paterno when, following the disastrous season-opening home loss to Toledo in 2000, he suggested a coaching change might be beneficial. Now he counseled the fans to be patient and finished his brief talk by vowing that Penn State would "kick Purdue's ass."

The Nittany Lions had been joined onstage by a student who had won a rally-related contest and, as his prize, now sat among the first row of players. He was wearing a baseball cap and Paterno, apparently thinking he was one of his players, kept gesturing at the puzzled youngster to remove the cap.

When it was his turn to grab the wireless microphone, Paterno slipped on the white dinner jacket that, in deference to the weekend's "White Out" theme, Jones had been wearing. The coach joked that, in the jacket, he might easily be mistaken for Frank Sinatra. A male fan screamed out, "I love you, Joe!"

"I love you too," Paterno instantly shouted back. "And I love these guys!"

Paterno, who insists his players dress in suits and ties on road trips even though their chartered-jet itinerary rarely brings them in contact with the public, removed the dinner jacket and donned a wrinkled Penn State T-shirt, tugging it over his head in such a forceful manner that it appeared to be a defiant gesture. He didn't care that his hair, finally graying, was a mess, that the tight shirt accentuated his belly, or that his high-pitched speech to a crowd peppered with tiny children was sprinkled with *hell*s and *ain't*s.

He had even abandoned his infamous pregame caution. While veteran observers had long been amused by his tendency to ennoble even the weakest of Nittany Lions opponents, this time he boldly predicted Penn State was going "to beat the hell out of Purdue!" He urged the fans to yell so loudly tomorrow that they'd drown out Orton's signals and audible calls and the "next time Number—what's his number?—next time Number 18 goes back there in the huddle, he ain't gonna change any plays!"

It was odd to see Paterno like this, so out of character, sputtering and shouting like some beer-soaked undergraduate. Sure this was a pep rally where a certain level of hyperbole was expected, but did he really believe the very un-Paterno-like things he was saying?

"I don't really look at it in a sense of something I like to do or don't like to do," Paterno explained later about his pep-rally persona. "But there just comes a time when a team needs to get a bunch of people to rally around them. That's what a rally is. To go there and say, 'Well, I hope we can win. The other guys are good and we've had tough luck.' What's that gonna do? I think you've got to make yourself go into those things and say, 'Hey, we're going into battle.' Not just the football team but the whole Penn State community."

"We got, what, six games left?" he now asked the crowd. "We can win 'em all. We're as good as anybody in America! . . . There's only one Heisman Trophy winner who's going to be on the field tomorrow and his name is Zack Mills."

Players smiled, bemused by their coach's violation of one of the rules he constantly harped about. He was guilty of an emotional outburst in public.

Now Paterno slammed his fist on the podium like some enraptured preacher and screeched at the top of his lungs to the delighted crowd:

"You know I'm frustrated. I really am. Because these guys are working their tails off. They're on the verge of being something, but they lick themselves. Tomorrow we ain't gonna lick ourselves, *all right!* Tomorrow we're gonna beat somebody! We're *tired* of losing! You're *tired.* I'm *tired.* And"—pointing to his players, who sat behind him—"they're more *tired!*"

Penn State's students, reminded by omnipresent advertisements and by D'Elia's designated dormitory criers, who roamed the halls early Saturday rousing them from sleep, responded heartily to Paterno's midseason pleadings. The following day, more than thirty thousand of them entered Beaver Stadium wearing the same kind of white T-shirts Paterno had put on at the rally, purifying large swatches of the east and south grandstands.

The sartorial togetherness enlivened their spirits. They stood and noisily shouted long before the 4:30 P.M. kickoff. That's not to say there weren't cynics among them, those more colorfully attired who felt the "White Out" theme was aptly symbolic of a program trying to obscure its recent past.

The wildly positive atmosphere brought to mind the glory days. Smiling, eager fans took early laps around the outside perimeter of the stadium, glancing occasionally at the fall colors illuminating Mount Nittany. Tailgaters were plentiful and loud. Among those stopping at the Paterno statue for photographs, the anticipation was as thick and redolent as the barbecue sauce some of the tailgaters smeared on ribs and chicken.

Happy Valley was, if only for a day, happy again. That's why several spectators and State College residents had been upset that morning when they picked up the *Centre Daily Times* and found the special pregame Penn State insert had Purdue's Orton on its cover. The perceived slight was minor when compared to everything that had been written about Paterno and his teams in recent years. But on this day, for those trying to restore Penn State spirit, it seemed inappropriate.

"I was shocked and disappointed to see the front page covered with pictures of Purdue's quarterback Kyle Orton," wrote Bernie Ryan of State College in a letter to the newspaper. "I realize he is one of the top quarterbacks in the country and a Heisman contender, but why would Penn State's hometown paper highlight him on the cover? I would expect to see pictures like that on an inside page. Granted, Penn State has had a rough couple years, but why not highlight some of our stellar student-athletes on the front page, as you have done in the past? These young athletes are not professionals and need our encouragement."

The answer was simple and likely not the one Ryan and his fellow boosters wanted to hear.

"The decision to feature Purdue quarterback Kyle Orton on the cover of the pregame edition," explained an editor's note that followed, "was necessitated by the fact that several Penn State players, with whom interviews had been requested, were not made available."

Homemade signs had virtually vanished from Beaver Stadium in recent seasons. But amid the white background several could be spotted. PURDUE PURDON'T, read one, while another was a message for the Boilermakers' quarterback, ORTON: WELCOME TO LINE-BACKER U. OUCH!

As the old coach led his team from the stadium tunnel minutes before the game, he veered unexpectedly toward the students. With raised arms wildly flailing in an attempt to pump them up further, Paterno resembled an aged cheerleader. He prompted even louder shouts as he slapped hands with students in the front row.

Later, during the game, when his younger self might have been knee-deep in strategic calculations, he frequently turned to whip up the crowd. That action, captured by ESPN's omnipresent cameras, disillusioned at least one Purdue fan.

"On October 9, I tuned in to the Penn State–Purdue football game," L. Robert Smeltzer of Carol Stream, Illinois, wrote the *Chicago Tribune*. "Ignoring the fact that I am a Purdue alum, I wanted to watch one of the finest field generals in my seventy-plus years. I was inundated with shots of coach Joe Paterno inciting the Penn State students to make enough noise to prevent Purdue quarterback Kyle Orton from turning his superb talents for defensive assessment into audible calls at the line of scrimmage. Paterno continued this exhortation during the game with frequent arm motions to solicit even more noise from the spectators. His apparent motive was his assessment that his team was not as well coached and able as Purdue, and the only way he could win was to employ unsportsmanlike conduct. I would like to see the Big Ten censure Paterno's conduct and establish a rule against such practices."

The behavior showed how much Paterno had invested in this game—his time, his energy, his talents, his voice, his heart, his soul, even his dignity. He felt it was all worth it because he knew Penn State would beat Purdue, work like hell during the bye week, and come back strong for the final five games.

He had drawn a line in the sand. The turnaround would start here.

The excitement surrounding the game had caused a mental "White Out" of sorts among many Penn State fans. In their enthusiasm, they had managed to overlook the gigantic performance gap between these two teams. Penn State was still 2–3 and hadn't beaten a good team yet. They would be without Michael Robinson again. They couldn't pass the ball. And because of that, they couldn't run it either.

Purdue, led by Orton, was 4–0. The ninth-ranked Boilermakers had annihilated Notre Dame in South Bend, 41–16, the previous week. They had the nation's No. 1 offense, averaging 47 points a game. They had outscored Syracuse, Ball State, Illinois, and Notre Dame by a combined 189–53. And, incredibly, they had not yet committed a single turnover.

"They are a great football team," said Paterno, using virtually the same words he had employed to describe Minnesota a week earlier. "They are one of the better football teams we have played since I have been at Penn State. . . . They are averaging [549 yards] a ball game. . . . If we give him [Orton] three or four turnovers, they will beat us 50–6. You just have to play solid football and hang in there, go to the ball and tackle the receiver when he catches it, try not to let him beat you deep, keep everything in front of you and pray."

It looked like his prayers may have been answered when on the game's second play, Mills hit Hunt on a 20-yard pass. But a false-start penalty wiped it out and the Nittany Lions soon punted.

Penn State's game plan for Purdue was overloaded with passes. Paterno understood that, given his team's virtually nonexistent aerial game, Purdue, like everybody else, would be geared to stop the run. So he rode his wide receivers hard all week, telling them Mills might throw fifty passes and that it was about time they caught a few.

"I think it's basically the fact that if you have an extra guy to block," he said of the front-loaded defenses the Nittany Lions had faced, "and you don't have a man to block him, then you have to throw the ball . . . it's either that or go back to the single wing."

Tom Bradley's defense, which had Connor now in the middle in place of the injured Shaw, was doing a good job of limiting Orton to short throws. With 5:57 left in the first quarter, Ben Jones's 50-yard field goal gave the Boilermakers a 3–0 lead.

Following a few more costly Penn State penalties, Purdue made it 10–0 when, with nearly ten minutes remaining until halftime, Brandon Jones scored on a 2-yard run.

Paterno's sideline performance quickly turned frantic. He became even more animated and irritable than usual. He looked disgusted at Penn State's penalties and, particularly when Purdue had the ball, beseeched the crowd to make more noise. When a first-quarter punt return was nullified by a block-in-the-back penalty, he was livid, running down the official during a time-out to deliver a stern, hands-on-the-hips lecture.

Then, on the Nittany Lions' drive that followed Purdue's touchdown, Austin Scott was tackled after a 1-yard gain when a wide receiver missed a block. Paterno lunged toward receivers coach Mike McQueary and screamed at the first-year assistant who, arms folded across his chest, stoically accepted the public rebuke.

Two plays later all was forgiven. Mills, who looked healthier and more accurate than against Minnesota, finally hooked up with a wideout for a big play—even if it came as a surprise to Paterno.

On a first-and-10 at Purdue's 37, the Lions quarterback retreated and lofted a deep floater toward Terrell Golden, who was racing toward the end zone. Cornerback Brian Hickman had the receiver blanketed but the ball sailed just beyond his reach. Golden, dropping to his knees as he did, made the touchdown catch.

Penn State's bench and the enormous crowd erupted. Golden, caught up in the spirit that had been building on campus all week, violated one of Paterno's best-known principles, performing a brief and relatvely subdued celebratory shuffle.

The end-zone dance prompted a 15-yard penalty on the ensuing kickoff. Paterno, visibly angry again, grabbed Golden as he passed and chastised him. Golden stood still until the coach was through, then broke away and resumed his celebrating with teammates. He would not get back into the game until the final minutes of the fourth quarter.

"He was not punished because of that," Paterno insisted several days later. "Having said that, that's none of your business. If I felt he should not have been in that game because he hot-dogged and cost us fifteen yards (that's my business). . . . He's a young kid and he'd better learn, but that's not the reason I kept him out. . . . I kept him out because he hadn't even been in the plans."

Actually, the coach said he hadn't even been aware Golden was in the game. The redshirt freshman from Norfolk apparently entered when another wideout pulled himself for a breather.

"I was shocked when he was in there [and] when we threw the ball to him," said Paterno.

The touchdown energized the Lions, who then tied the game at 10–10 on Gould's 38-yard field goal with under a minute left in the half.

During the intermission, Paterno cautioned his team about their habit of permitting long scoring drives to start the second half. And then Purdue became the fourth straight opponent to do it. Orton finished off a nine-play, 80-yard drive by hitting Taylor Stubblefield, left wide open on a mistake by cornerback Anwar Phillips, on a 40-yard touchdown pass four minutes into the third quarter.

"I can't explain it," said Bradley of the start-of-the-second-half syndrome. "We even played a couple of defenses we hadn't played in the first half, thinking maybe they were onto something we had been doing."

Before the quarter ended, Gould added a second field goal, a 27-yarder, cutting Purdue's advantage to 17–13.

A brief rainstorm arrived early into the fourth quarter, just as Orton threw his first interception of the season. That pass, intended for Kyle Ingraham, was picked off by Lowry and returned to Penn State's 43. The Lions, with Mills connecting on five passes, moved to the Boilermakers' 6. There, on a fourth-and-5, came the most important play of the game, perhaps of the Nittany Lions' season.

Paterno sent out the field-goal unit, hardly an illogical decision at the time, since Penn State at last looked capable of moving the ball. Mills took the snap but arose, pulled the ball into his chest, and rolled right. Guard Tyler Reed missed a block on linebacker Stanford Keglar, who lunged and dragged Mills down at the 3, 1½ yards short of a first down.

"We thought we had it," Paterno said of the faked field goal. "We had practiced it all week. They gave us a look, and I thought we had it. And it would have given us a chance to score. Obviously, if it works it's a great play."

Still, Penn State got the ball back quickly when Phillips intercepted another Orton pass at Purdue's 42. This time, Paterno called for the field goal and Gould missed a 45-yarder. An uneasy hum spread through the stadium. These fans had seen this all before.

Sure enough, Purdue marched downfield in a time-killing drive (5:34) that concluded with a 46-yard field goal by Jones. With only 2:48 to play, the Boilermakers led by a touchdown, 20–13.

A comeback still seemed possible when Kinlaw returned the ensuing kickoff 65 yards to Purdue's 33-yard line. But four straight Mills incompletions wasted his effort.

One more stand by Penn State's defense got the Lions the ball back at their own 30 with 1:15 to go. This time they could manage just 20 yards before a fourth-down Hail Mary pass from Morelli—inserted on this play for his arm strength—was batted down near the end zone.

It was over. Another defeat.

Penn State had gotten production and plays from the passing game. Mills (twenty-nine of forty-nine for 293 yards, a TD, and no interceptions) had been sharp. Wideout Gerald Smith caught five more balls, Rubin three, and the scuffling Phillips two for 53 yards. Tight ends Smolko and Hunt had seven receptions apiece. And there was Golden's TD.

The defense had been impressive again, limiting Purdue to 348 net yards (200 below its average) and 20 points (27 under its average). The kicking game had improved, except for the long field-goal miss. Paterno had done all that he could.

And yet here he was again, hoarse, frustrated, and weary, dragging himself off the field after another loss. His tenth in eleven Big Ten games. His eleventh straight against a ranked opponent.

As he entered the postgame news conference, Paterno's dark, downcast eyes averted the roomful of reporters. His optimism was spent and wasted after what he would call "one of the most disappointing losses in my coaching career."

Already, while slouching into his chair behind the podium, he had declared his players off-limits for interviews, soliciting groans from sportswriters who, facing two long weeks until the Nittany Lions' next game, had hoped to fill up their notebooks.

"They're emotionally drained," he explained. "I know I am."

Paterno was as transparently disheartened as he had been buoyant the previous night. People who had been observing him for three, four, five decades said they could not recall seeing him so low after a loss.

"Yeah, we played better in spots," he allowed at one point. "We played a really good football team. And Wisconsin was a really good football team. And Minnesota was a really good football team. But we're Penn State. We're supposed to win those football games. Yes, we're better today than we were a week ago. But we're not good enough. And I'm tired of not being good enough. It's as simple as that."

The postgame scene inside Penn State's locker room was just as dreary. The players had been buoyed by Paterno's enthusiasm all that week. Now they and their coach had disappeared beneath the surface.

"Guys were upset," said Mills. "There were guys crying in the locker room—very, very down. This was a game we felt we should have won. [Coach Paterno] was very upset. . . . I haven't seen him like that too much."

When the stadium finally had emptied, Paterno and son Jay decided to walk back to the head coach's home. As they passed through the dark Beaver Stadium parking lots, the bravest of the thousands of dedicated but disappointed tailgaters who lingered there shouted out to them.

"Good game, Joe. We're getting better."

If the words were meant to soothe the devastated coach, they instead had the opposite effect. He felt like shouting angrily at the well-wisher. *This is what my program has become,* he thought. *Expectations are so low that a tough loss is good enough?*

"Where do you vent your anger?" Paterno said when recalling the incident. "You know what you want to do, and you're working like a dog to get it done, and it doesn't happen. What do you do, sing songs? You're angry. If you had said to me after the game, 'Hey, you sound like you are angry.' You're damned right I was angry. Who was I angry at? I was angry at you and everybody else. I was angry at my wife. People wanted to talk. . . . I felt like [cursing them]."

The parking-lot encounter reminded Paterno of a moment from 1967, his second year as Penn State's head coach. A few days following a 17–15 loss to Rose Bowl–bound UCLA, whose quarterback was Heisman Trophy–winner Gary Beban, the Quarterback Club welcomed the coach with a standing ovation. An embarrassed Paterno upbraided the State College supporters.

"I said, 'If you are going to give me a standing ovation because we got licked, I'm in the wrong place. If you think I'm gonna jump with joy because we lost some games and it's not going to affect me, I'm in the wrong place and you're [supporting] the wrong team. I'm not going to be satisfied until we win those games. That is where I'm going to go.'

"People say to me, 'Well, you're getting beaten down.' I'm not getting beaten down. I'm getting PO'd."

CHAPTER 14

JOE PATERNO IS NOT EASILY INTIMIDATED.

Just ask the six Penn State presidents he has won over and over-shadowed. Or the wealthy donors he has talked into multimillion-dollar gifts. Or the star players and assistants who have battled and argued with him through the years—and lost. Or the opposing coaches who have tried to get the best of him in recruiting or game planning—and lost. Intensely competitive, Paterno relishes any sort of challenge. The bigger the better. He's self-confident, maddeningly cocky, and unconcerned by the opinions of others.

But if ever there was a fellow coach who could make Paterno sweat and doubt himself, it was Paul "Bear" Bryant. "Even his peers in the coaching business felt in awe of him," said Paterno. "He had such charisma. Whatever it is that makes great generals, he had it. Tons of it. He was just a giant figure."

Paterno was a young Penn State assistant in the mid-1950s when, at a coaches' convention, he first encountered the drawling legend. Returning to the hotel one night, he boarded an elevator and pushed the button for his fourth-floor room. Before the doors closed, a quartet of very familiar faces entered—Oklahoma's Bud Wilkinson, Notre Dame's recently retired Frank Leahy, Georgia's Wally Butts, and Bryant, then at Texas A & M.

The eager young coach was awestruck. He rode past his floor and went all the way to the twelfth with his elders, hoping they might invite him to tag along. Though they never acknowledged his puppy-dog presence, he had been impressed by the powerful physical aura that surrounded the men, particularly Bryant. "Self-confidence," he later said of him, "hung in the air around him like a fine mist." Later in the week, Paterno attended a lecture where Bryant was the speaker.

"Bryant got up and gave one of the best clinic speeches I had ever heard," Paterno recalled a half century later. "He didn't have a lot to say, but he said a couple of things. Talking about game plans—'Keep your plan small. Have a plan for everything.' " The latter would always come naturally to the details-obsessed Paterno. He constantly refers to notes he makes for himself and others, a trait he traces back to Bryant's advice.

Their paths would cross again. In 1959, when Paterno was still an assistant to Rip Engle, Penn State defeated Bryant's second Alabama team, 7–0, in the inaugural Liberty Bowl in Philadelphia. Between 1975 and 1982, Bryant and Paterno faced off four times as head coaches. Alabama won all four games. He called Bryant "the greatest defensive coach of all time" and was convinced the older man had his number. The feeling intensified after he was outfoxed by Bryant in the heartbreaking 1979 Sugar Bowl loss. Even in Penn State's championship season of 1982, Bryant could not be bested. The Nittany Lions' lone loss that year came to Alabama.

When that 1982 Crimson Tide season concluded with a December 29 Liberty Bowl victory over Illinois, Bryant retired at sixty-nine. Four weeks later, a day after chest pains sent him to to DCH Regional Medical Center, he died of a heart atack.

Paterno was sobered by the news of his coaching idol's death. While less-involved observers might have looked at Bryant's demise as a warning against the stresses of the profession, Paterno got another message. For him, the old coach had died because he'd walked away from the occupation that had given meaning to both their lives.

Penn State's coach was fifty-six at the time of Bryant's death and though he occasionally had forecast his departure at some undetermined future date, Paterno hadn't seriously contemplated retirement.

After that, always citing Bryant's demise as the reason, he never really would.

Four years after his death, Bryant still loomed large in Paterno's mind. The 1986 Nittany Lions had opened their season with six wins against unranked opponents, including Temple and Rutgers. On October 25 in Tuscaloosa, they met second-ranked Alabama, now coached by Ray Perkins. But all that week, and especially once his team arrived in Alabama, Paterno's head was filled with thoughts of the late coach. They were so potent that, on game day, he could almost see that craggy face beneath a houndstooth hat on the opposite sideline.

Penn State won easily that day, 23–3, its first victory ever on Alabama's home field. It was as spiritual a triumph as Paterno had experienced. For him, the vibes about Bryant and the flawless play of his team against a quality opponent in a hostile environment had served as an omen: Another national championship, he now believed, was not merely possible in 1986. It was likely.

After more than two decades as a head coach, Paterno had begun to recognize college football's cyclical nature. Unless a program was willing to cheat, by covering for academically underperforming athletes, or cut corners by recruiting polished junior-college or transfer players, it was impossible to contend for a national championship every year. There was a seasoning process that had to take place for all but the most exceptional high-school players. His best players on his best teams often were seniors. Seniors graduated. And their places were subsequently taken by underclassmen who hadn't played enough to have developed.

Paterno believed he ought to be able to produce two or three strong contenders a decade, maybe one great team every eight or ten years. By understanding that and remaining patient, he could avoid taking transfers or playing freshmen, whose minds, he believed, were better focused on adjusting to college life and whose bodies needed to adapt to the rigors of the college game.

"Every four or five years we end up with a pretty good football team," he said. "I've always tried to put us in a position where we're building toward a team that could be a contender for a national championship. Sometimes it works. Sometimes it doesn't. It takes a while. We don't get rich quick. We don't take junior-college kids. We try not to take kids that don't belong here. . . . I just have felt, *Let's do it right. Let's be solid. Let's build.* And if we're not good this year, at least we're not making sacrifices on the future in order to win X number of games this year."

That timetable played out perfectly after the 1982 championship. Penn State went 8–4–1 in 1983 and 6–5 in '84 (ending a streak of thirteen straight bowl seasons). The 1985 Nittany Lions were a surprising 11–0 and ranked No. 1 until their quest for another national title ended in a 25–10 Orange Bowl loss to Barry Switzer's Oklahoma, a program that did not put the same emphasis on Paterno's standards, to say the least.

The 1986 season—the one hundredth for Penn State football— looked both promising and puzzling to Paterno. Two thirds of Penn State's letter winners would return. Fifteen of them were fifth-year seniors. The defense, led by linebackers Shane Conlan and Trey Bauer and a hard-hitting secondary, was as good as any he coached.

But he had questions about the offense, particularly the passing game. Quarterback John Shaffer was an outstanding leader who had lost only one start since junior high. But he was not shifty in the pocket and was, at best, only an adequate passer. The roster also was devoid of any standout wide receivers. Penn State's top pass-catcher in 1985 had been Ray Roundtree, with a paltry fifteen receptions for 285 yards.

Paterno had by then retreated to a more comfortable coaching staff. He had turned 1982's winning formula on its head. The '86 Lions weren't going to play wide-open football. They were going to have to get points the old-fashioned Penn State way—relying on tailback D. J. Dozier and an offensive line anchored by all-American Chris Conlin.

The jokes and complaints about Paterno's conservative nature resurfaced. This Penn State offense, the critics scoffed, was just like the popular new golf balls that, branded with the coach's face, were being sold all over State College that fall: It was guaranteed to go right up the middle three times out of four.

The schedule had worked in Penn State's favor that year. After playing the nation's toughest schedule in the late 1970s and early 1980s, the Nittany Lions' lineup was, for various reasons, much less formidable. In fact, it looked an awful lot like those that had once earned Penn State national scorn. It included Temple, East Carolina, Rutgers, Cincinnati, Syracuse, West Virginia, and Maryland.

In fact, the only ranked team Penn State would meet before its Fiesta Bowl showdown with Miami was Alabama, No. 2 at the time. But just four years removed from a national title, the Lions' reputation had grown substantial enough that poll voters were conditioned to rate them highly, regardless of the opponent. Penn State began the '86 season ranked sixth, moved into the No. 2 slot in early November after the win in Tuscaloosa, and clung to it until the Fiesta Bowl.

The 1986 bowl season marked the last great splash of college football's independents. The growth of cable TV and television-rights fees was leading to the formation of many new conferences and the expansion of older ones. Between 1978 and 1994, the Pac Ten added Arizona and Arizona State; the Big Eight became the Big Twelve with the addition of Texas, Texas A & M, Texas Tech, and Baylor; South Carolina and Arkansas joined the SEC; the Mountain West and Big East began play, and the venerable Southwest Conference folded.

When Miami and Penn State finished unbeaten and ranked Nos. 1 and 2 in 1986, they became the first two independent teams to occupy the polls' top spots at a regular season's end since 1946 (Army and Notre Dame).

With no bowl commitments, the two schools found themselves in an enviable position. They could sit back and wait for the best offer from all those eager to televise a true national-championship game. By landing them both, a midlevel bowl could instantly become a major.

The most ambitious of those second-level bowls was the sixteen-year-old Fiesta Bowl in Tempe, Arizona. To get Miami and Penn State, its organizers, backed by NBC, agreed to double the game's payout (guaranteeing each school $2.4 million), move the game away from the New Year's Day football traffic to January 2, and schedule it in prime time.

The appeal of a Penn State–Miami game was unmistakable. Viewers, whether watching TV sitcoms, movies, or sporting events, were drawn instinctively to conflict. And in the media's shorthand profiles of these two programs, conflict seemed inevitable. The contrasts couldn't have been clearer.

The Hurricanes had risen to national prominence in the early 1980s under coach Howard Schellenberger with a flashy, pass-dominated attack led by quarterbacks like Jim Kelly and Bernie Kosar. On the field, Miami was characterized by speed, big plays, and trash talk. Thirty-four members of this team, including Kosar, defensive tackle Jerome Brown, and wide receiver Michael Irvin, eventually would be drafted by the NFL and twenty-eight would play in the league. Off the field, Miami possessed an outlaw image that befit the 1980s' *Miami Vice* reputation of its hometown, the capital of cocaine and Uzis. The Hurricanes, as Irvin noted, were ranked No. 1 "by the AP, UPI, and FBI." Among the various legal difficulties that surrounded the program that season were incidents involving drugs, handguns, questionably leased automobiles, shoplifting, fradulent phone calls, and physical battles with campus police.

Penn State, with its vanilla offense, dull uniforms, Boy Scout image, and the lofty ideals inherent in its head coach's philosophies, provided the perfect foil for these bad boys. It didn't take long for the media to cast the showdown as college football's version of a morality play. Here was Good versus Evil for the highest stakes possible. And it would all play out in prime time.

The contrasts extended to Paterno and Miami coach Jimmy Johnson. Johnson, slick and shifty, was a coaching maverick with a restless ambition. Though he was just forty-three, the former Arkansas lineman already had worked at Louisiana Tech, Picayune, Wichita State, Iowa State, Oklahoma, Arkansas, Pitt, and Oklahoma State.

That was eight more schools than appeared on the sixty-year-old Paterno's resume. And Johnson was among those coaches—many of them clustered in the South and Southwest—who saw Penn State's coach as annoyingly self-righteous. When asked during Fiesta Bowl week if he would recommend that the NCAA adopt overtime, that dislike surfaced. "I could do it," Johnson said, "but I think that it would have more clout if St. Joe proposed it."

Johnson by then had seen that week's *Sports Illustrated*, with Paterno on its cover. The magazine had named Penn State's coach its Sportsman of the Year for 1986. In a glowing article by Rick Reilly that served as St. Joe's formal canonization, he was portrayed as the game's last white knight.

"In an era of college football in which it seems everybody's hand is either in the till or balled up in a fist, Paterno sticks out like a clean thumb," Reilly wrote. "His standard of excellence is so season-in, season-out consistent it borders on the monotonous: win ten, eleven games; send off another bunch of future doctors, lawyers, and accountants. In the heyday of the Bosworth Ethic, when talking trash is hot and shaking hands before the coin toss is not; when the Texas coach gets fired for winning just seventy-five percent of his games, the Maryland coach runs a 9.9 100 to chat with a referee, and the Cal coach lets his Fruit of the Looms do his talking; when it takes a paralegal just to make out the sports page, we need the guy in the PhotoGray trifocals more than ever."

For his part, Paterno could be equally dismissive of Johnson. In his autobiography, published two years later, he criticized the Miami coach in unusually harsh terms for failing to rein in his players' controversial behavior that week. After all, Paterno wrote, "[Johnson's players] were representing the University of Miami and supposedly higher education."

No one would be surprised when this updated version of the Friday night fights attracted 52 million viewers and a 25.1 rating—records for college sporting events that have survived till today.

Privately, the publicity-hungry bowl organizers must have been delighted when Miami showed up in just the right costume. Upon the team's arrival that week, a dozen players exited the plane in camouflage fatigues. While Irvin, Brown, and others seemed to relish their role as villains, they also appeared genuinely disturbed by their opponents' "goody-black-shoes" image. And whether it was some psychological ploy or not, they went out of their way that week to denigrate them.

"We played for the national championship on September 27

[against Oklahoma]," said defensive tackle Dan Sileo. "As far as I'm concerned, Friday's game is just the end of the season."

Irvin said that if the all-American Conlan covered him, he'd "run right past him."

And when Brown was asked what he thought of Dozier and Shaffer, he scoffed: "I think they're nothing."

Meanwhile, Penn State's players, dressed in their traditional coats and ties, got through most of the week's interviews and banquets without reciprocating—until both squads attended a steak fry that, ironically, had been designed to bring them together in a spirit of sportsmanship. And, curiously, it was not Miami but Penn State—and, in particular, punter John Bruno—that precipitated The Tempest in a T-bone.

Each team had been asked to present a humorous skit after the meal. When it was Penn State's turn, Bruno joked first about Johnson's helmet of immovable hair. The Hurricanes didn't laugh. Next he and teammates performed some mocking Heisman Trophy poses, aimed at Miami's Heisman-winning QB Vinny Testaverde.

Then Bruno uttered a foolish joke that inadvertently pointed to the disparate racial makeup of the two teams. While Paterno's teams traditionally had been predominantly white, Bruno suggested there was harmony on this slightly more intergrated squad. "We even let the black guys eat with us once a week at the training table," he said.

After Bruno's racial joke, the Miami players were furious and wanted to leave. Johnson insisted they stay, at least until the skits were finished. Some stood up and defiantly removed their sweatshirts to reveal more camouflage. When Penn State's skit concluded, Johnson said he "gave them the high sign and they left in unison."

On his way out, Brown shouted, "Did the Japanese go and have dinner with Pearl Harbor before they bombed them? No. We're out of here." The Hurricanes' mass exit and Brown's remark—though not any of Bruno's—were what filled the newspapers the following day.

Paterno probably would have blanched at the comments, but the coach, obsessively preparing for the game, had not been there to hear them. Later, in his autobiography, his only comment on the tawdry affair touched on Miami's "disgraceful walkout."

"People trash us because we all left together," Johnson said. "But Joe Paterno didn't even attend."

John Junker, the Fiesta Bowl president, was there. And in an interview with *The Miami Herald* seventeen years later, he defended the Hurricanes' behavior at the dinner.

"One of my memories that is terribly underreported . . . the Penn State players were making fun of [Miami], doing Heisman poses and doing them in less than respectful ways," he said. "That never got reported by anybody because of the level of rhetoric it got to. I always thought it was a little unfair. Miami definitely got the rough end of the deal. There were two sides to that coin, and the one side doesn't often get looked at."

Eerily, that night's chief protagonists, Bruno and Brown, would be dead within six years. Bruno would succumb to cancer in April of 1992. Two months later, Brown was killed in a Florida car crash.

The antagonism continued through game day. Then, Miami clearly was the instigator.

When Penn State's buses pulled up outside Sun Devil Stadium a few hours before the game, some Hurricane players, hurling four-letter words, blocked their paths to the locker room. Paterno eventually had to step between them. Then, during warm-ups, several Miami receivers ran through a circle of stretching Nittany Lions defensive backs.

Paterno had held his tongue during the week. Not long afterward, though, he remarked that Johnson, who had occasionally complained about not getting enough respect, might win more praise if he'd address "the sideshow of bully tactics, thuggery, and goonery [that] stole the attention from his true skills."

Throughout the pregame sideshow, Paterno remained convinced that his team, a 7-point underdog, could win. As was his habit before bowl appearances, he had thrown himself and his staff into preparing a game plan that would catch their opponents off-guard. And for all the talent they had on both sides of the ball, the key to beating Miami, he believed, was confusing Testaverde. For weeks, he and defensive coordinator Jerry Sandusky had been devising schemes to accomplish that.

They came up with several new zone coverages, some of which dropped eight men back and relied on a three-man front to pressure the quarterback. By game time, Sandusky had so much confidence in his veteran unit that, when Penn State won the opening toss, he persuaded Paterno to kick off.

While Miami had brief bursts when it gobbled up big chunks of yardage in the game, it was clear that when Penn State went with their new zone packages Testaverde was baffled. After a few Miami first downs on the opening drive, Testaverde tossed an interception to safety Ray Isom. The Hurricanes eventually grabbed a 7–0 lead when fullback Melvin Bratton scored shortly after Shaffer's second-quarter turnover. Penn State responded immediately with a sustained drive, capping the 74-yard march with a 4-yard bootleg by Shaffer. Thanks in part to Bruno's outstanding punting (he averaged nearly 44 yards on nine kicks), the score remained 7–7 until the Hurricanes hit on a 38-yard field goal early in the final period.

Then Conlan, who would be named the game's MVP despite knee and ankle injuries, picked off Testaverde for a second time, returning the pass 39 yards to Miami's 5. Two plays later, Dozier, who ran for 99 of the 162 offensive yards Penn State accumulated on that night, put the Nittany Lions ahead with a 6-yard scamper into the end zone. With 8:13 to play, Penn State led by four points, 14–10.

On the night, Testaverde would throw for 285 yards and Miami would run for another 160. But he also threw five interceptions and the Hurricanes could manage just a single touchdown—and that was the result of a Shaffer fumble deep in Lions territory. In addition, Penn State defensive linemen Tim Johnson, Donnie Graham, and Mike Russo were able to penetrate constantly despite a Tempe desert heat that, as the game wore on, seemed to wilt Miami's offensive line.

The clock was down to 2:24 when, facing a fourth-and-6 at Miami's 27, Testaverde and receiver Bennie Blades combined on a 31-yard pass play. Paterno was impressed by Johnson's daring call. "In my experience, whenever I've taken a big gamble like that and made it, I've usually won. . . . I was scared," he admitted afterward.

Testaverde at last appeared to have found his confidence. He hit Blades again, then Brett Perriman, then Irvin three times in succession to reach the Penn State six-yard line. *Oh, God, here they come,* thought Isom.

Paterno anticipated that Miami now would turn to its tailback. Fast and big (six-one, 235 pounds), Alonzo Highsmith had run for 111 yards in the game. But Testaverde was hot and he convinced Johnson that he could throw for the winning score.

A first-down pass failed. Tim Johnson then sacked the Heisman winner for a four-yard loss. Testaverde missed Warren Williams on his cross-field, third-down throw. There were eighteen seconds left and it was fourth down. A single play would now decide the national championship.

Eight Lions defenders dropped back to the goal line to defend what had to be another pass. Penn State's players had noticed that on long third- and fourth-down tries, Testaverde tended to fix on his intended receiver early. And this time he was looking at Perriman.

When the ball was released, linebacker Pete Giftopoulos stepped in front of the receiver and cradled the pass, Miami's seventh and final turnover.

With that play, Paterno and Penn State had a second national championship in four years.

And on that night, no one—not the players in the joyful locker room, or the record audience watching on TV, or the alumni celebrating at parties across the country, or the students and fans back in State College, or the writers heaping praise on the coach and his program—could have imagined that nearly twenty years later, there still would not be a third.

CHAPTER 15

WHEN THE PURDUE BUBBLE BURST, the impatience that even the most loyal Penn State fans had held in check began to spill out. The flow of discontent with Paterno and his program would widen over the course of the bye week and beyond until, by the end of the Nittany Lions' next game, an October 23 homecoming matchup with Iowa, it would be an angry torrent.

The continuing futility had dimmed even the homecoming spirit. Tickets for those games used to be impossible to find. Penn State's widely scattered alumni—an estimated 440,000—made sure that if they could attend only one game every season or two, it would be homecoming. This year, in the days before the game, more than five hundred tickets remained unsold.

Paterno wasn't surprised. He knew how the fans felt. How could anyone possibly be excited about this team? "Having lost three games in a row," he said, "if anybody is optimistic, they are probably cuckoo."

At this point, he certainly wasn't hopeful. The Purdue loss still stung him badly. Twelve days later, during his October 21 radio show, the coach's lingering disappointment remained transparent.

That Thursday night call-in show, *Nittany Lion Hotline,* was broadcast around the state weekly, between 6:00 and 7:00 P.M. It emanated from a makeshift studio in a coaches' meeting room at the Lasch Building, just a few steps from Paterno's office.

Calls tended to come from a small circle of Penn State diehards. Though the show's producer, Jeff Tarman, the former AD's son, insisted he did not screen them, their questions invariably were polite and un-critical. This year, in fact, they had been so supportive of the troubled coach that the show frequently resembled an electronic get-well card.

In the State College area, that night's broadcast began just after an appeal for local residents to attend an 8:00 P.M. "Believers for Bush" rally in Mount Nittany High School. Curiously, the autumn's super-charged presidential campaign, into which the coach would visibly thrust himself, had diverted some attention from the Paterno debate.

Like the rest of the nation, Penn State's campus was unusually en-gaged and bitterly split by the Bush–Kerry contest. And as the Novem-ber 2 election neared, each candidate's supporters grew progressively louder, more strident, more confrontational. The two sides sniped con-stantly at each other—via posters, radio talk shows, and letters and op-ed pieces in the *Daily Collegian*.

The night following Paterno's radio show—after the homecoming floats had paraded down College Avenue—controversial filmmaker Michael Moore would speak at the Bryce Jordan Center, an event sponsored by the College Democrats. Outraged conservatives arranged a campus appearance by right-wing radio talker Michael Gallagher for that same night.

Paterno, the son of a rabid FDR supporter but now a prominent Pennsylvania Republican, managed to steer clear of the turmoil, though not from the presidential politics. The coach was scheduled to appear at an on-campus Bush rally on October 29, one at which he would share the stage with the current president's father and daugh-ters, Barbara and Jenna. Paterno and the elder Bush had formed a friendship over the years, with the coach having seconded his nomi-nation at the 1988 GOP convention.

The football coach's politics, though far more centrist than the younger Bush's, didn't win him any points with those Penn State fans who supported Kerry. Paterno, in fact, had received part of the blame when, a few months earlier, two prominently liberal Penn State pro-fessors, Henry and Susan Giroux, fled to a Canadian university, com-plaining about the stifling political climate in State College.

According to an article in the liberal journal *Axis of Logic*, "The fact that [the couple was] allowed to walk away from Penn State . . . ironically coincided with the school investing untold amounts of money to retain Joe Paterno, Penn State's football coach and apologist for the policies of George W. Bush."

(In April, three days after the Blue-White Game, Paterno's youngest son, Scott, had won the Republican primary in Pennsylvania's Seventeenth Congressional District, an area south and east of State College. Despite the advantage of his famous name, he would be soundly defeated in the general election.)

In what was evidence of another altered tradition this season, the busy coach no longer arrived at his radio show at 6:00 sharp. It was 6:15 when he entered the room on this night. And as soon as he sat in a chair at the head of a conference table and slid on the headphones, it was clear the bye week had not been long enough.

He looked washed out, as pale and shaken as he had on the cover of the latest *Blue White Illustrated*. That post-Purdue photo of the downcast coach was accompanied by a headline that aptly described his dilemma: "Sick of Losing: Emotional Joe Paterno Searches for Answers."

Before taking calls, Paterno told host Steve Jones he wanted to thank the fans who had been so enthusiastic at the Purdue game.

"They were fabulous," he said. "And we had everything going for us. That's probably why I was so frustrated after the game. The crowd was into it. I thought we played hard. We didn't make a couple of plays you've got to make when you get in that league. It's been a frustrating year that way."

The first few calls were from the Philadelpia area, somewhat surprising since Penn State's in-state appeal had always been stronger elsewhere. There was, in fact, only one station in the state's largest city that carried Nittany Lions games. There were three in State College alone, two each in tiny Wellsboro and Lewistown.

When the initial caller, Todd, from the Philadelphia suburb of Lansdale, greeted him with "Good evening, Coach, how are you?" Paterno couldn't let the innocent pleasantry pass without again revealing his frustrations.

"Well, I'll tell you, Todd, we'll find out. I'm getting to the point where I'm punching walls."

Jerry, a sycophantic regular from Philadelphia, was next. Before the caller could pose one of his upbeat questions, Paterno interrupted.

"Hey, Jerry, you want to come up and you and I will cry together?"

Later, the coach candidly admitted how deeply the Purdue loss continued to impact his psyche. "I'm still having trouble," he said.

No matter the question, Paterno's answers kept boomeranging back to the crushing loss. He couldn't understand it. At one point, he sounded as if he were blaming the officiating. In that regard, he hadn't been able to stay on the wagon, even though, with the advent of instant replay in the Big Ten this season, he had vowed to kick the habit.

"The holding penalties and the lining up offsides bothered me a little bit. . . . They called us for one of the tackles lining up in the backfield because he is in an up-stance and his helmet didn't break the ground," said Paterno. "I was looking in there all day and I was trying to get them to call the same thing on Purdue because Purdue was doing the same thing. It was across the field that it was called and I couldn't get the guy on my side to call it. . . .

"I don't know how good a coach I am, to be frank with you, but the one thing anyone who ever played for us [will tell you], if they hold in practice, I'm all over their backs. I don't want to hold. But there are coaches who teach holding. And I'm naive if I tell you they're not. . . . There's nobody in position in the officiating crews that can call the tight end holding. The side judge can't see it. The referee's not looking at it. The umpire is looking at the inside guys. The guy who is twenty yards down the field is supposed to call it and he can't see it. So some guys teach holding. . . .

"One of these days all of us—the coaches in this league—are going to have to sit back and say, 'Hey, what's going on with the officiating?' Because really it's not very consistent. . . . We turn in a tape every week to [Big Ten supervisor] Dave Perry. And in it there are six, seven blatant holding situations. What happens? [He says,] 'You're right, Coach.' But the same guys show up every week."

• • •

In all the autumns of Paterno's life, there hadn't been many when he had to endure two weeks without a football game. But after Penn State's addition a decade earlier, the Big Ten was left with an uneven eleven members. So each got a bye week during the conference schedule. The Nittany Lions were idle from October 9 to October 23.

His routine interrupted, his determination temporarily deflated, Paterno approached the downtime as if it were a spiritual retreat. There would be contemplative walks, inspirational films, and plenty of soul searching.

After meetings on Monday, October 11, he decided that for the first time in a long while he'd walk home from his office. For most of his career, the coach had made the trip on foot. This season, thanks to his renewed ardor, there just hadn't been time.

"It's the first time I've been able to really take a walk without worrying about having to look at my watch," he said.

On this head-clearing jaunt on a sunny afternoon, he took a detour, ambling over to Eastview Terrace. Though the cluster of handsome new brick dormitories in the campus's southeast corner had opened that summer, the coach had not yet seen it. "Beautiful," he now pronounced the project.

Arriving at home that afternoon, he went to his den. Instead of picking up a novel or watching an old movie, he decided to look at some videotapes—of both his team and of Iowa. His wife was right. He couldn't relax.

Paterno typically did not meet with reporters during bye weeks. However, the coach belatedly realized that, by keeping his players from talking and by answering questions for only seven minutes himself, he had imposed a hardship on writers who needed to produce several Penn State stories a week.

He told Nelson to let the media know he would be be available on Tuesday, October 12, to answer questions. He also wanted to use the occasion to apologize. But just as his radio-show answers would the following week, the apology quickly turned into a lament on the loss.

"I didn't feel very comfortable with the way I handled some things after the game on Saturday," he began. "I know you folks have a job to do and something has to come out of the game, win or lose. It was one of the most disappointing losses I have ever been around. That is one of the reasons I tried to keep the kids away from everybody.

"We really thought we were going to win that football game. We practiced well, prepared well, and the kids did what we asked them to do. . . . We did everything and we didn't win the football game. That is kind of frustrating to me. I don't feel any better. I would be dishonest if I told you I feel better."

The rest of that first week proceeded like any other—practices Tuesday, Wednesday, and Thursday afternoons and a brief morning session on Friday. After the Friday workout, he dismissed the players for the weekend, urging those who could to go home and visit with family and friends.

Paterno then drove to State College's airport, where he was to board a university jet for a flight to Pittsburgh. A luncheon rally for that city's Penn State supporters was set for a downtown hotel. Paterno and Nittany Lions basketball coaches Ed DeChellis and Rene Portland were to speak.

At the last minute, the coach had second thoughts. Hort, his son-in-law, though improving, had just been released from the Altoona hospital and still had some rehabilitation issues to confront. (Hort would attend the Iowa game. "He looked great," reported family friend Kay Kustanbauter.) Paterno felt that he ought not to abandon his family under those circumstances. He told DeChellis and Portland he wasn't going. Instead, he spent the afternoon with Hort's children.

That night Paterno took those players who stayed on campus to see *Friday Night Lights*, a film about a successful Texas high-school football program based on Buzz Bissinger's Pulitzer prize–winning book. The coach, who rarely employed such rah-rah methods, had been trying to boost his team's spirits all season and the film's ending, he had heard, was an inspirational one.

"This year I spent a lot more time trying to get these guys to believe in themselves and not to get discouraged," he said later. "[Doing] those kinds of things that you don't do when you're winning. When you're winning, you try to keep them under control. I have a saying, 'You're never as good as you think you are when you're winning and you're never as bad as you think you are when you're losing.' So when you're winning it's easy to keep them under control. When you lose, it really almost comes to the point of 'Here we go again.' It's an ongoing fight."

Paterno rose early on the football-free Saturday, took another walk, and then morphed into a couch potato. He watched football all day, Ohio State versus Iowa, Michigan State versus Minnesota, flipping back and forth constantly. Then he wrote some letters to recruits.

Though he was a longtime member of the aptly named Our Lady of Victory parish, Paterno rarely attended Mass there on Sundays during football season. He spent most of this one at home with his family. On Monday, his familiar game-week routine resumed.

Paterno and his assistants had initially agreed to try and lighten the mood at the workouts the previous week. These young players had been devastated, and the three-game losing streak had put a lot of pressure on their padded shoulders.

"We've had a little fun," he said when asked about Monday's practice, "and hopefully we'll be able to do some things that will help us go from where we are just losing to where we are just winning, because we are not going to dominate anybody."

The more he looked at film of the Purdue game, however, the worse his demeanor became. He snapped constantly at Mills and at his aides. And he was particularly incensed at the offensive line, whose performance against Purdue, he said in a very un-Paterno-like assessment, was "horrible."

The Nittany Lions' running game had picked up an unthinkable 18 yards on seventeen carries, the worst performance in his Penn State career. A blocking assignment was forgotten on the faked field goal, the game's pivotal play. And Mills had been pummeled by Purdue's pass rush.

"Coach was on them probably the most out of everybody," said Mills of the linemen.

That testiness lingered at his October 19 press conference, especially when he was asked how he planned to utilize Robinson, who had been cleared to return.

"You can ask all the questions you want about how I am going to use Michael Robinson and I'm going to give everybody the same answer. You'll find out on Saturday. I'm not going to get up here and tell you what I am going to do with Michael Robinson. Why should I? Michael Robinson is going to be in the football game and in a lot of different ways. Hopefully, he will be a strong factor in the outcome of the game. I'm not going to be explicit as to what he is going to do and where he is going to be. Why help the other guy?"

The reporter, ignoring the one-question rule at his own peril, persisted, reminding the coach that it was a logical question and that he wasn't "asking for state secrets."

"What *are* you asking for?" Paterno said. "I don't know whether he is going to play wide receiver, tailback, or quarterback. I know where he is going to play, but I am not going to say. It's possible he could play any one of those places, so what are you asking? Tell me what you are asking. Do you want me to tell you where he is going to play? Is that what you want me to tell you? I'm not going to tell you."

One last query on the subject set him off further: Could Paterno offer a few reasons why he continued to call Robinson one of the nation's best players?

"He can do everything," Paterno shot back. "He's a great football player. I have coached great football players for fifty-five years. If I tell you that Michael Robinson is one of the best football players I've ever coached and one of the best in the country, don't question me."

On the day before the Iowa Game, *Cold Pizza*, ESPN's morning show, came to State College for a live segment on Penn State and Paterno. If school officials had hoped the nationally televised piece might provide a boost to their ailing football program, they must have been disappointed.

Cold, gray, and misty, the morning's weather hid the still colorful mountains from TV viewers. The human backdrop for cohost Thea Andrews's outdoor interview with the coach—band members and cheerleaders in neat rows outside Beaver Stadium—looked cold and artificial. And Paterno, apparently baffled by its name, came across as an antique on a show aimed at a young, hip, and edgy audience.

"What are you?" he asked Andrews on the air in an incredulous tone, *"Cold Pizza?"*

Assured that, yes, that indeed was its name, Paterno remained uncomprehending.

"*Cold Pizza? Cold Pizza?* My father would kill you all. He never ate a cold pizza in his life!"

The odd exchange was, in the eyes of his critics, just what you'd expect from a seventy-seven-year-old coach out of step with a changing world. He was so old that in the Iowa game, Paterno would pass one name from football's ice age—Pop Warner—and move into second place behind another—Amos Alonzo Stagg—in games coached all-time.

Paterno did offer an interesting theory for Happy Valley's powerful appeal during the interview. He gave credit to State College's size and isolation.

"Homecoming is special at most universities, but it's especially special here because of the fact that, you know, we're a small town," he said. "We're not a big city. The kids come to school here and they have to be together. There's no outside activity, really. It's university life. And they get so close they really look forward to coming back to school and revisiting with friends."

And then came the inevitable question from Andrews about his job status.

"People say, 'Why do you stay in coaching?' and I say, 'Well, what are you doing on Saturday?' Tomorrow morning I'll get up early and I'll twitch and do some other things and won't let anybody talk to me. And then I'll come over here and walk out on the stadium with a hundred and seven, a hundred and eight thousand people and it's exciting and it's fun to be part of. . . . [I'll be here] as long as I'm healthy and as long as I think I can do the job."

In these difficult times, Penn State's spectacular football tradition didn't always help. In fact, the glorious past often served only as a painful counterpoint to a troubled present.

That night, for example, Penn State honored Lydell Mitchell, the ex–running back from the Class of 1971 who had just been elected to the College Football Hall of Fame, with a dinner at the Nittany Lion Inn. More than one hotel guest, passing by the basement ballroom where it was held, noted that when Mitchell played, the Nittany Lions usually rushed for more than 17 yards.

Penn State AD Curley greeted Mitchell's guests, many of them big-time donors, at the ballroom door. Later he and his Iowa counterpart, Bob Bowlsby, walked down the hall to the weekly media reception. A representative from the Outback Bowl was there as well. Paterno was not.

The light rain continued into the night, soaking those students and alums who packed College Avenue for the Eighty-fifth Homecoming Parade. All day long, sorority pledges sat atop the cold sidewalks, a tradition by which they held the best viewing spots for their older "sisters." By early evening, they had been joined there by fellow students, middle-aged alumni, State College residents and their children, and the merely curious.

Occasionally, small groups of students carrying plastic cups filled with beer or some undetermined clear liquid weaved through the crowds. Sometimes the raindrops falling on their heads were enhanced by beer or water dumped down—intentionally or inadvertently—by those occupying the balconies of College Avenue apartments. No one seemed to mind.

The floats and marchers from 170 university organizations passed in a sentimental fog. When the parade concluded, spectators walked to Old Main for a rally at which Sue Paterno, the event's grand marshal, spoke briefly.

"Welcome back," said the coach's wife, "to the home where your heart was and always will be."

Then they all joined together to sing Penn State's fight song.

In the mismatched voices of the wet alumni, it wasn't difficult to detect a longing for the past.

Penn State had scored 27 points in its three Big Ten losses. During the two off weeks, the offensive coaches continued to be the focus of criticism, particularly by those still reluctant to point fingers at Paterno.

New speculation bubbled to the surface. Returning graduates said they'd heard from this player or administrator, from that parent or booster, that Galen Hall, trapped between a pair of Paternos, was terribly unhappy. The *Centre Daily Times* even felt the need to publicly address—but not debunk—a rumor that Hall already had decided not to return in 2005.

"Hall has been called an offensive genius and has been successful at both the major college and NFL levels. Something tells me he could handle this Penn State gig all by himself," Wilkes-Barre's Kellar wrote that week.

Observers wanted to know why Hall, unlike the majority of college football's offensive cordinators, was stationed on the sideline during games and not up in the press box. Shouldn't it be the coordinator and not quarterbacks coach Jay Paterno who benefited from the lofty view?

"We've discussed that as a staff," Paterno told the press. "And I think it's up to Galen as to whether he thinks he can do a better job upstairs or downstairs. I've left it up to him. I have tremendous faith in Galen Hall. There isn't a finer offensive mind anywhere in the country. We've talked about maybe just changing the whole operation and that might be something we do even as close as this Saturday."

Those who liked to blame Jay for all the program's ills saw Hall as a victim. Nepotism or not, the son made an inviting target. From the time he'd been named quarterbacks coach before the 2000 season, Penn State's offense had never placed higher than 54th nationally (out of 117 schools) in passing yards. Four years later, the Lions' attack was now more inept than ever.

But when the game with Iowa began on Saturday, Hall and Jay Paterno remained in place.

That cold, foggy morning a scalper stood at the corner of Park Road and McKee Street, silently flashing his tickets, a desperate gesture that unwittingly mocked the coach whose home was so close by.

Other scalpers were stationed all around Beaver Stadium, trying to unload tickets. Big SUVs, their bumper stickers betraying their political allegiances, rolled past without stopping.

Alongside most of the seventeen hundred RVs in the parking lots, tailgating parties were under way. Penn State grad Jason Mahla of Bel-camp, Maryland, hosted sixty guests at his, serving them shrimp, ranch burgers, lamb, and deep-fried Oreos. He had begun setting up at 2:00 A.M.

Once inside for the noon game, this crowd appeared even older than normal. Fans cheered politely when a host of paunchy Blue Band alums in white T-shirts—D'Elia had called for yet another "White Out"—marched onto the field.

Some spectators who had not been back for a Penn State game in several years were disappointed that they could no longer see Mount Nittany from inside the stadium. Had they been able to, though, they'd likely have been dismayed by the sight of new housing developments creeping up its sacred slopes.

When Paterno and the players emerged for the pregame workout, the old coach walked over to the student section and again tried to rouse them to noise. Then he turned back toward the field, from which one of his grandchildren ran toward him for an embrace.

Despite another sea of white shirts forming in the student section, these spectators were much more subdued than before the Purdue game. Despite the weekly hopes for a season-turning victory, there were limits to how often optimism could be summoned and renewed.

Iowa's players walked out of a tunnel at the opposite end of the stadium and were greeted by the small contingent of yellow-and-black-clad supporters stuck in the stadium's northeast corner. Despite their 4–2 record and No. 25 ranking, the Hawkeyes came into the game a damaged team.

Iowa had lost its two top running backs—Marcus Schnoor and Al-bert Young—to early-season knee injuries. The Hawkeyes were down to their Nos. 5 and 6 backs for Penn State. Still, it was somewhat surprising that the oddsmakers had made scuffling Penn State a 2 1/2-point favorite.

This homecoming matchup contained a little extracurricular interest too. Iowa coach Kirk Ferentz, a forty-nine-year-old who had played high school football in western Pennsylvania, was often mentioned as a possible successor to Paterno. Smart and articulate, Ferentz possessed a well-groomed, razor-cut image that counted for so much at Penn State. His eighty-four-year-old father had passed away the previous Friday and he had been back in Pennsylvania since Wednesday night. He didn't accompany Iowa to State College, but instead joined the team there on Friday night.

When his visiting Hawkeyes last defeated Penn State, 42–35, in 2002, they had run the ball forty-nine times. But now, without his best runners, Ferentz had transformed Iowa into a passing team. Nimble sophomore QB Drew Tate had thrown eighty passes in routs of Michigan State and Ohio State over the past two weeks.

Paterno was more concerned about Iowa's defense. End Matt Roth was a terrific pass rusher, and even two weeks later Mills was still sore from all the hits he'd taken against Purdue. Unhappy with the play of the right side of his offensive line, the coach had shifted sophomore tackle Levi Brown to right tackle in place of junior Andrew Richardson and inserted senior Scott Davis at right guard in place of Reed. Brown, said Paterno, might fare better against Roth.

Before the game, Anthony Adams, the ex–Penn State defensive tackle now with the San Francisco 49ers, addressed the Nittany Lions defenders, many of whom he'd played alongside. His speech suggested that the locker room might be separating along an offensive–defensive fault line.

"He said we should go out there and go all out," said defensive lineman Tamba Hali, "we shouldn't worry about the offense. [He said] the game is really in our hands because we have to play the game, too, and we should not really be too concerned about what our offense wants to do on the field."

The opening series offered an immediate glimpse of what was to follow.

Iowa failed to move the ball and on fourth down, a snap sailed over the head of punter David Bradley and into the end zone. Bradley retreated rapidly and intentionally kicked the ball out of bounds, the safety giving Penn State a 2–0 lead after just 1:26.

When Iowa's next possession ended with a 28-yard Bradley punt, Lowry's 33-yard return left the Nittany Lions with a first down at the

Hawkeyes' 24. But after two penalties and Roth's sack of Mills, Gould was forced to try a 51-yard field goal. It fell short. Iowa took the lead, 3–2, on a 27-yard field goal by Kyle Schlicher with 1:42 left in the first quarter.

Early in the second quarter, Mills threw the first of four Penn State interceptions, with Iowa safety Sean Considine returning it to the Nittany Lions' 10. A loud chorus of boos began to submerge whatever homecoming cheer remained. The negative noise resurfaced a short time later when Schlicher added another 27-yarder for a 6–2 Iowa lead.

Mills's next pass was nearly picked off. Then, just five minutes after his first, he further emboldened the boobirds by heaving another interception, killing a drive that had advanced to Iowa's 34. The quarterback, who took a nasty lick on that second interception, would complete just four of twelve first-half passes for 33 yards.

Both the booing and the offense worsened in the second half. On Penn State's first play, a groggy Mills threw the ball to no one, eliciting another crowd reaction. But Penn State got another golden opportunity when Donnie Johnson blocked a Bradley punt and the Lions recovered at Iowa's nine. This time, runs by Hunt and Robinson and another Mills incompletion preceded another missed field goal by Gould from 25 yards.

On the Penn State sideline, Paterno hunched over, put his hands on his knees, and shook his head. His offense's incompetence was so complete that it seemed to suggest Iowa might be stealing the signals, which were being relayed to Mills from the sideline. "We had a couple of times when they yelled out the play before it started," said Smolko. "They were definitely well prepared for the game." That may have been so, but it didn't explain their ineptitude the previous three games.

Robinson replaced Mills, who was experiencing dizziness, late in the third quarter, prompting cheers for one of the few times all day. With Hunt carrying the load, he moved Penn State deep into Iowa territory again.

But on a second-and-goal from the 9, Penn State was called for an illegal-procedure penalty. Then Robinson threw an incompletion. And on third down, his pass was intercepted by Antwan Allen, who was tackled at the Hawkeyes' 8.

What followed was the ultimate indignity in a season filled with them.

Iowa couldn't move the ball and an illegal-procedure penalty left the Hawkeyes facing a fourth-and-17 at their own 1 with just over eight minutes to play. Bradley had struggled on his punts and Ferentz was reluctant to risk one from the back line of the end zone. His only other option was a safety. That might be sound strategy with a big lead, but with only a four-point advantage, if Iowa took one, Penn State could then win with a field goal.

The Iowa coach knew he had no reason to fear Penn State's offense. Mills was out. Robinson looked rusty. Who else was there?

So he ordered the safety that made it a 6–4 game.

"The decision was pretty obvious," Ferentz would later say. "I'd rather give the safety and then play field position, you know, ride our defense. That was a pretty good thing to do today."

Paterno agreed with his counterpart's call, even though it was a slap in the face. "We weren't going anywhere," he said.

Ferentz's call paid dividends immediately. Robinson's first pass on Penn State's subsequent possession was intercepted by Jovon Johnson at Iowa's 40.

Penn State got the ball back again after Iowa's offense sputtered. This time, again on the first play, Robinson fumbled it back to Iowa— three turnovers on three plays—at the Nittany Lions' 14 with 2:30 to play.

Much of the crowd had departed by then but for those who remained, there would be one final embarrassment.

With 1:23 still to play and facing a fourth-and-2 at Penn State's 6, Ferentz passed up a field goal that would have given Iowa a 5-point lead, insurance against a possible game-winning 3-pointer by Penn State. That risky decision became moot when Penn State defenders jumped offsides, the penalty yielding the Hawkeyes the first down and allowing them, beneath a final ceiling of boos, to run out the clock.

• • •

The game's final statistics were stunning.

Iowa had managed just ten first downs, 168 total yards, and two field goals—all of which surpassed Penn State's figures.

The Nittany Lions' six first downs were the fewest ever for a Paterno team. They had gained less than 100 yards rushing (51) and passing (96). They had fumbled three times, thrown four interceptions, and turned the ball over five times.

All against an Iowa defense that had surrendered 435 passing yards and 44 points to Arizona State a month earlier.

CHAPTER 16

AS POORLY AS the Nittany Lions had performed on offense against Iowa, the four points they managed were four more than they scored with unhappy fans.

After this one, it seemed there ought to have been another category of postgame statistics, one that more accurately reflected all the humiliations Penn State—and by extension its supporters—had endured: The boos. The baseball-score loss on homecoming weekend. The five turnovers. Ferentz calling for a disrespectful safety. Another quarterback concussion. The national snickers. The incompetent offense of historic proportions.

In Paterno's first thirty-five seasons as head coach, the Lions had never lost four games in a row. They had now done it three times in four years. The players' growing futility was evident in the Nittany Lions' locker room following the Iowa loss. The frustration, bewilderment, anger, and embarrassment were so thick and overpowering that several players again broke down and cried. And this time Paterno had run out of words with which to console them.

"Coach had a tough time with words after the game," said defensive tackle Scott Paxson. "I think he's thinking what everyone is kind of thinking, where do you go from here?

"He's not used to this," said defensive end Lavon Chisley. "This would be hard for any coach to deal with, but it's especially hard for a coach like him."

The defense had played so well again—and the offense so poorly—that a locker-room schism seemed unavoidable. "It seems like that's the lullaby of this season," cornerback Zemaitis said of the disparity between units.

During the game, defensive lineman Hali could be seen railing at the offense on the sideline. "I always get frustrated at the beginning of the game," he explained, "and I get up and start yelling and say, 'We're going slow out there, let's get it going!' "

Penn State's offense had scored two touchdowns in four Big Ten games. It had turned the ball over twenty-one times. Its rushing totals in its five losses were mind-boggling for a Paterno team—233 yards on 115 carries, barely 2 yards an attempt.

Waiting in the media room for the coach, the sportswriters joked cynically, about the offense, about the rare 6–4 score, about Paterno's apparent inability to recognize his team's failings.

"I guess Robinson will have to give back the Heisman," one writer mocked.

Finally, wearing a sweatshirt beneath a windbreaker, Paterno walked into the room. His entrance triggered a stacatto snapping of camera shutters from the balcony above. It was probably a hopeful sign for the program that the families and recruits who watched from up there still wanted his picture.

"I don't know if we could have played much poorer," Paterno began. "There have been a lot of tough ones. This one would certainly be right there with them."

The question-and-answer session that followed was largely unrevealing and painfully familiar. When it was over and Paterno had departed, Penn State players, some of whom still had red and swollen eyes, touchingly patted their coach on the shoulder as they passed in the adjoining hallway.

"He's frustrated," said Hali. "It's not his fault. I mean, people keep saying we need to get rid of him. You get rid of him and what does it change? The team? We've still got the same players. We're the ones that have to make the adjustment. We're the ones that have to play the game, that have to win. All the help we can get from our coaching staff, we're still the ones that have to win."

They were growing increasingly sensitive to criticism of their coach. All it did, from their perspective, was layer another level of pressure on them. They didn't want to go down in history as the Penn State team that drove off Joe Paterno.

"I feel bad," said Paxson. "He's a great coach. All the winning seasons he's had, and now he's got to go through this. People on the outside are telling him he should give it up. But if people were allowed to come to practice to see Joe [they'd see how much he still cares]. He slaps us in the face. If you jump offsides, he grabs you by the helmet. He's all over you. I don't see a guy who is going to hang it up. I see a guy I want to hide from."

Spectators, dizzied by the scope of Penn State's impotence, lingered in the parking lots long afterward.

Some of their car radios were tuned to the local postgame call-in show on 970–AM. Fans, drinking beer in little clusters, listened intently and nodded their heads in agreement while cohost Phil Grosz lambasted Penn State's "stone-age offense."

Grosz, a lifelong Pennsylvanian whose gray-blond hair appeared to have been styled beneath a bowl, also published *Blue White Illustrated*, the weekly tabloid for Nittany Lions fans. In his column and on the radio, he had been urging Paterno to become a Bobby Bowden, a CEO-type coach who delegated all the offensive and defensive details to powerful assistants.

The parking-lot fans' ears perked up when caller Skip Dreibelbis—a State College resident, a onetime high-school teammate of Jay Paterno's, and an ex–Penn State football player—offered his sobering assessment.

"The program has taken a real turn for the worse," Dreibelbis began. "And it's really been disappointing to me as a former player. . . . It's no reflection on the players. My heart goes out to every single one of those guys. They deal week in and week out with Joe's little hissy fits. He gets in a tirade and carries on. But they deal with that. They go out and they work really hard. You've got to blame the leadership of this team.

"I've talked to former players who played in the NFL and who've come to Joe and said, 'Hey, I'd like to get a chance to do a little bit of coaching.' Joe won't take them in. Don't have enough coaching experience. You know I like Jay as a person. He was a great holder for me and a nice guy. But doggone, Jay's only played maybe one quarter of football and it was in high school and he's out there coaching quarterbacks. And there's Mike McQueary, who played [quarterback] all through high school and college, and he's coaching tight ends.

"Sooner or later someone has to take the bull by the horns and say enough is enough. Last year was the worst in Penn State history and what do they do? Give him a new contract and a bonus. Let's start holding people accountable."

Cohost Jerry Fisher, a devoted Penn State loyalist whose father had been the Nittany Lions' boosterish radio voice for decades, had walked through the parking lots before the game. There he asked fans if they thought the inevitable decision on Paterno's future ought to be left to the coach or the administration.

"Ninety percent are saying that Joe is the one that needs to make a decision," said Fisher, "but that he needs to make it soon."

A few days later, Paterno did nothing to aid his supporters' case. When asked if he thought his players were too tight, he veered off into another frustrated riff about bad luck and bad officiating.

"Those kinds of things happen to us," he said. "It's very easy to generalize and easy to start to panic about different things. . . . [But] I think we can get started. We were ahead two to nothing on Saturday. We couldn't take advantage of it."

For his critics, the bizarre allusion to the 2–0 score proved just how far Paterno's expectations had slipped. Once he had wanted a national championship so badly that he publicly criticized a U.S. president who had declared Texas No. 1. Now he was satisfied with a 2–0 lead?

By that last week in October, Paterno's age, abilities, and status were being debated so passionately in State College that the subject even found its way to the coach's dinner table.

Following the homecoming humiliation, the Paternos, as they did after most home games, hosted a dinner at their house. Among the old friends in attendance was Don Bellisario, a seventy-year-old Penn State grad who had gone on to Hollywood, where he had produced, among other shows, *Magnum P.I.*, the Tom Selleck series.

"[Bellisario] said the worst thing ever invented was dates," Paterno recalled. "I was teasing him about how long he was going to produce and write for television . . . and that is how he responded to that. He looks great at seventy and you wouldn't believe he was seventy. I don't feel seventy-seven. That's not my problem. My problem is not winning games. That's my problem."

His players had problems of their own. The civility that always had surrounded Penn State football appeared to be vanishing in the toxic vapor of another four-game losing streak. There had been more boos during the Iowa loss than in entire decades of Nittany Lions football. Mills, who was the target of most of them, probably had been vilified more than any Penn State player who ever set foot in Beaver Stadium.

"That wasn't right," said fullback Paul Jefferson. "I don't think Zack deserved that. [A loss is] never one person's fault."

Angry fans continued to berate the senior quarterback in e-mails and nasty, anonymous telephone messages.

"One e-mail said, 'You need to go up there and tell [the coaches] you don't want to play anymore, and let some one else play,' " Mills recalled. "I got a message on my phone that said basically that I suck. . . . I haven't got to the point to e-mail people back, but I've been close."

Robinson said he got the same question over and over from fellow students who once had been too shy to approach him but now felt emboldened enough to ask: "What's wrong with the offense?"

Tight end Smolko noted that he sat silently on campus buses, listening as fellow students disparaged his team. "There's not much good for anyone to talk about anymore," he admitted.

"It's frustrating," linebacker Shaw said of the negative buzz on campus. "You start to think if we were doing better, life would be a lot better and people would like us better."

"It's hard on everybody," said Chisley. "Nobody came here to lose."

Paterno, who was shouldering plenty of the blame himself, tried again to deflect criticism from his players and assistants in the days before they traveled to Ohio State.

"You guys are being critical of the wrong people," he told sportswriters. "You should be critical of me. I'm the boss. I hate it when you guys are critical of kids or critical of the staff. I know what's going on and I know what kind of coaches I have. If I didn't think they were doing their job, I would do something. I'm not sure how critical we should be of anybody. I think we should look back and realize that we're playing against some people that are good football teams and [we] may be playing with some kids that are a little bit outmanned or a little bit outexperienced or something like that. That's the attitude I have to take."

Paterno continued to take hits from the media. And some of the writers and talk-show hosts now demanded that Morelli play at Columbus on Saturday.

It seemed logical. Mills was ninety-fifth in Division I-A passing efficiency and was still groggy from the concussion. Robinson had turned the ball over the last three times he touched it. And unless the Nittany Lions somehow won their final four games, they weren't going to be going to a bowl anyway. So why not play the promising freshman? Hadn't Paterno said that his decision not to redshirt him was made because he hoped to give the young QB some experience? Here was his chance.

Apparently, given the coach's emphatic answers at his weekly news conference, either his thinking or his assessment of Morelli's ability had changed.

"Do you think Anthony Morelli is adequately prepared to play against Ohio State should you need him?"

"No."

"Why not?"

"He isn't adequately prepared."

"Does he not know the plays?"

"He isn't adequately prepared."

The truth was somewhat different. The coaches had inserted some plays for Morelli into the Ohio State game plan. But Paterno was hoping not to have to use him. He didn't want to get Morelli killed. The offensive line had already allowed two mature quarterbacks to endure serious beatings.

"I think they lost a little confidence in themselves because they have had some breakdowns in key situations," Paterno said of the line. "I just think we have to get a little bit more confident, consistent, don't make so many mental mistakes, concentrate a little bit better, and not get discouraged if you get licked every once in a while, because we are going to get licked every once in a while."

Pep rallies. Inspirational movies. Soft words. Harsh words. Nothing Paterno had attempted could get his team over the hump. But he was too stubborn and too competitive to stop trying.

Two days before the Ohio State game, at the end of a long and grueling practice, he addressed the team in a T-shirt. It was a replica of a shirt that Boston pitcher Curt Schilling had worn during the just-completed American League Championship Series, when the Red Sox overcame a 3–0 deficit to defeat the New York Yankees in seven games. The shirt's message read WHY NOT US?

"Why not us?" the coach, who grew up in Dodger-crazed Brooklyn despising the Yankees, asked the players. "We got four games left. We can win 'em all and wind up with a winning record and a bowl game. Don't worry what people think. You think anybody but the Red Sox thought they were going to come back and win?"

The following day Paterno spoke at another rally, though this one was for the Bush campaign. The president's father, George H. W. Bush, and daughters were, along with the coach, the star attractions at a Robeson Center gathering Friday afternoon.

In introducing Jenna and Barbara Bush, Paterno told the fifteen hundred spectators that the Bush family was "everything you ever wanted in people—courage, conviction."

When former President Bush, eighty, spoke, he alluded to Paterno's age and troubles.

"I think it's OK when you get to be an older man," Bush said. "I love him. I love him like a brother."

There was some talk of Scott Paterno's congressional campaign at the gathering. Privately, Paterno acknowledged his son wasn't going to unseat the popular incumbent, Democrat Tim Holden. So he had already let reporters know he wouldn't be attending Scott's postelection party, scheduled for the Four Points Sheraton in Harrisburg late Tuesday night.

"It's the middle of football season," he said. "I've got too much work to do."

Not long after the Bush rally, the coach and team traveled to Columbus. That night at their hotel, the Marriott North, which stood near the confluence of several new highways, ESPN *Classic* showed a replay of the 1995 Penn State–Ohio State game, won by the Buckeyes, 28–25.

Though it had been just nine years, the differences were striking. Paterno seemed far less agitated and restless along the sideline. And the '95 Penn State team looked bigger, faster, and infinitely more sure of itself. Anchored by future Pro Bowler Jeff Hartings, its offensive line, even when Ohio State stacked the box with eight and nine defenders, consistently cleared huge gaps for tailback Curtis Enis.

The hotel lobby was surprisingly empty that night. Typically, Penn State fans buzzed inside and outside the team hotel, hoping to see, chat with, or get autographs from players and coaches. But there just didn't seem to be many Penn State fans here. Who could blame them? Who wanted to travel to watch a team that had lost nine straight road games? Besides, late October in Columbus was hardly springtime in Paris.

"I've talked to travel agents back home who said that Penn State's move to the Big Ten has hurt their business," said David Jones, a *Harrisburg Patriot-News* columnist who had covered Penn State for more than a decade. "I mean, look at the road trips you get. Bloomington? West Lafayette? Iowa City? Champaign? Who wants to go to those places? Especially not when your team stinks."

The search for ways to explain Penn State's descent was again the topic at the weekly media reception. In Suite 116 at the Marriott, several reporters, photographers, and the bottle of Jack Daniel's waited in vain for Paterno.

The sessions were gaining a momentum of their own. In the absence of the coach, they had become forums for the exchange of opinions and speculation.

Wilkes-Barre's Kellar had been told that a group of parents had informed Curley that unless Paterno stepped aside, they'd see that their sons transferred; Jones heard that Paterno and Jay had been accosted by angry fans as they'd walked home after the Iowa loss; and a source in Old Main told Reading's Scarcella that administrators had contacted Sue Paterno in an effort to gauge her husband's state of mind.

As for reasons for the program's struggles, this week they focused on recruiting. They included Paterno's inability to recruit the "speed states"—Texas, Florida, and California; the fact that the staff had only two black assistants and needed another to aid in recruiting; and the move to the Big Ten, which introduced rivals into territory Penn State used to dominate.

But just days earlier an anonymous Big Ten assistant had told *ESPN.com* that any suggestion Penn State wasn't getting top talent was "a myth."

"We recruited a lot of their kids, and to be honest, we really wanted some of those guys," he said. "A few of them looked like Superman. But you watch them on tape now and you're like 'That's so-and-so? Man, what happened?' These kids aren't developing. It's actually like they're regressing athletically when they get there. That tells me the problem isn't just the coaching in practices, but in the weight room too."

What none of them knew, though, was that the nation's No. 1 recruit, speedster Derrick Williams of Greenbelt, Maryland, would be driving with his family to State College the following afternoon for an official visit. On Sunday, the Williamses would meet with President Spanier, and with Penn State players and students. They would enjoy lunch at Paterno's house. And though the decision would not be revealed for another two months, they would be won over.

Even as the terrible autumn continued for the Nittany Lions, the seeds of a new season of hope were being sown.

• • •

When Penn State's team entered Ohio Stadium early the next morning, a gray and rainy day was about to turn sunny and extremely windy. Though Ohio State also had recently refurbished and expanded its historic football stadium, the game-day atmosphere in Columbus was far more commercial than that at Penn State. Airplanes trailing banners from local car dealerships flew overhead. Commercials played constantly on the giant stadium scoreboard. Sponsors' signs and logos were ubiquitous. And in the narrow streets and tiny parking lots surrounding the stadium, a chaotic festival of capitalism was in full flower.

Those circumstances reflected a couple of chilling statistics for anyone concerned about the commercialization of college sports. Ohio State athletics, after redoing the stadium and constructing new state-of-the-art basketball, hockey, baseball, and track-and-field facilities, owed more than $220 million. The $90-plus million 2004 sports budget—the nation's largest—required annual debt-service payments that topped $16 million.

Once Paterno accompanied his team onto the field for pregame warm-ups, he was extremely busy. These road trips gave all his admirers in those places an opportunity to get close to him. And now his age and uncertain future lent some urgency to their efforts.

He talked with Ohio State coach Jim Tressel while photographers, sprawled on the grass below, snapped their photos. He chatted with Buckeyes assistants, one of whom introduced him to his son, a Buckeyes walk-on. He posed for pictures with the chain-gang crew and with some traveling Blue Band members. And he tested the footing on the wet surface.

Mills was dressed for the game but would not play, which delighted his many critics. Even Jack Ham, the former all-American linebacker at Penn State who now served as Jones's color analyst on radio broadcasts, was privately critical. While telling sportswriters he admired Mills's character a great deal, Ham described the quarterback's arm as "candy-ass."

Just before the game began, a Penn State fan released a clot of blue-and-white balloons. They rose quickly into the dark sky, buffeted back and forth by the winds, before drifting slowly out of sight.

If nothing else, the Iowa loss had prompted Paterno to make a few dramatic changes. Concerned that the Hawkeyes might have been stealing sideline signs, the coach mandated that plays would be shuttled in. And for the first time, Hall would be stationed in the upstairs coaches' box, alongside Jay Paterno. With the eyes of countless reporters on them, the two men in the glass-enclosed booth kept their attention focused on the field.

"We felt like [Hall] could do a little better job upstairs," Paterno explained. "He had always been upstairs when he was an assistant. The play calling was done exactly the same way. They consult on different things. It was a good change of pace and Galen didn't have to listen to me bitch on the sidelines, so it was a good break for him."

The perception grew stronger that Penn State's byzantine playcalling system—Hall calling the running plays, Jay calling the passes, all with the input of Dick Anderson and, ultimately, Paterno himself—was a hopeless muddle. Asked who had been calling the plays against Iowa, Robinson laughed and said, "God."

Paterno insisted he had little to do with the play calling once the games started. He said his main input had been to try to keep things simple, to remove plays from the game plan, not add them.

But with an offense that ranked 107th out of 117 Division I-A teams in scoring and passing efficiency and 86th in rushing, the pressure on the staff intensified. Reports of a rift between Hall and the younger Paterno continued, reports the head coach continued to deny.

Only Bill Kenney, who, along with Anderson, coached the line, remained on the sideline among the offensive staff. So it was he who had to endure Paterno's frequent questions and complaints.

"Bill Kenney has to take all the brunt now," Paterno joked.

Despite the show of self-deprecating humor, Paterno continued to bristle about the negative sniping at his offensive staff, criticism that stung all the worse when it was directed at his son.

"I just don't think it's fair," he said. "If there's a criticism to be made of the coaches, I think I'm the guy to do it. If I allow people to criticize the offensive coaches or criticize the defensive coaches for something here, something there, I don't think you can have a good organization," he said. "I really don't."

On a Penn State football blog, one fan summed up the feelings of many.

"The fans want Oe Paterno," he wrote. "That's Joe Paterno without the Jay."

Ohio State was experiencing a down year too. The Buckeyes were 4–3, 1–3 in the Big Ten. Penn State, however, had lost five straight at Ohio Stadium, not having won there since 1978.

The game began with Robinson at quarterback. And when the first play was a rollout run by the junior, a Penn State photographer in the press box yelped with joy. He had won a $40 bet, correctly anticipating that Robinson would run right on his first play under center. "He does it every time," said the photographer.

Without Mills, Paterno's game plan was heavy with runs. Keeping the ball on the ground, the Lions moved to Ohio State's 31 on their opening possession before Robinson's sideline pass was intercepted by Buckeyes cornerback Ashton Youboty.

There were no passes and no first downs on Penn State's next drive. But Kapinos's punt was returned 67 yards for a touchdown by Ted Ginn Jr. Ginn raced untouched into the end zone, displaying the kind of breakaway speed the Nittany Lions sorely missed. For the game, the Buckeyes' return teams would outgain Penn State's by a total of 192 to −1.

"Those guys," said Kapinos, who fanned on Ginn late in the return, "are freak athletes."

Robinson's next pass, a screen to Terrance Phillips on a third-and-7 from his own 23, was intercepted too. Strong safety Tyler Everett returned it 24 yards for a score. With 3:41 left in the opening quarter, Ohio State had run four plays, gained five yards, and accumulated no first downs. And the Buckeyes led, 14–0.

Robinson, who had ended the previous game with two interceptions and a fumble on his final three plays, had thrown two interceptions in three attempts in this one.

No one could blame the defense. While Penn State now had given the ball away twenty-three times this season, its defense had permitted only two touchdowns and three field goals on those turnovers.

Paterno was experiencing his standard sideline agita—reacting angrily when Rubin dropped what would have been a first-down completion on a third-and-15 pass from Robinson; repeating the tantrum when Phillips dropped another one later; throwing his hands up in the air after the second interception; collaring Kenney for a heated exchange. ESPN, which televised the game, kept track of his pacing, calculating that the coach logged more than four miles during the course of the game.

At one point, when he made the decision to go for a first down on a fourth-and-short, Paterno disgustedly waved "go ahead" to his players, as if this woeful offense had forced him to abandon all his cautious instincts.

After the two lightning scores, the Ohio Stadium bell tolled joyously for the crowd of 104,947. But for Penn State and its season, it sounded ominously like a death knell.

A three-yard TD run by Tony Hunt in the second quarter (only the third Penn State TD since September 18) was negated immediately by Branden Joe's four-yard scoring run on the ensuing drive.

The Nittany Lions' defense had controlled Ohio State's attack throughout the game, but the Lions still trailed 21–7 when Paterno made another bizarre fourth-quarter decision. With under ten minutes to play, his team trailing by 14 points and facing a fourth-and-goal at the Ohio State 3, he decided to go for a field goal. At that point, the possibility that the Big Ten's worst offense might score twice more in the closing minutes seemed as remote as a Ralph Nader victory in the coming Tuesday's national election.

"I thought we were playing really good defense with 9:30 to go," he later explained. "I figured we'd get on the board, put some pressure on them rather than have to score twice, and get a two-point play to win. That's one of those things you're never sure you're right, but I think I'd probably do it the same way again."

Gould's 21-yarder made it 21–10. Penn State would have one more possession before time ran out—in that day's game, and on their faded dreams of the postseason.

The Nittany Lions had now lost five straight games for just the second time in Paterno's career, the other streak having come a season earlier.

"Each one," said linebacker Posluszny, "gets worse and worse."

Robinson had run twenty times for 90 yards, but completed only seven of twenty-one passes for 69 yards and two interceptions. "I stunk," he later admitted.

The defenders were frustrated again. They had allowed Ohio State just 202 yards and one touchdown and now were, statistically, the nation's seventh-best defense. Their average yield of 275.4 yards a game was Penn State's lowest since 1978.

Yet, at 2–6, the Lions were guaranteed a fourth losing season in five years and, much to the dismay of alumni who had once been accustomed to a winter's vacation at a warm-weather bowl site, another December at home. That meant the graduating seniors would become the first class in the Paterno era to go through school without a bowl victory.

"I never would have thought I would have lost as many games as I have wearing a Penn State uniform," said junior guard Charles Rush.

"Each week we're so close," said Paxson, "so close, but we just find a way to lose."

Someone asked Robinson what he would have said if, when he was a freshman, he had been told what awaited him in the seasons ahead.

"It's a lie," he imagined. "You're crazy."

The postgame performance wasn't one of Paterno's best either. No one bought his explanation on the field goal. He said Hall's being upstairs "didn't make any difference to me." He admitted to planning to play Morelli despite having said the freshman wasn't ready a few days earlier. And when asked why safety Andrew Guman, who had badly bruised his chest, didn't play late in the game, the coach responded that he hadn't even been aware of his absence.

When Paterno and Tressel came together at midfield for the postgame handshake, Brent Musberger, the ESPN broadcaster, advised his audience to pay attention to their exchange.

"Because when you're a coach," he said, "you never know if this will be the last time."

CHAPTER 17

WHILE PATERNO HAS been widely praised over the years as "the conscience of college sports," his thought-provoking suggestions have nonetheless been as widely ignored. Since he first gave voice to the concept in the late 1960s, his Grand Experiment has done little to improve national graduation rates or to prevent academic scandals at Minnesota, Tennessee, Georgia, and elsewhere. His nearly forty years of prodding about the need for a postseason play-off system to replace the arbitrariness of the college-football polls has produced little change. His warnings about freshman eligibility have gone unheeded.

The reason, as he eventually came to understand, was that big-time college football was a formidable commercial industry, a multibillion-dollar enterprise supported by corporate sponsorships, tax breaks, and TV money. For all the nobility of purpose Paterno and some of his colleagues espouse, the desire for change among American colleges has never been as potent as the hunger for cash and the lure of football success. There were rare exceptions, such as when the national powerhouse University of Chicago abandoned football to concentrate on academic success, or when the Ivy League was formed in 1956 and its members subsequently eliminated athletic scholarships. Like politics today, the sport is driven increasingly by an endless need to raise money. The circular nature of that process prevents substantive change: Victories attract big crowds and generous donors. Big crowds and generous donors provide the revenue to build and maintain state-of-the-art sports facilities. Those facilities attract the top recruits. And the top recruits produce the victories.

Take Paterno's loudly trumpeted belief that the football season is too long for busy student athletes. Regular seasons have grown from nine games when he started at Penn State to twelve. And for teams involved in conference play-offs and bowls, it can be extended even further, to thirteen or fourteen.

"People don't seem to understand," Paterno has said. "A kid comes into a big-time program and a place where you demand he goes to class, you demand he takes legitimate subjects, and then you say to him, 'OK, but don't screw up on Saturday. You're going to play. You better do your homework. You better be in meetings. You better pay attention. Take a tape home. Do the whole bit.' . . . I hate it. . . . I think we need to make up our minds. Are we here to educate kids? Or are we using these kids to make money?"

Many coaches agree with him. So does the watchdog Knight Commission on Intercollegiate Athletics, which in 1991 characterized football's lengthy schedule as "one more extension of the overcommercialization of college sports." Finally, in 2000, the NCAA decided to compromise, limiting regular-season schedules to eleven games, except in years when there was a fifth Saturday in either September or October. But when Penn State played eleven games in 2004, its Big Ten and other scheduling obligations meant the Nittany Lions had only six at home instead of the typical seven. The loss of that single Saturday cost the athletic department more than $3 million in revenue. Other schools also were penalized financially, and so, not surprisingly, the NCAA soon was pressured to reinstate permanent twelve-game schedules. Paterno had tilted at another windmill and lost.

His frustrations with the misappropriated priorities of college athletics, however, always were ameliorated by his obsession with coaching. Whenever the dollar signs threatened to overwhelm him, he would lose himself in Xs and Os. Still, there were times when Paterno's administrative headaches wouldn't go away. Football is the linchpin of

Penn State athletics. Its revenue, as Paterno never fails to note, supports the other twenty-eight sports. That being the case, in the early 1980s university administrators decided that the man in charge of football ought to be the man officially in charge of all athletics. So at President John Oswald's request, Paterno, for two hectic years, served as the school's athletic director.

"We were in a little transitional situation," Paterno recalled. "The reason I took it over was . . . we had been to four or five straight New Year's Day bowls as an independent and I was trying to get some facilities done and we didn't have any money. It was a lot of late nights until three or four A.M. . . . There still were some things that were not right. It wasn't anybody's fault, but that is just the way it drifted a little bit. So I took it over."

By then, Paterno could see a shifting sports landscape. New, made-for-TV basketball leagues like the Big East, which began play in the 1979–80 season, were thriving. More significantly, football conferences and the big independents wanted to make their own TV deals. The NCAA's monopoly on those contracts was being challenged in the courts. In anticipation of its nullification—which eventually came from the Supreme Court in 1984—the Southeastern, Southwest, and Atlantic Coast Conferences were moving openly toward expansion. They recognized that the bigger and broader they and their audiences became, the more they could demand in TV-rights fees. (The size of the bonanza was unimagined at the time. Between 1996 and 2000, the Big Ten, Big East, ACC, SEC, Pac Ten, and Notre Dame would earn $373 million from televised football.) Suddenly, football independents like Notre Dame, Miami, Florida State, and Penn State were being hunted like prized high-school tailbacks.

By the early 1980s, Paterno knew Penn State football had to get into a conference if it wanted to ensure a steady flow of television revenue. So he tried to persuade the school's traditional rivals to form an eastern all-sports league. But several, especially those where basketball was far more powerful than at Penn State, balked. In particular, Pitt, Boston College, and Syracuse did not want to abandon lucrative Big East basketball to join a conference with the Nittany Lions. Another of Paterno's dreams was dead.

Not long after that disappointment, he relinquished the AD's job, though certainly not the power. He turned it over in 1982 to his hand-picked successor and close friend, Jim Tarman. And when Tarman retired in 1993, another Paterno loyalist, Tim Curley, became AD.

Its vision for the East thwarted, Penn State looked westward, toward the Big Ten.

Paterno continues to insist that the real impetus for Penn State's move into the Big Ten came from the university's administrators and not its football coach. But it's impossible to examine the scenario and not see Paterno's fingerprints.

Had Penn State's request to join the ninety-four-year-old conference been left to the ten coaches and athletic directors, it's doubtful the move would have occurred. Paterno knew how his colleagues thought, and he realized there was no way those competitive individuals were willingly going to welcome a program like Penn State's, one that had the potential to upset the balance of power among perennial strongboys like Michigan, Ohio State, and Wisconsin. So he helped orchestrate an end run.

President Oswald, on whose watch the first negotiations took place, was a native Minnesotan who had long been an admirer of the Big Ten schools and their broad-based, politically supported, research-driven academic agendas. While leading a major transformation at the University of Kentucky in the 1960s, he had looked to those large midwestern schools as models. At Penn State, with Paterno's urging and essential imprimatur, he did so again.

To Oswald and Paterno, the Big Ten looked to be a perfect fit. Rural central Pennsylvania was far more midwestern than northeastern in its outlook on life and sports. Penn State's fans had a soft edge when compared to those in Philadelphia, New York, or Boston, whose markets were dominated by professional sports. The league's stadiums and national reputation were larger than those of Penn State's traditional eastern rivals. And all of its members but the private Northwestern were big, research-oriented state schools with academic missions similar to Penn State's.

Still, as eager as the league's presidents may have been to add Penn State and its promise of financial bounty, they needed something that would lessen the concerns of their top athletic people. What eventually clinched the deal was the realization that an expanded Big Ten would include the millions of viewers in the Philadelphia and Pittsburgh TV markets, no small point when negotiating future network contracts.

While there were potential drawbacks, most were relatively minor. The most immediate hurdle was scheduling, because game commitments were made years in advance. Travel expenses would jump tremendously for all the schools. State College's tiny airport couldn't yet accommodate the kind of large jets in which Big Ten football teams traveled. Nittany Lions fans, accustomed to making relatively short drives for Penn State road games in Annapolis, Morgantown, Philadelphia, New Brunswick, Syracuse, or Pittsburgh, would instead have to get to Chicago, Madison, or Minneapolis.

Nonetheless, with Paterno's considerable input, Oswald and his successor, Bryce Jordan, continued secret, sporadic negotiations with Big Ten presidents for years until, in December of 1989, the marriage was formally announced. Football would make the switch in 1993 and the other sports, then members of the Atlantic Ten, would convert sooner. On hearing the surprising news, Michigan's legendary coach Bo Schembechler telephoned Paterno and called his new league rival "a sneaky son of a bitch."

Paterno warmed to the Big Ten instantly. For a man in his midsixties who had been at one school all his coaching life, it was a welcome change. "It's like starting a second career," he said. He ratcheted up his exercise routine, walking farther, lifting weights, watching his diet more closely. The Penn State coach, who needed only a victory in the Pasadena classic to complete a grand-slam sweep of the major bowls, began wearing Rose Bowl ties to games and various social functions. He took to videotaping every televised Big Ten game and studying it intently. "I go to sleep watching those tapes," he said in 1992.

He would soon awake to a new dawn for Penn State football.

• • •

Finally, after a nearly four-year wait, the Nittany Lions played their first Big Ten game at State College on September 4, 1993. In anticipation of the move, Beaver Stadium had been expanded again. The addition of an upper deck in its north end zone added 10,033 seats and raised the stadium's capacity to 93,967. So great was the anticipation of Big Ten success that a record 95,387 attended the conference opener, a 38–20 triumph over Minnesota.

Anyone who feared that the switch to a league renowned for its physical, earthbound style might make for boring football was comforted immediately. Penn State rolled up 504 yards in offense that day, while Minnesota quarterback Tim Schade threw 66 passes for 478 yards.

"It feels pretty good," Paterno said after the long-anticipated debut. "I went into the game with a little anxiety."

Penn State's star in that Minnesota game had been wide receiver Bobby Engram. Engram had sat out the previous season after he and fellow wideout Rick Sayles were implicated in an off-campus burglary. An unprecedented spate of off-the-field problems in 1992 had hit Paterno's program. In addition to Engram and Sayles, defensive back Brian Miller was charged with cocaine possession, and Sayles, O. J. McDuffie, and Mark Graham faced disorderly conduct charges after a bar fight.

The unusually serious nature of some of the arrests led to speculation that Paterno's standards were slipping. The *Centre Daily Times* editorialized that the incidents tarnished "the reputation of the team and the individuals." They also revived talk about the perceived hypocrisy of Paterno, who was happy to criticize other programs but apparently couldn't control his own.

"Penn State gives the impression that its kids walk out of chemistry class and say, 'We only have sixteen credits this fall, let's play football,' " said ESPN football analyst Beano Cook, the former Pitt sports-information director. "My only resentment is those holier-than-thou statements, those self-serving statements. I don't get mad at Miami, because they don't try to represent themselves like Penn State does. Penn State is no different than Miami, Michigan, Texas. It's a business. Notre Dame is no different. It's money. It's big time."

But winning can cure a variety of sins. And the immediate success that accompanied the Lions' entrance into the Big Ten quickly quieted all the concerns.

In the past, Paterno's best offenses seemed always to lack one crucial element. Maybe it was the strong-armed quarterback in '69, the NFL-quality wide receiver in 1973, the kind of sure-handed tight end missing since Ted Kwalick in 1968, or an offensive line that was solid from end to end. But in 1994, there were no weaknesses.

Paterno had an offense that would be unparalleled in Penn State history. The unit would establish fourteen school records, lead the nation in total offense (520 yards) and points (47.8) per game, produce five all-Americans—Engram, quarterback Kerry Collins, guard Jeff Hartings, tight end Kyle Brady, and tailback Ki-Jana Carter—and four first-round NFL draft picks, including Carter, the No. 1 overall pick in the 1995 draft.

"You don't see any NFL offenses like that," a shell-shocked Michigan State quarterback Tony Banks said after the Nittany Lions thumped his Spartans, 59–31.

The offense had begun to take shape early in 1993. During that season's third game, a 31–0 shutout victory at Iowa, Paterno replaced junior quarterback John Sacca with junior Kerry Collins. Collins scuffled at times, but following a loss at Ohio State on October 30, the Nittany Lions would not lose another game for twenty-three months. They would finish 10–2 overall, 6–2 in the conference for their first Big Ten season, and thump Tennessee, 31–13, in the Citrus Bowl.

In 1994, the Lions won their first five games—over Minnesota, Southern Cal, Iowa, Rutgers, and Temple—by an average score of 51–17. When Penn State rallied for a stirring 31–24 victory at No. 5 Michigan in Week 6, it moved to the top of both national polls and moved students in a way that took State College authorities by surprise.

Police said more than ten thousand students, many of them fueled by a day's worth of drinking, gathered around campus for a spontaneous celebration after Penn State's win at Ann Arbor gave it the No. 1 spot. Near midnight, some in the roaming pack entered Beaver Stadium, where they tore up sod near the fifty-yard line and in the end zones.

The damage was repaired before an October 29 homecoming matchup with No. 21 Ohio State. A year earlier, in Columbus, the Buckeyes had manhandled the Lions, 24–6, and then taunted them afterward, mocking them as "pussies" who were undeserving of Big Ten membership. "That was really a low point for me," Collins would later recall.

This time, before a record Beaver Stadium crowd of 97,079, Penn State's players avenged their humiliation. The final score would be 63–14, but only because Paterno, as always, called off his dogs in the fourth quarter and sent out the second- and third-team units. It was Ohio State's worst defeat since an 86–0 shellacking by archrival Michigan in 1902.

But there may have been an explanation beyond revenge. Undefeated Nebraska was No. 2 in the polls that week and its victory over No. 3 Colorado concluded before the start of the Penn State–Ohio State game. While Paterno never admitted to any such calculation, his team understood that it would need an impressive victory to counter Nebraska's win.

Afterward, Paterno adamantly refused to touch on the subject of rankings and routs. "You guys can talk about it, you have papers to sell," he said. "I don't have to talk about it and I'm not going to."

Apparently, 63–14 wasn't impressive enough. While Penn State held on to the lead in the *USA Today*/CNN coaches' rankings, Nebraska jumped into the No. 1 spot in the next Associated Press writers' poll. Some observers made the connection between the Nittany Lions' lopsided victory and the tight battle in the polls, accusing Paterno of intentionally running up the score on Ohio State—even though he had substituted liberally in the final minutes.

A week later, however, the polls and the criticism must have been on his mind. His reluctance to pile it on an outgunned Indiana team probably cost him a third national championship.

Following the victories over Michigan and Ohio State, the Nittany Lions leveled off emotionally against Indiana. Before and during the game, Paterno chastised them for being lethargic. The Lions played solidly against the 5–3 Hoosiers, but nowhere near their spectacular standards. Collins threw for 213 yards and two scores and Carter collected 192 yards on the ground, 80 of which came on a touchdown run with six minutes left that gave Penn State a comfortable 35–14 advantage.

It was then that Paterno might have doomed his chances for a third national title. While his need to win was overpowering, he never wanted to embarrass a coaching colleague. Up by 21 points with less than half of the final quarter remaining, he began to make wholesale substitutions.

"What I owe to my team is to make sure everybody plays and works hard and I have an opportunity to play them," he said. "I think that for me to take some kids who look forward to playing on a Saturday and not play them when I think the game is in control because I want to make sure that we win by X number of points so we can preserve a place [in the polls] would be irresponsible."

Indiana scored twice in the game's last three minutes. The second touchdown came with the clock at 0:00, on a successful Hail Mary pass into the end zone. Hoosiers coach Bill Mallory then, for some reason, ordered a two-point conversion try. When it was successful, the final score was deceptively close, 35–29.

The built-in flaw in the polls, of course, is that no single voter can see every game, or even a majority of them. They are left to digest reputations, prejudices, newspaper reports, TV highlight shows, and raw scores. Voters who hadn't seen or read about the Indiana game assumed the Nittany Lions had barely squeaked by the lowly Hoosiers. And since Nebraska had won easily, 45–17, against Kansas, they moved the Cornhuskers to the top of both polls.

If it seemed a minor setback at the time, it soon became an enormous one.

At Illinois a week later, the high-rise hotel where Penn State was headquartered lost power on game day, forcing players to climb up and down steps, and eat pizza instead of their prearranged brunch. Given the school's taste in uniforms, it wasn't surprising that the fifty pies hurriedly ordered for the Nittany Lions were all plain.

When the game began, the Lions quickly fell behind the 6–3 Illinois, 21–0. With 6:07 to play, they trailed 31–28 and had the ball on their own 4-yard line. But Collins, who completed thirteen of fifteen passes in the fourth quarter and all seven on this final drive, moved them 96 yards down a fog-shrouded field for the winning touchdown and a 35–31 lead with just fifty-seven seconds left. No other Paterno team had ever come back from a deficit as large as 21–0.

"If there's a quarterback playing any better than Kerry Collins, he's got to be out of this world," Paterno said afterward.

"That," said a surprised Collins when told of his coach's comment, "is high praise from someone who doesn't give high praise."

Penn State then ran out its remaining regular-season schedule—winning 45–17 over Northwestern and 59–31 over Michigan State. Nebraska, meanwhile, defeated Iowa State (28–12) and a mediocre Oklahoma team (13–3) to finish its regular season 12–0.

Had Penn State still been an independent, it might have met the Cornhuskers in the Orange Bowl. This time, as Big Ten champs, the Nittany Lions were committed to the Rose Bowl, where they would play twelfth-ranked Pac Ten champ Oregon. That gave the Cornhuskers an enormous advantage. They would face No. 3 Miami in the Orange Bowl. So even if the Nittany Lions won big in Pasadena, the only way they were going to capture another national championship would be for Nebraska to lose.

The statistics compiled and the awards won by his offense even impressed Paterno. "Some of those numbers," he said while preparing for the Rose Bowl, "are amazing." Carter had rushed for 1,539 yards, a single-season figure topped only by the legendary Lydell Mitchell at Penn State. He had scored twenty-three touchdowns, averaged 7.8 yards a rush, and finished second to Colorado tailback Rashaan Salaam in the Heisman Trophy balloting. Collins was fourth in the Heisman voting, won the Maxwell Award as the nation's top player and the Davey O'Brien Award as its best QB. He completed 176 of his passes for 2,679 yards, both school records. Engram captured the Biletnikoff Award as the nation's top receiver and caught fifty-two balls for a record 1,029 yards. Brady, the tight end, averaged 13.5 yards a catch.

The Rose Bowl proved to be an enormous treat for Penn State football. Fans who had wearied of the Lions' New Year's trips to Florida or New Orleans flocked to Pasadena for the team's first trip there since 1923, when the entire traveling party, team and all, totaled twenty-nine people. The partylike atmosphere surrounding the school's second Rose Bowl seventy-one years later is still recalled as one of the greatest moments in Penn State football history.

The game was entertaining, if ultimately fruitless. Carter burst 83 yards for a touchdown on the Nittany Lions' first play from scrimmage. Penn State, its all-white uniforms contrasting sharply with Oregon's garish green-and-gold outfits, pulled away from the Ducks in the third period for a 38–20 triumph.

In just its second league season, Penn State had become the first Big Ten school to finish with a 12–0 record. Paterno, meanwhile, now had assembled an undefeated team in each of the four decades he'd coached, captured all four of the major New Year's Day games, and won a record sixteen bowls overall.

But Nebraska had won that day as well, 24–17, over Miami. There was some hope among the Nittany Lions that the close Orange Bowl result and Penn State's easy Rose Bowl victory might combine to cause poll voters to rearrange the two top spots. In the end, though, sympathy for Cornhuskers coach Tom Osborne, who had yet to win a national title, was likely a more significant factor. Nebraska held on to its No. 1 ranking.

For a fourth time, a Paterno team had finished unbeaten and not won a national championship. This time, though, his complaints were few. "If I could do something about it, I'd do it," he said. "If I could rant, scream, and yell and get people to change their votes, I'd do it. But it's over. I don't think it was fair. I think we were as good as anybody. I wouldn't say we were better than Nebraska, but we were as good."

The Rose Bowl season did have its rewards beyond the field for Penn State. While researchers consistently found that athletic success did not translate into increased alumni contributions, a 2000 Western Economic Association International study determined that there was one exception—a football bowl victory. Contributions to the Nittany

Lion Club increased sharply the following year, as did requests for season tickets. Before long, the school announced plans for yet another Beaver Stadium addition. And a Penn State professor, who established that each Nittany Lions win was worth an additional fifteen hundred applications, calculated that in 1996 the number of applicants jumped by fifteen percent, a phenomenon he attributed to Rose Bowl–driven publicity.

For a while, Penn State would be remarkably successful in the Big Ten. In their first five seasons, Paterno's teams would go 31–9 in league play and 51–10 overall. But then something changed.

Some say Penn State's descent into a conference also-ran came about because the week-to-week competition was stiffer. Others pointed to the recruiting inroads other Big Ten schools had made in Pennsylvania, New Jersey, and Maryland. Whatever the reason, from 2000 through 2004, Penn State went 16–24 in the conference.

And on Penn State Web sites and chat rooms, in response both to their team's recent record and a new national rush toward conference realignment, a cry that must have made Paterno chuckle went out from some Nittany Lions fans:

Let's get out of the Big Ten and form an eastern conference.

CHAPTER 18

JOE PATERNO LIKED TO SAY that newspaper reporters used to be among his best friends. Even now, when the wall of separation between press and State was as thick as ever, he was willing to make time for *The New York Times* or *USA Today*.

A coach's relationship with the men and women who cover him and his team on a regular basis might seem trivial or a little too "inside baseball" for the general public, until you consider that it was the media who introduced America to Paterno. It was the media who chronicled his controversial stands over the years and who voiced its approval of his methods. And it was, of course, the media, with the considerable aid of the coach himself, who constructed the legend of Joe Paterno.

But they never really had much access to Penn State football except through the coach. Practices were off-limits. So were assistant coaches. You could request interviews with players, but very often they weren't granted. As a result, the beat writers became dependent on maintaining a good and happy marriage with Paterno. And for the most part, through all the years of Penn State success, they did.

When the Nittany Lions began their recent decline, however, the relationship suffered. Criticism became necessary and often Paterno, while insisting he didn't read the papers or watch TV, bristled. Things worsened considerably during the 3–9 season in 2003 and in 2004.

"I get to the point where I don't read it," Paterno had said of the coverage. "I read the news section of the local paper and I get the Sunday *New York Times*, and they never rip on us in the *New York Times*. . . . I've told Zack Mills and Michael Robinson and all these guys, 'If you don't read it, it doesn't exist.' "

The sessions with reporters generally were conducted with civility, and Paterno usually cooperated good-naturedly. But while his answers frequently were expansive, they became less and less revealing over the years. He gave reporters what he wanted to give them and didn't care what they did with it.

"I wouldn't enjoy reading some of the crap people write," he would say after the 2004 season. "Newspaper guys have got to sell newspapers. They're in a tough business. They're competing against talk shows and television and all those guys who are talking all the time, so I can appreciate where they're coming from. They're trying to get a story. They're trying to get some interest. . . . And one of the ways to do it is create some controversy. Whatever they say or do doesn't really make any difference to me."

But clearly it did. That strained relationship, he later admitted, turned out to be the reason he had stopped attending the cocktail receptions on Fridays. Paterno said that he once enjoyed providing writers with insights into his thinking and strategy. He knew they had a tough job to do and, he said, he genuinely wanted to help them. But as he got older and the reporters younger, they often came to cross-purposes. Because he revealed less, the writers asked less. Eventually, according to the coach, the sessions grew to be little more than a bunch of people sitting around a hotel suite watching sports on TV.

"And then I got to the point where I don't trust some of them," he explained. "I just literally don't trust them. I used to trust them. I didn't care if they said something and we had a couple beers and wanted to clown around. I don't trust a lot of these guys right now. That's maybe my fault but I just don't trust them. They're just looking for a controversy. . . . The environment has changed so much. It isn't what it used to be for me. Friday nights were a waste of my time because I didn't enjoy it. And it was a waste of their time because I wasn't about to tell them anything."

What seemed to really get under his skin was the fact that many of the most critical writers on the Penn State beat were so young and inexperienced. Heather Dinich, the *Centre Daily Times*'s beat reporter, seemed to bother him more than the others, probably because Paterno subscribed to her paper and because she was twenty-seven, a half century younger than himself. Dinich frequently questioned the coach's methods in print, and whether he read it or not, word got back to him.

"I sit there and I've got to answer questions from a young lady who's never played football," he said, without naming Dinich. "She's got all the answers. She's twenty-seven years old and she's quizzing me. 'Why did you this? Why did you do that?' Challenging this and that. Fine, she wants to make a reputation. She wants to do a job. But I'm not going to pay attention to her.

"I don't want to be bothered by that. If Bobby Bowden wrote me a letter, and said, 'Joe, I watched your game and you ought to do this, this, and this,' well, then I'd listen. Because every once in a while some coach will write me and say, 'Hang in there. Do this.' Try to give me something helpful."

The more Penn State lost, of course, the more necessary it became for the writers to ask the questions that irritated him most. Generally, they were smart enough and respectful enough to drape them in a polite tone.

At one of Paterno's late-season weekly teleconferences, for example, Bob Flounders of the *Harrisburg Patriot-News* phrased his one allotted query like this:

"Coach, what is your definition of progress for this team in the final two games, and if the team doesn't meet it, do you deserve to be back?"

Paterno had been playing this game a long time. As he frequently told friends, he was adept at avoiding questions he really didn't want to answer. This clearly was one of those.

The coach said he hadn't heard the second part of the question, then began answering the first. Flounders, ninety miles away in Harrisburg and limited to one question, interrupted and started to ask it again.

Paterno cut him off, "Oh, yeah," he said, "you were asking me about progress." He then started talking about the Nittany Lions' strong defense and how his team had hung together despite the adversity.

"So," Flounders recalled later, "I finally decided I needed to be a little blunt because either he was trying to pretend like he didn't hear my question or he simply didn't want to answer it. So I said, 'Do you deserve to be back next year?'

"Knowing he would turn seventy-eight in December, it was a legitimate question. . . . I tried to ask the question delicately, tying it to improvement over the final two games, but it was clear to me Joe was intent on avoiding it. So I took the direct approach after two failed tries because I believed Joe had some explaining to do regarding the decline of his program."

The directness of the question caught Paterno off guard. There was a slight delay, a moment of collective disbelief among those in the hushed media room with the coach. The emperor had been asked if he were wearing any clothes. Paterno appeared to mentally sift through his options before, in a tone that combined hurt, disappointment, and anger, he spat out a most uncharacteristic reply.

"You write your own story," he said. "I really don't appreciate that question, to be honest with you. After fifty-five years to have somebody tell me that, I don't appreciate that."

The online transcript of the interview session posted on Penn State's Web site later that afternoon omitted that exchange. But it made it into newspapers all across the state the next day.

Flounders, whose paper circulates in the heart of Nittany Lions country, calculated that he received nearly a hundred responses.

"I would say roughly ninety-five percent of the people were glad the question was asked," he said. "I was surprised. I expected a lot of hate mail, but it was just the opposite."

When an attorney in York, Pennsylvania, read about the question, Paterno's reaction, and the Web site's censoring, he decided the time had come to act. Joseph Korsak, a 1971 Penn State graduate and longtime football season-ticket holder, contacted the *Daily Collegian*. He paid $350 for a half-page ad that appeared the day before the Northwestern game.

"He had his little hissy fit and they just erased it," Korsak explained. "He's treated like a dictator in a banana republic."

In large, bold type, the advertisement proclaimed, TIME FOR JOE TO GO. Above that phrase, in smaller print, were nine stinging words: "The talent is there. The coaching is an abomination."

"I've been going to Penn State games for years," Korsak later said. "The people I sit with have been complaining about the coaching for a long time. But nothing happened and it dawned on me that Paterno was being treated like the uncle with cancer. We weren't addressing the issue, we were talking around it. So I wanted to bring focus to the discussion."

And though he didn't read the papers, the coach had somehow spotted Korsak's ad too.

"The hardest thing about anything you do in life is you can get overcome with a lot of people who really don't know what the situation is," Paterno would say. "Some guy puts an ad in the paper that says 'Fire Joe Paterno' and pays three hundred and fifty dollars and now everybody knows who he is. I mean, the guy's a celebrity."

If nothing else, the ad seemed to give voice to those last few in the Penn State community who had been holding their tongues on the subject.

On a student-run radio station in State College, The Lion 90.7–FM, two young men were talking about music the day the ad appeared. When asked a question, one of them hesitated.

"Sorry," he said, "I had an Alzheimer's moment."

The other interrupted. "You mean a Paterno moment."

The chatter on sports talk shows became overheated, "More venomous," said Jed Donahue, the host of one in State College. "It's the toughest coaching situation I've ever seen, pro, college, or high school."

On ESPN Radio's nationally syndicated *Dan Patrick Show*, which was heard in State College, the subject had been discussed so thoroughly that week that by Friday it was all played out.

"I'd have some more former Penn State players on if I thought they'd say anything about Joe other than 'He deserves to get out when he wants to,' " Patrick said that day. Then he played an audio clip from Washington Redskins defensive tackle Brandon Noble, who said exactly that.

Paterno said he was touched by such shows of support.

"I know there's been a lot of media that's been critical of me and the coaching staff and the team and certain players," Paterno said that week, "but I've just had so much mail and people who stopped me on the street and say, 'Hey, hang in there a little bit.' It's been very encouraging."

His friends and neighbors in State College displayed compassion on those increasingly rare occasions when they encountered the workaholic coach. It was, he said, "people from out of town that hassle me."

"Once in a while alumni come back and bring kids that want their pictures taken with me," he said. "That's flattering. In fact, I go around looking for people to take pictures with me these days."

The day he was insulted by Flounders's question was also Election Day. Paterno had been to the College Heights polling station earlier that morning. There he was able to vote, presumably, for George W. Bush, but not for his own son, Scott, whose Seventeenth Congressional District did not include State College.

Politically, Paterno's moderate Republicanism was probably more in line with Nelson Rockefeller's than George W. Bush's. "Joe is a liberal person who has conservative values," his brother George told biographer Michael O'Brien. President Ford and others had tried to convince him to run for office over the years, but he had always declined. His close affiliation with the GOP, however, had earned him criticism from those who felt it was inappropriate behavior for a coach at a public university.

"I won't get into politics," he said to the press that day, "but I just hope we pick the right guy. . . . I woke up this morning on Election Day thinking about my dad. My dad was a diehard liberal Democrat. I had a younger brother who died in infancy who was named Franklin after Franklin Roosevelt. If he knew he had a grandson running in the Republican Party for Congress, he would jump out of that grave, call me up, and give me every dirty Italian word you could ever think of."

Scott Paterno, as his father had anticipated, lost to Holden. He got 112,242 votes (thirty-nine percent) to the victor's 170,449 (fifty-nine percent). Bush, meanwhile, won Centre County but lost Pennsylvania by a wide margin.

That week a caller to his radio show jokingly suggested that perhaps the Paterno name had hurt Scott. If Penn State had been 6–2 instead of 2–6, he said, maybe the thirty-one-year-old candidate would have fared better.

"Thanks a lot, buddy," Paterno replied in good humor. "No, he had a tough opponent. I think it was a good experience for him and he gave it a good fight and I'm proud of him. I've got five great kids and all of them have got a little moxie. . . . I used to tell them all the time that a turtle can't cross the road unless they stick their head out. So they're all willing to stick their heads out.

"The guy he ran against is a good guy. He's a good congressman even for . . ." His voice trailed off, apparently before he could say "a Democrat." "He's a five- or six-term incumbent. He knew it was going to be tough. . . . I called him and told him when Abraham Lincoln lost his first election somebody said to him, 'How do you feel?' And he said, 'I'm too big to cry and it hurts too much to laugh.' "

Lincoln's words, curiously, could have been applied just as easily to Joe Paterno's situation.

For Paterno, one of the most difficult defeats of the 2003 season had come at Northwestern.

The coach believed many Big Ten schools took liberties—in recruiting or with academics—that he would not permit at Penn State. To friends, he frequently pointed to the Maurice Clarett mess at Ohio State as an example of doing things the wrong way. Clarett, a sensational freshman running back on Ohio State's national 2002 national-championship team, had been suspended after accusations that he received preferential academic treatment and no-work jobs. He also pleaded guilty to lying to police about an alleged theft of $10,000 in merchandise from his car.

But Northwestern, in his view, was a program very much like his own. Three times since 1998 the Evanston, Illinois, school had been awarded the American Football Coaches Association's academic achievement award for a hundred-percent graduaton rate. Maybe Penn State wasn't always going to play at the level of an Ohio State or Michigan, but Northwestern ought to be a different story.

"Northwestern is a school that does it the way we do," Paterno said. "We have to be able to compete against that. There are some schools that you can step back and say, 'Well, that's a whole different program than what we have.' You can't do that with [Northwestern]."

That challenge provided him some motivation for what was otherwise a meaningless game.

In what was becoming a weekly ritual, Paterno on Monday again sought to lift his players' heads. He told them to ignore all the negativity swirling around State College. He said they ought to approach their final three games the way the Irish, and not the Italians, approached a wake.

"At the Irish wake, at least you have a little fun," he said. "At Italian wakes, all of the women are crying all day. We're playing football in the fall. The leaves are out. Everything is great. It's such a beautiful day and you're young. Let's go out and play a football game. Have some fun and forget about what the media is saying."

Paterno had been encouraged that week when the father of a recruit visiting campus told him he still "had something special here." He also knew by then that he had a good shot at landing Justin King and Derrick Williams. While he couldn't tell his team the recruiting specifics, he let them know help was on the way and urged them to keep the faith. The program's difficulties were overblown. Penn State, he told them, was this close to a turnaround. And it could start with the Lions' final three games, against Northwestern, Indiana, and Michigan State, all of them winnable.

Outside Beaver Stadium on Saturday, fans hawked unused tickets right up until the noon kickoff. The crowd would be announced at

100,353, the smallest attendance for a Big Ten game since the latest stadium expansion. That total reflected tickets sold. In reality there were far fewer fans there.

In the face of the program's steep decline, Penn State continued to make every effort to maintain its base of support. Just that week, Greg Myford, an executive with the Palace at Auburn Hills, the Detroit Pistons' arena, had been hired for a new athletic-department position, associate AD for marketing and communications. And D'Elia, seeking to generate some excitement in the midst of another lost season, had declared a "Code Blue."

Despite their disappointment over the season, most of the students arrived wearing that color, though some also brought beach balls, apparently as insurance against boredom. A few of them also had bags to place over their heads as a silent protest. And at least one female student, with sunshine and temperatures in the fifties, had written MORELLI across her bare midriff, a naked plea to see the youngster in action.

The game was being televised at noon by ESPN Plus on a regional basis. Penn State's record had made them unappealing for national audiences. As a result, as the season progressed, smaller regional telecasts and noon starts became the norm. While noon was somewhat early for college students' tastes, it was a boon to university police.

"We love the noon starts," said Spanier. "Who's going to start drinking at nine A.M.? Games that start later, at, say, eight P.M., are far more challenging. With an eight P.M. kickoff, there's a lot more time to drink before the game and then afterwards everybody heads downtown to the bars."

Even so, every campus police officer, as well as scores of state troopers and law-enforcement officers from the borough of State College and surrounding communities, were in or outside the stadium that day. With more than a hundred thousand fans on football Saturdays, the area surrounding Beaver Stadium became Pennsylvania's third largest city.

Also surveying that population from perches high atop the multi-level press box and the new suites on the stadium's east side were several plainclothes policemen.

"[Their] job, while everyone else is watching the game, is to look out at the parking lots, checking around to see if there are any problems," said Spanier.

Northwestern, at 4–4, 3–2 in the Big Ten, was no juggernaut, but the Wildcats didn't have to be to beat this Penn State team.

Randy Walker's team ran the kind of vanilla offense Paterno once had—a big offensive line opening holes for a talented running back. Senior Noah Herron was third in the Big Ten, averaging 111.6 yards a game, nearly as many as the Nittany Lions managed as a team.

Penn State would be without safety Andrew Guman, whose chest and rib injuries against Ohio State kept him out. That meant ten of the eleven defensive starters were underclassmen, an encouraging sign for a unit that already was one of just four Division I-A teams—Texas, Auburn, and Wisconsin were the others—to have limited all of their opponents to 21 or fewer points.

On offense, Mills was back at quarterback. That meant Robinson would be shifted all around again, a strategy that by this stage of the season appeared to be doing little but diminishing his effectiveness.

Paterno had upset all the Morelli backers further by implying earlier that Robinson would most likely be his quarterback in 2005. What was the use of recruiting high-school superstars, the thinking went, if they were going to languish on the bench? But this week the coach appeared to waver on his commitment.

"That [finding Robinson a permanent position] is a legitimate decision I'm probably going to have to make down the road," he said. "I can't tell you what it is right now."

Morelli was on the sideline as Robinson lined up as a flanker on Penn State's first play. For an offense that was under such fierce attack, things could not have started less encouragingly. On a pass play set up by a double reverse, Robinson, a right-hander, got the ball running to his left. Stopped by the defense, he reversed field and, while trying to elude a defender, heaved a weak floater toward Tony Hunt. Northwestern's Dominique Price easily picked it off. It was Robinson's fifth interception in just over one and a half games, and it was the Lions' twenty-fourth turnover in nine games.

This time there was no hesitation. Loud boos immediately rolled through the stadium even though the Lions had run just a single play. What kind of atmosphere would there be if they were trailing in the fourth quarter?

Northwestern responded immediately after the interception. A 51-yard pass from Brett Basanez to Jonathan Fields set up Terrell Jordan's 1-yard touchdown run and the Wildcats led, 7–0.

Penn State's next drive provoked more catcalls when fullback Paul Jefferson dropped a catchable third-down pass to end it. The game became a punters' battle until Paul Cronin, subbing for Guman, intercepted a Basanez pass and returned it 14 yards to the Wildcats' 22. Six plays later, with thirty-seven seconds remaining in the half, Mills found Smolko on a game-tying 2-yard scoring toss.

Early in the second half, in what had become another recurring theme, there was more confusion and anger visible on Penn State's sideline. Following cornerback Gio Vendemia's recovery of a fumbled punt at the Wildcats' 14, the offense huddled around McQueary and Kenny. Meanwhile, the twenty-five-second clock continued to run. Finally, Paterno rushed in to break up the gathering, but the Lions had to spend a time-out. In the chaotic aftermath, McQueary and Kenny screamed loudly at each other.

"The torture of watching this team is exceeded only by [the torture of watching the] players carrying out the marching orders—when they get them on time," Rudel would write in *Blue White Illustrated*.

Herron, who would finish with 175 yards on thirty carries, and the Wildcats' offensive line began to weary the Nittany Lions' defenders. On the third play of the fourth quarter, Herron capped an 83-yard drive with a 1-yard plunge that put Northwestern in front, 14–7.

Penn State's last drive started at its own 20 midway through the final period. Mills's passing moved them downfield and, on a 24-yard strike to Robinson, got them a first down at Northwestern's 18. But there the pass-catching problems that had wounded the Lions all season resurfaced.

Kinta Palmer missed a pass on first down. Then, on third down, Robinson broke free near the Wildcats' goal line. Mills's pass hit him in stride but the receiver could not hold on, squandering what would have been a game-knotting TD. On fourth-and-10, Mills inexplicably threw a short pass to a well-covered Hunt. It gained only four yards.

Spectators booed, screamed, and fled to the exits.

Northwestern took over with 3:27 left and Penn State out of time-outs. The Nittany Lions would not get the ball back.

Morelli had warmed up a few times on the sideline and fans, spotting him, began yelling that he be inserted. He never was.

"I was very close," said Paterno. "It just didn't seem like the right time."

Mills completed twenty-one of thirty-four passes for 183 yards, but could produce only seven points.

On the sideline, Adam Taliaferro, in street clothes and able to walk now with only a slight limp, shook his head in dismay. He joined his former teammates as they trudged into the stadium tunnel, heading for the locker room.

Many of the fans leaning over the tunnel walkway, even those regulars who generally did nothing more provocative than ask for a wristband, barked angrily at the players, particularly when Mills passed.

"You suck, Zack!" screamed one.

In the stands, just yards away from where he walked, a few students started a chant of "Joe Must Go! Joe Must Go!"

"As far as we know, he's staying," said Smolko. "There's no reason for him to be leaving. I don't see it happening. And even if it is, we don't know. . . . He's about the same way we are. He just doesn't know what to think and what to expect and what the reasons for the outcomes of our games are."

The person to whom many of Paterno's detractors continued to gripe was Graham Spanier.

Penn State's fifty-six-year-old president, as his university biography noted, was an unconventional administrator. A magician, musician, and pilot, Spanier believed in hands-on involvement. He had performed with the school's marching band, its musical-theater group, and glee club. He even once made an appearance as the Nittany Lion mascot.

Spanier, the husband of a Hemingway scholar, also had run with the bulls in Pamplona. He had approached that 2001 adventure with an academic's precision. By studying the bulls' tendencies, identifying the safest route, and familiarizing himself with the event's history, he managed to dodge the rampaging bovines and the swarms of red-scarfed revelers who surged through the Spanish city's cobblestoned streets every year on the Feast of San Fermín.

Paterno's game-plan alterations earlier that morning hadn't helped. Penn State was minutes away from a sixth consecutive loss. Now, on the Northwestern possession that would conclude Penn State's 14–7 loss, Spanier again found himself scurrying from danger. Only this time, there was no way he could have prepared.

As he hurried along the Beaver Stadium sideline, directly in front of sections jammed with Penn State students in blue T-shirts, he was moving with considerably more dread than on his Spanish dash. And the horns of the dilemma that confronted him were every bit as threatening as those on a fifteen-hundred-pound bull.

"Hey, Spanier, get rid of Paterno!" yelled one student in Section EB. "It's over."

As more among the disgruntled crowd recognized the Penn State president, they began bellowing their own complaints. Spanier, accelerating his unathletic stride, moved uncomfortably past the shouts, past the straggly back row of Nittany Lions reserves, past security guards and the ex-players and hangers-on who had wangled field passes for the game.

"Make a change, Spanier!" came a loud cry from the front of Section EC. "Make a change!"

His late-game jaunt through this gauntlet of frustration had been a mistake, like waving a red flag in front of thousands of irritated bulls. Spanier should have known better. For weeks, wherever he went, he had heard the same thing. He couldn't outrun all the negative buzz about Paterno.

Nine games into another disappointing season, Spanier still had no easy answers. That's why he had stopped discussing the issue in public.

At that moment, on his rapid sideline walk, Spanier found himself flanked, both figuratively and literally, by two Joe Paternos.

To the president's left was the seventy-seven-year-old coach, his body tilted sharply forward in a posture of surrender as Penn State neared its sixteenth defeat in twenty-one games. This Paterno appeared tired, confused, vulnerable. As his Lions' last-gasp drive died with a pair of dropped passes, he lowered his gaze, dejectedly planted his hands into the pockets of his khaki pants, and leaned his graying head into an intensifying wind.

Not far off to Spanier's right, however, in a stone grotto just outside the stadium's student section, stood a much sturdier version. Smiling, upbeat, vigorous, this bronzed Paterno was vibrantly middle aged, his index finger was thrust skyward in a permanent reminder that he had made Penn State No. 1. The Paterno sculpture, in fact, was such a fetching representation of the iconic coach that even in these dark days fans regularly lined up to pose for photos alongside it.

This was the uncomfortable geography Spanier occupied. Marooned between the puzzled old man and the bronze legend. Two Paternos inextricably linked. Attempting to push the coach aside after fifty-four years and 341 wins would be no less difficult for him than lifting the seven-foot-tall, nine-hundred-pound statue.

Not that he wanted to push him aside. Paterno's departure, no matter when and how it came, was going to be a costly one. No one could raise money like the old coach.

The silver-haired Spanier, wearing an expensive gray suit and a practiced smile, moved quicker now. As he did, more students and fans targeted him. Somewhere around Section EF a few faint chants of "Joe Must Go! Joe Must Go!" arose.

Since 1995, when Spanier, a former University of Nebraska chancellor, first assumed the presidency, Paterno's age and status had been an issue. By 2001, a 5–6 season that began with four consecutive losses, he had felt the need to address the topic in his annual letter to alumni. Though not referring specifically to Paterno, Spanier noted that age was rarely an impediment to achievement. Michelangelo, he pointed out, was seventy-one when he painted the Sistine Chapel.

The discontent ebbed a bit when Penn State went 9–4 and appeared in a New Year's Day bowl in 2002. But the 3–9 mark in 2003 and six consecutive losses this season had resurrected it with a vengeance. Alums who were proud of Paterno's principles were weary of his teams' football failings. And with each new disappointment, the questions and the questioners had become more intensely unpleasant. Hundreds of letters and e-mails calling for a coaching change arrived in Spanier's office each week.

"You know you've got an outstanding human being, there's no question about what he's done for Penn State," Spanier said later. "But then you've got people complaining about 'We lost the game.' Or 'He made a bad call.' Or whatever. . . . When you're winning, everybody is happy about everything. But when you're losing some games, we find out that there are some fair-weather fans out there. And there are some people who have never been friends and it gives them more of a case to get on them. So you have to be able to sort through that and see the big picture.

"It's very hard, how you answer letters like that and how you deal with it. As president I don't have the luxury of not answering them. And in that respect, it was a little different this season because we did get more mail than we've ever gotten."

Spanier and Steve MacCarthy, vice president for university relations, had a fairly pat answer for most of the anti-Paterno correspondents.

"We usually said something like 'We're very sorry you feel this way. We'll certainly keep your thoughts in mind, but we're going to make our decisions in terms of what's in the best interest of the university.'

"That's the main message I send to people," said Spanier. "That my job as president is to see the big picture and to make decisions in terms of what's in the best interest of Penn State. Once I start making decisions on some basis other than that, the university is not going to be run well."

Finally, Spanier reached his destination, clear of the grandstands and safely inside a stadium tunnel. There he greeted several potential football recruits, including highly prized cornerback Justin King from Monroeville, Pennsylvania, who were attending the Northwestern game with their families. When Penn State's 14–7 loss was officially complete, he escorted them all to Paterno's postgame news conference.

From a balcony that overlooked the interview room, Spanier, the athletes, and their parents watched as a gloomy Paterno—a bandage covering the cut he had suffered in his den early that morning—entered and slumped behind the podium to face another barrage of questions about a loss, his team, his future.

Spanier pressed against a balcony railing. He was listening carefully, leaning forward to absorb each question and answer, looming over the old coach like a concerned deity.

Among the spectators inside the stadium that day, though virtually no one recognized him, was Jackie Sherrill. The former Pitt and Texas A & M coach had once been Paterno's principal antagonist, the epitome of all that the Penn State coach believed was wrong with the sport. Once, when asked if he would pursue a career in politics, Paterno famously responded, "What . . . and leave college coaching to the Switzers and Sherrills?"

But Sue Paterno, a peacemaker by nature, sought to mend that fence. She invited Sherrill and his wife, Peggy, to that weekend's game and to a postgame dinner at their house.

Sherrill told a Pittsburgh newspaper that week that despite Paterno's jibes a few decades earlier, he was not looking for an apology.

"That's not an issue," Sherrill explained. "That has no bearing on my feelings for Joe. A lot of things were said. . . . When two people compete, things happen."

Sherrill, who knew he'd be spending a lot of time talking football that night, took notes during the game. He condensed them into a message on a yellow legal pad that he gave to Paterno that night after dinner.

"[It said], 'You guys are doing a good job and are getting the most out of your kids. Your scheme is good, the play calling is good, but your skill people have to rise up and get better.' "

When Paterno agreed with him, Sherrill imediately mentioned a few junior-college players he thought would help. The Penn State coach balked.

"We don't get rich quick," Paterno said later. "We don't take junior college kids. We try not to take kids that don't belong here. . . . And I've felt it was not fair to bring junior-college kids in and put them ahead of kids you've had.

"That's not to say junior-college kids aren't good kids. You always have to be careful when you say things like that. But I just have felt let's do it right, let's be solid, let's build. And if you're not good this year, at least you're not making sacrifices on the future in order to win X number of games this year. I've always tried to put us in a position where we're building toward a team that could be a contender for a national championship. Sometimes it works. Sometimes it doesn't."

As friendly as the two men now claimed to be, getting advice from his onetime bitter rival had to be one more mortifying experience for Paterno in a season filled with them. After all, the last time Sherrill had been in State College, he was coaching Pitt. His Panthers had won that day in 1980, 14–9, ending the Nittany Lions' dreams of a New Year's Day bowl appearance.

Now Paterno would have to endure another indignity.

When he and Jay got back to the McKee Street house hours after the loss, the elder Paterno asked where Sherrill was. The ex-coach, he was told, was down in the basement watching another college football game.

Paterno descended the stairs and, sure enough, there was the sixty-year-old Sherrill in a recliner, viewing the game.

Sitting in Sherrill's lap, snuggled against his chest, was Paterno's four-year-old grandson and namesake, Joey.

CHAPTER 19

THROUGHOUT THIS SIX-GAME losing streak there was speculation that Paterno and Spanier, or Paterno and the trustees, or Paterno and major contributors, had been meeting privately to plot exit strategies, pinpoint a successor, or plan a retirement announcement. But despite the widespread perception, there had been very little behind-the-scene intrigue.

"I had one meeting with a couple of people in the administration," Paterno said, "and I said, 'Hey, everybody just calm down. We're OK.' And that was it," Paterno would say. "Now, what was going on beyond that, I can't tell you."

At least two trustees, however, admitted privately that while they might not have met formally with the coach, they had had "casual" conversations with him about retirement during the season. They said he had rebuffed their efforts to convince him that, if nothing else, he at least needed to designate a successor.

"The more you bug him about it," said one of those trustees, "the more determined he becomes to hold his ground. He won't let anyone dictate anything to him, even if they're not really dictating anything at all."

Spanier, who had been responding to reporters' queries only via e-mail, finally addressed the subject after the season. He indicated for the first time then that while the ideal scenario would have Paterno determining his fate, he retained the final say.

"Clearly there are three key people in any decisions about any of our head-coaching positions," he said, "—the head coach, the athletic director, and the president. We talk about these things a lot together, but I've such immense respect for Joe Paterno and so much admiration for what he's accomplished and done for the university that I would want his voice to be a very strong voice in the scenario. Our preference is to have it be a decision that Joe makes."

In any event, the ongoing mystery exacerbated the atmosphere of uncertainty surrounding the coach. Rather than address the subject at hand, he continued to blame the sportswriters for creating the rumors. That was disingenuous. After all, he could have attended a few Friday-night receptions and assured everyone—off the record, if need be—that nothing was happening and that he wasn't going anywhere. Instead, in the information vacuum he permitted to exist, the whispers had become shouts.

"If I had gone there [to the media cocktail gatherings] and they would have asked me, they [wouldn't have believed] me anyway," he would later say. "It was at that point where they had assumed certain things were going on and they didn't want anybody to disrupt their assumptions. That's what went on all year. They assumed this, assumed that. . . . There was no way to change their minds. They couldn't change their minds. They were in too deep."

The conspiracy theorists searched for any sign, any statement, any hint, that indicated movement. And that Thursday, two days before the Indiana game, they thought they had their smoking gun at last.

The incident began when a pair of former Steelers, Tunch Ilkin and Craig Wolfley, the cohosts of an irreverent morning sports talk show on a Pittsburgh radio station, began lamenting the state of Penn State football with guest Leo Wisniewski, a former Nittany Lions offensive lineman.

In the course of their conversation, Ilkin mentioned that a source at the university had told him Paterno would be stepping down soon and that Bradley, his longtime defensive coordinator and top recruiter, would be replacing him. Wisniewski added that he had heard the same thing and that when he arrived in State College later that same day, he'd check out its veracity. Much of Penn State nation had been eagerly anticipating news like this for weeks. The rumor quickly hardened into accepted truth, as telephones, e-mail, and Internet chat rooms disseminated the news around the state and nation.

Back in State College, in his office on the first level of the Bryce Jordan Center, sports information director Jeff Nelson began fielding an avalanche of phone calls from frantic reporters. After making sure the news was not true and getting the OK from Curley, Nelson composed a terse release. It would be the first time he could recall that Penn State had formulated an official response to a rumor.

"Statements made on a Pittsburgh radio station earlier today regarding the future of Penn State football coach Joe Paterno," it read, "are unfounded and untrue. The meeting described in the radio report did not occur. The Board of Trustees has not met since mid-September. In his weekly news conference this past Tuesday, Coach Paterno reaffirmed his commitment to continuing to lead the Nittany Lion Football program. Any other statements to the contrary are untrue."

A short while later, Bradley, a Pittsburgh native, emerged from a coaches' meeting. Paterno hated cell phones, and his assistants always turned theirs off when they were with the coach. Now Bradley, as he always did, switched his phone back on to see how many calls he had missed.

There were fifty-three.

"What the hell?" he muttered. "I hope everything is OK."

Bradley quickly found out why he had become so popular. And in between returning the calls and answering the questions, his phone rang again. This time it was Paterno.

"Congratulations," the coach said, "on your new job."

"Thanks, Coach," said Bradley. "The first thing I'm going to do is give all my new assistants a big raise."

The two men laughed. Sometime soon the scenario they were now joking about might well become a reality. But today wasn't going to be that day.

"We've had a lot of laughs about it," Bradley said later. "Coach knew it was just a dumb rumor."

• • •

Losing had revived a debate long absent from State College: Was Penn State being hurt by what were widely perceived as its higher standards? That week Paterno implied as much when asked how he planned to resurrect his slumping program.

"There are a lot of ways to remedy different things, and some of them I don't want to do," he said. "I don't think it is the way Penn State wants to do it. There is a great wideout in the country now playing for one of the best football teams in the country, if not the best football team in the country. He's from New Jersey, and we never even looked at him because of the academics and things like that. We could take a step backwards, but that is not what I wanted to do for Penn State and I am not going to do it for Penn State."

The New Jersey receiver was soon revealed as Dwayne Jarrett of Southern California. He told the *Los Angeles Times* that Penn State had indeed offered him a scholarship but that he turned it down because they emphasized a run offense.

"I heard that thing Paterno said about me," Jarrett said. "I don't have any words, no reaction, to that. None at all. Penn State [offered] me a scholarship, but I wasn't too interested in going there."

Whatever his academic record, Jarrett would catch fifty passes in 2004 for 734 yards and twelve TDs as USC won a second straight national championship.

Depending on how you viewed Paterno's remark, it was either an honest assessment of where Penn State stood, or an example of the attitude that had irritated so many of his coaching competitors over the years. If Penn State only took choirboys, rivals moaned to one another, how come so many of them had ended up in trouble last year?

Yet Paterno certainly appeared to be clinging to his principles. A week earlier he had shot down Sherrill's junior-college-player suggestions, and he admitted that it had been at least four seasons since he had asked Spanier to grant him an academic exemption for a recruit.

Football had made Penn State's fabulous growth over the last half century possible. But administrators, though benefiting enormously from the success of Paterno's program, traditionally tried to minimize the cause-and-effect. Penn State was much more than a football factory and that's how it wanted to be seen.

In a 1986 interview, then-president Bryce Jordan told CNN's Larry King, "I think if you polled them [Penn State's alums] on their feelings, they are every bit as proud of the success of the Penn State artificial heart as they are of the great success of the football team."

That was for public consumption. The university's true feelings were expressed in a private memo from the university's public-relations staff to Jordan just before that '86 interview:

"Penn State football success, for example, has enabled the university to realize additional recognition for its academic programs," it read. "It has provided a visible vehicle for us to talk about academic standards and achievements. . . . Athletics-generated publicity has a positive effect on high school students in the very critical area of student recruitment, apart from athletic recruitment. . . . It provides entry for nonathletic university components to approach potential contributors in connection with fund-raising efforts."

Eric Walker, who in 1956 had succeeded Milton Eisenhower as the university's president, learned that immediately. Upon accepting the position, Walker asked renowned scientist and mentor Vannevar Bush how to go about building a great university.

"Three things," Bush told him. "More buildings, an outstanding faculty, and a great football team."

Following the Northwestern game, Paterno vowed to do some soul searching.

"The problem with my soul searching," he said a few days later, "is that I couldn't find my soul."

While he was kidding, it was true that failure tended to make Paterno more introspective. And these days, with his being questioned and criticized at every turn, that tendency was inflamed.

He'd never thought that, with his esteemed record, he would have to justify himself to reporters young enough to be his grandchildren. But he did. He had never thought he'd be asked how he felt about hearing Penn State fans boo his players, chant "Joe Must Go!"

or deride his quarterbacks coach–son on radio talk shows. But he was. He'd never imagined that his brains and will wouldn't be enough to turn around a struggling team. But they weren't.

On Monday, two days after the Northwestern defeat, seeking a literary metaphor for the situation he and his team faced at the end of this miserable season, he thought of *Hamlet*. When Paterno addressed his players that day, he quoted a part of the Danish prince's soliloquy, letting them know that their "outrageous fortune" required an existential decision: Would they surrender to the unpleasant reality of 2–7? Or fight to salvage their dignity?

A day later, Shakespeare's words surfaced again when the coach's weekly teleconference began with a query about his own confidence. Had it been shaken by a second straight disastrous season? Paterno's response initiated a series of answers that, overflowing with literary allusions, recollections, contradictions, and ramblings, may have hinted at his mental turmoil.

"You would have to define what you mean by *shaken*," he began, paraphrasing the Danish prince. "Obviously, I go back to *Hamlet*, 'To be or not to be, that is the question. Suffer the slings and adversity of outrageous fortune or take arms and fight the enemy? By doing so eliminate the problem.' I have a lot of confidence in my staff and a lot of confidence in this football team. Things haven't gone, obviously, the way you would like them to go.

"Sometimes people think it's the planning, the plays, and sometimes the coaches or what have you. Yes, I get shaky once in a while. I would be less than honest if I told you I didn't. That doesn't mean that I lose faith. Even Christ said, 'Take this away from me.' "

The reference to Christ's words on the cross sounded like an admission that Paterno had thought about quitting. So he was asked again, in a much less direct fashion this time, if his recent record didn't warrant questions about whether he should return in 2005. His answer was lengthy, serpentine in its logic, and as enlightening as anything he would say publicly all season.

"There's no question about it. I have never disputed that. You have to understand that I have not spent this many years at Penn State or worked this hard to get Penn State football to a certain level [to just leave]," he said. "I could have had fifteen jobs that would have been more lucrative and a lot of different things through the years in pros and college. I won't get into all of that stuff, but I have always felt that Penn State was a place that I was comfortable with and I wanted to bring my family up here, make the university and football as good as I could make it.

"I go back to my dad when I decided to coach. My dad says to me, 'What are you doing, thinking about coaching?' My dad wanted me to be a lawyer. He graduated from high school, graduated from college, and then graduated from law school and passed the bar. He loved the law and always dreamed about my being a lawyer or my brother George being a lawyer. George did go to law school for a year. When I got into coaching and I came home and said, 'I think I'm going to make coaching my career,' he said, 'Well, do you think you can have an impact on anybody?' I said, 'Yeah, I think I can have an impact. I think I can have an impact on this university. I think there are some people around here who don't realize how good they are and I am going to work my butt off to try to make them understand that Penn State can be a special place.'

"I've spent fifty-five years doing that. If you think that I am going to back out of it because I am intimidated, you are wrong. If you think I am going to stay when I think I am not doing a good job, you are wrong. Those things have to develop and have to evolve. Right now, I think we can get this thing done and do a good job. We obviously have to recruit some people. We have to recruit some skilled people. I have said that before. I don't want to hang around here and pull Penn State down. I have a great staff of coaches. I could walk out of this thing. I could call and tell you today I'm going. What does it mean to me? It doesn't mean a thing to me. What impact does it have on the program, the coaches, and is it the best thing for Penn State? They are the things that I think about all the time.

"It has nothing to do with Joe Paterno unless Joe Paterno feels he can't get the job done. I think about it, but I really feel comfortable as long as I can go to practice and have some enthusiasm. I think the squad responds to some things that we challenged them with. I don't see any reason to say, 'I'm going to get out of here this year, next year, or whatever year.' I don't mean that to be cocky, stubborn, or anything like that. I'm just trying to do what is right."

The drumbeat for Morelli got louder in the days leading up to Indiana.

It wasn't unusual for fans of a losing football team to clamor for another quarterback, particularly at the end of a season. And besides, what else did Penn State fans have to look forward to?

The ballyhooed quarterback's continued inactivity baffled fans. Paterno wasn't hesitant about playing the linebacker Dan Connor, another freshman who was by now a solid starter. Why did he stall with Morelli? Certainly, with the way Mills and Robinson had performed, he deserved a shot.

Conflicting loyalties may have helped explain Paterno's indecision. He felt that he had an obligation to stick with a veteran player like Mills, especially now that the quarterback had become the boobirds' favorite target. But he also also felt he had a duty to get Morelli some work.

"I haven't been hesitant because of Anthony," he explained. "I've been hesitant because I have an obligation to Zack Mills. Zack has worked through some things and Zack is a good quarterback. . . . Is Anthony Morelli better than Zack Mills? No, not now. He might be. I was going to play him last week. I kept telling him, 'Warm up, Anthony.' He is the most warmed-up quarterback that never played a play in the history of football. I have to make my mind up that we are going to play him a certain time in the football game and give him a shot. I think I owe it to the kid. I owe it to Zack not to give in to what some people think is the right thing to do, because I don't think it is the right thing to do. Yet, for the good of the future of the team we should take a look at what Morelli can do."

All that raised another significant question for Penn State's future. If Morelli, whose redshirt year was gone, were going to get some playing time, did that mean he'd be the quarterback next season, when Robinson would be a fifth-year senior? That certainly was the preference among Nittany Lions fans.

"I don't think that the permanent position for Michael Robinson is wideout," said Paterno when asked about his plans for '05. "Right now he is a wideout because I want Zack to end up his career as best we can do and I want to give Anthony Morelli a chance to show us what he can do. Michael Robinson in the long run may end up being the best quarterback of the entire group we have, because he can do some things that the other kids can't do. It depends, again, on whether we can recruit some skill people."

To many Penn State supporters, it seemed like he just kept talking in circles. It was maddeningly frustrating.

If you parsed his words carefully, Paterno appeared to be implying that Morelli might not be as good as everyone had anticipated.

"I see the pimples," Paterno explained. "You don't see the pimples. I know when they [freshmen] are good, when they are bad, and what they can do. You have to evaluate that as to whether they are better than the people you are playing. If they are better than the people you are playing, obviously, at times we have used freshmen because we think they are better," he explained. "However, I have to be loyal to my people. I have to be loyal to my coaches and I have to be loyal to my team. Unless I am sure that the guy who is younger will help our football team more than the guy that has paid all the dues and has worked hard, I am very reluctant to change. We have had a lot of good years with that philosophy. . . . I don't think it's fair that some guy comes in here and you guys all read about him and he is so-and-so this, and so-and-so that. But that doesn't mean he's that good. It just doesn't mean he's that good."

Until the basketball coach left Bloomington in disgrace, Bobby Knight and Paterno, both admirers of General George Patton's military strategy, occasionally got together when Penn State visited Indiana.

The bawdy Knight used to like to kid with Paterno. Watching the Nittany Lions coach walk away once, he yelled, "Joe, you know what I never noticed about you before?" Knight said. "You've got no ass."

And before there was a Paterno statue at Beaver Stadium, the famously volatile Knight once advised him on how to earn bronze immortality. "Throw a chair across the field, Joe," he said. "They'll build a fucking statue of you."

Knight was gone now, but basketball remained the sport of choice on Indiana's campus. The Hoosiers' football program could never get off the ground. Gerry DiNardo, now in his third (and last) year as Indiana's coach, had an 8–25 record. Indiana had won one Big Ten cochampionship in the last fifty-eight years. That came in 1967. Since then, the Hoosiers' conference record was 97–194.

So it said something about the state of Penn State football when the Nittany Lions (2–7, 0–6) came into this game in sole possession of last place in the Big Ten. Indiana, which had never beaten Penn State in nine tries, had a 3–6 record that included one conference victory, a 30–21 upset at Minnesota.

The Big Ten standings weren't the only grim reminder of Penn State's fall that day. It was here in Bloomington where Penn State had squandered—needlessly, in the minds of many—its last shot at a national title in 1994.

On this crisp and windy Saturday, Senior Day for the Hoosiers, the game attracted a tiny crowd to Memorial Stadium, just about half of what the 1994 game drew. The Nittany Lions' sudden lack of appeal, coupled with the traditional end-of-season ennui produced by Indiana football, resulted in a crowd of 24,092. It was the tiniest gathering for a Penn State football game since November 13, 1976, when only 19,627 saw the Nittany Lions win, 21–7, in Miami.

The previous year's meeting with Indiana had been Penn State's last conference win, and homely Memorial Stadium was where the Lions got their last road victory, 58–25, on November 16, 2002, nearly two full years ago.

"Penn State should never be on the level of a Northwestern or an Indiana," said Lions cornerback Zemaitis. "I don't care if any of those programs hear what I have to say. That should never happen. Every time we go against Northwestern and Indiana, it should be a constant 'W.' "

As had been their habit, the Nittany Lions immediately embarrassed themselves when the game began. Rodney Kinlaw fielded the opening kickoff in the end zone and then fumbled it. He retrieved the ball and appeared ready to kneel down for a touchback. But, his head swiveling from side to side in search of guidance, he froze. Finally, with Indiana defenders bearing down on him, Kinlaw attempted to run. He got only as far as the 5-yard line.

"The kid just got a little nervous," said Paterno.

Two series later, Mills threw another interception, his eleventh (against seven touchdowns) of the season. That turned into a quick Indiana score when, on the Hoosiers' second play, wide receiver Courtney Roby took an option pitch from quarterback Matt LoVecchio and raced 26 yards for a touchdown. With 8:41 left in the opening quarter, Penn State trailed 7–0.

That week Bradley had told friends that he was concerned about the mental state of his nationally ranked defense. They were performing superbly, but, largely because of the ineffective offense, Penn State was losing week after week. "We can't keep playing like this without seeing results," he had said.

This time the offense responded. After the Penn State contingent in the stands cheered derisively when Hunt downed the next kickoff in the end zone, Mills led the Lions downfield. He ended the drive by completing a 33-yard pass to a sprawling Robinson in the corner of the end zone.

The officials initially ruled Robinson out of bounds, but an instant replay reversed the call and Penn State had tied the game at 7–7.

As Paterno often pointed out, it was the kind of play that Robinson, alone among his wide receivers, could make. The coach also was happy with the replay. And why not? Every replay ruling this season had gone in Penn State's favor.

"The replay is great," he said after the game. "I mean that sincerely. Nobody would want to lose that football game because of bang-bang calls, including the officials. So I'm glad we have it and I hope we get it around the country."

Finally, as the second quarter neared its conclusion, Paterno inserted Morelli into the game. It quickly became apparent why the freshman had not yet played any significant time. He looked unsure of himself.

His first pass went incomplete. His second was intercepted by Kyle Killian and returned 46 yards for a touchdown that, after the extra point was missed, left Indiana in front, 13–7.

Morelli threw two more incompletions on the next series and was sacked (injuring his ankle) before finally completing one to Hunt for 13 yards on a third-and-18. With just under five minutes to go in the half, Paterno reinserted Mills.

"I asked E. Z. [Smith] how Anthony was in the huddle, and he said he was a little slow getting things out and getting things processed," Mills said after the game. "But that's to be expected with him. That is the first time he's been in there in a tight situation in the middle of the game."

In the third quarter, Mills led the Lions on an eleven-play, 81-yard scoring drive. Penn State led, 14–13. Indiana regained the edge, 16–14, on a Bryan Robertson field goal early in the fourth. But Hunt scored on a two-yard run with five minutes left in the game to put Penn State ahead again. A two-point conversion pass was missed and the Lions' lead was 22–16.

Then came a series that both Paterno and his son predicted could one day be viewed as the moment when Penn State football was reborn.

A 29-yard Matt LoVecchio pass to Travis Haney moved the ball to Penn State's 42. After three running plays, the Hoosiers faced a second-and-9 at the Lions' 30. LoVecchio threw a sideline pass to Chris Taylor that cornerback Anwar Phillips read perfectly. The Penn State defender stepped inside the receiver and the pass hit him in the chest—and bounced to the grass.

"Here we go again," said Paterno as he threw up his hands in disgust. "Holy God."

His lack of faith was reaffirmed on the following play when LoVecchio and Haney successfully hooked up. Phillips, "using both hands and every breath," managed to run down the receiver at Penn State's 1. With two minutes to play, Indiana had a first-and-goal.

Along the sideline, a fellow coach asked Bradley if he thought they ought to go to Paterno and ask him if wanted the defense to allow Indiana to score quickly, saving more time for a possible comeback drive. Bradley declined.

"You know what," he said, "if I don't believe in them, then they're not going to believe in themselves."

As the Penn State defenders waited at the line of scrimmage, they could hear Indiana players buzzing excitedly in the huddle. "If you're a football player, you live for goal-line stands," said Connor.

Tailback Taylor tried the middle of the line on first down but was stopped by lineman Ed Johnson for no gain. Indiana tried the same play on second down and this time Posluszny, who led the Lions with thirteen tackles that day, stopped him for a yard loss.

Now, after a Penn State time-out, Indiana took the snap, LoVecchio rolled right on an option. Had he pitched it to Taylor, the tailback likely would have scored, but the quarterback held on and Wake and Lowry stopped him near the 1. That set up fourth-and-goal.

Penn State called another time-out and as defenders huddled up deep in its end zone, Hali thumped his chest and yelled to his teammates, "It's in here! It's in here!"

Bradley wasn't sure which defense to call. "I've got four [defenses] ready to go and I'm thinking of all four calls. They came in with what we called the Hoosier formation, a stacked-I [three running backs]. So we were in a pretty good defense for the last play."

The Lions substituted linebacker Shaw for cornerback Phillips and lined up. Taylor got the ball again and again tested the middle of the defense. Posluszny and Connor met him high and Chisley got him low before he could reach the end zone.

"At that point," said Connor, "it's kind of like two rams smashing into each other. At that point, it's all about heart."

The defense and the sideline erupted as if Penn State had just won another national title.

"It makes me feel good that, being two and seven, they still believe in themselves down there on that goal line," Bradley said. "That tells me we've sold the kids on what we can become."

Those defenders were operating under some pressure too. They realized that, with fifty-five seconds left, their offense wasn't likely to march the ball downfield for a go-ahead score.

"We weren't looking forward to the offense coming back on the field," said Hali in a blunt assessment. "This was the last play to us. If we stop it we win. If we don't stop it, we don't have hope anymore."

• • •

While the sense of relief was palpable in the stadium storage area that served as Penn State's postgame media room, there also was a feeling that a victory over the hapless Hoosiers was hardly a cause for celebration.

Paterno smiled and looked relaxed, though reporters had to strain to hear him. "Geez," he responded when asked to speak up a little. "We won a football game. What do you want me to do, jump up and down?"

Robinson, who caught six passes for a career-best 99 yards, said, "Indiana's a great team but we expect to beat Indiana. Nobody came to Penn State to be in the position we're in."

Mills, who completed eleven of eighteen passes for 169 yards, spoke words that sounded odd coming from the QB of a 3–7 team. "It's great," he said. "But who'd we beat? Indiana isn't a Big Ten powerhouse."

Paterno even lifted his ban on freshmen talking to the press. Connor, developing into a star, and Rubin were given permission to enter the interview area.

"I was shocked," Connor said later. "I was nervous. I was asking guys what to do."

As far as Penn State's future went, perhaps the day's most significant statistic was the fourteen carries and 74 yards that Austin Scott had accumulated. That seemed to suggest that the talented sophomore running back was out of Paterno's doghouse at last. After sitting out the Boston College game, he had not carried the ball more than six times in any game.

"I would like to talk [to Paterno] to see where I'm at, see what I need to do, see what they want of me," Scott said. "It's kind of hard when you don't know what someone expects of you or what someone wants of you."

Paterno, not for the first time, acknowledged to the media that he needed to devise some sort of exit strategy. He just didn't say when.

"I think eventually I have to put a plan together so they know what I'm thinking," Paterno said. "I don't know when that time is going to come. I've been so busy trying to get us where we can win a game."

CHAPTER 20

LARRY JOHNSON SAT AT HIS DESK in the Lasch Building on Tuesday night, midway between the Indiana and Michigan State games, and wrote. And wrote. And wrote. Penn State's defensive line coach was composing handwritten letters to a recruit. He would write fifteen of them that night. All to the same youngster.

A personal note was the hottest trend in recruiting. "Kids don't even look at printed material," said Fran Ganter. "They just get too much of it. And the coaches counsel these kids, 'Go where they want you the most.'"

On Tuesday and Wednesday nights, when practices and meetings were over, Paterno's assistants cranked out these notes. They wrote them on official Penn State football stationery or on postcards that displayed a packed Beaver Stadium on an autumn Saturday. Typically, they were just exclamation-point-filled reminders to let the high school player know he hadn't been forgotten:

> Dear Bronco: Hope you're doing great and that you're still thinking about coming to Penn State! Coach Paterno and I are really excited about that prospect! Why don't you plan a visit here? We'd love to see you and your family! Remember, WE ARE . . . PENN STATE!

Ganter, now a first-year football administrator after decades as a Paterno assistant, said that as glad as he was to be free of eight-hour staff meetings, he missed the note writing even less.

Paterno pitched in, too, composing notes and long letters to the top recruits. A letter he sent Derrick Williams, the speedy Maryland wideout/running back who was rated by many experts as the nation's top 2004 recruit, was three pages long, and filled with underlined phrases and emotional entreaties.

Bradley, by his own estimate, had written thirty such notes in recent weeks to Justin King, the hotly recruited cornerback from Monroeville, a small town near Pittsburgh. Less than a week earlier, King, whose stepfather, Terry Smith, had once been recruited by Bradley and played for Paterno, phoned the defensive coordinator.

"Coach," King said, "I just called to tell you I've decided to go to Michigan."

Bradley was silent.

"Just kidding," King said. "I'm coming to Penn State."

Paterno strongly hinted to the press and his players that Williams might soon be following.

"We might have a great [recruiting] year this year, because we have had some people commit that a lot of you don't know much about, and some who have committed that have not announced," the coach said. "I think we are on our way to building a very solid squad down the road."

King's signing, the prospect that Williams might come, too, and the inspirational victory at Indiana served as a finger in the dike. The spate of late-season good news didn't stop the rumors about Paterno's future, but it certainly slowed the criticism.

An online petition started by Doug Skeggs, a '99 graduate, after the Iowa loss and meant to be sent to Curley and Spanier had garnered nearly four hundred signatures in the first three days. "The program is almost a laughingstock," Skeggs would say. "I just think it's time [for Joe] to go. It's true. And it's sad." A day before the Indiana victory, the petition's signature total had hit 570. After the Nittany Lions' victory, it was virtually ignored. By January, there would be only 587 signatures, some of them clearly bogus.

Paterno and his staff couldn't help but feel that a corner had been turned, that a team unsure of itself at last had discovered some confidence.

"It's like we tell recruits," sophomore linebacker Paul Posluszny said that week. " 'Don't be discouraged about the record. That's about to change.' "

Jay Paterno predicted that people would one day look back on the goal-line stand in Bloomington as four of the most important plays in Penn State history. The win at Indiana had given the head coach the kind of I-told-you-so moment that Republicans were feeling that week in the afterglow of President Bush's reelection.

"I know everybody has a better way to do it than I have," Paterno told reporters. "I know you guys have your own ax to grind and I understand that. But you are never going to change me or the way we run this program. . . . I think [a recognition of that kind of steadfastness] happened in the election. A lot of people just think that families and certain values are important. I am not saying that is right or wrong. But I know where I'm coming from and when we talk to kids, they know where I'm coming from. That I have not changed. When I am here in the year 2015, I will be telling you the same story. . . .

"If I came over here with all of the letters I've got in the last six weeks, I would have a stack that high from fans and everybody else saying, 'Stay with it,' and the whole bit. It's very important to me. Nobody likes to sit alone and have to make decisions that everybody interprets. Every decision I make is interpreted. That's fine. But when you make those decisions and you try to eliminate all of the outside pressures and then when people respond and say, 'Hey, Coach, we're with you,' that makes you feel good."

Some superstitious Penn State fans contend the team's troubles began when Beaver Stadium was renovated prior to the 2001 season, blocking off the view of Mount Nittany. But the view of Mount Nittany didn't just vanish. It was sold.

The 11,500-seat addition that enclosed Beaver Stadium's south end zone and cut off the fans' view of the picturesque mountain included a multilevel Mount Nittany Club. The club's spacious fourth-level concession area is enclosed by glass. High-end ticket-holders, paying a premium for the privilege, can sit there at tables with their hot dogs and sodas and gaze south at Mount Nittany, much as their less fortunate brethren used to be able to do from seats inside the stadium.

There, late on the Wednesday morning following the Indiana game, the tenth and final 2004 luncheon of the State College Quarterback Club took place. Hundreds of men and women roamed the spacious club carrying black plastic plates teeming with sandwiches and potato salad. And even though it was a school day, there were a few youngsters present. Membership is open to all. For a $50 annual fee, plus a $12 charge for each luncheon, Nittany Lions fans got a buffet, a brief talk from Paterno and one or two players, and the opportunity to ask questions. Though the sessions typically were off the record and closed to the media, Paterno had granted a reprieve that week to a few writers from large, out-of-town papers, including *USA Today*'s Malcolm Moran, who was writing a profile of the coach that would appear later that week.

Quarterback Club members typically fell into one or more of three categories: Penn State fanatics from central Pennsylvania, local businesspersons, or alums. Many, like President Jim Meister, were all three. The organization, which also conducted a postseason awards banquet, dated back to the 1930s, when the luncheons were held in a basement room at Old Main.

These were the most loyal of Penn State supporters, the ones who reupped for season tickets year after year, the ones who steered their children and grandchildren to school here, the ones who continued to support Joe Paterno and his football team no matter what. They certainly were not the ones who had booed Zack Mills much of the season. And as it turned out that day, Mills, about to play his final game, addressed them.

When Steve Jones introduced the quarterback, the club members stood and applauded heartily for more than a minute. Mills, who had missed the week's first two practices to attend his grandmother's funeral in Maryland, was clearly moved. He spoke briefly about his Penn State career and then solicited questions.

An elderly woman wanted to know what he had learned from Paterno. He reeled off a list of qualities and admitted that while he understood ninety-five percent of what the coach had tried to convey in his five years at Penn State, it would probably take him another five years to dissect the rest.

That was followed by an awkward moment, one that seemed to jar this audience's conception of what went on between Paterno and his players. Asked if he could cite his funniest moment with Paterno, Mills couldn't think of one.

Mills's reaction reflected Paterno's demanding, hands-on style of coaching. It simply didn't lend itself to warm and fuzzy relationships. Few players, as 1980s receiver Gregg Garrity once pointed out, liked Paterno when they played for him. But, as Mills suggested, there weren't many who didn't love and respect him after they graduated.

"He's a lot like your parents," said Charlie Pittman, who had been a star Nittany Lions halfback in the 1960s. "It's sometimes difficult to appreciate them until you've grown and become a parent yourself."

When it was his turn to address the luncheon, Paterno looked as relaxed as you'd expect someone to be when speaking to a roomful of familiar faces. Some of the attendees today had been coming to these affairs for as long as the coach had been in State College.

His performance was more aging Catskills comic than coaching legend. Wearing an old blue suit, Paterno had one hand stuck in a pocket and the other wrapped around a cordless microphone. He paced across the stage on those remarkably skinny legs that didn't seem capable of supporting a man of his energy and casually tossed off observations, jokes, and promises in a way that amused and delighted the captive crowd.

He touched on some by-now familiar themes—complaining about the Big Ten officiating, praising his successful recruiting, noting how Maurice Humphrey's expulsion had been a disaster, and predicting great things from his team in the next year or two. "We've got ten, eleven [freshmen] who aren't playing who are as good or better than anybody we've ever had up here," he said, a remark that did not elicit any follow-up questions as to why all that talent wasn't being employed in this 3–7 season.

There were some surprises, too, as when, just a few weeks after saying Michael Robinson might be his most talented quarterback, he mentioned that Robinson was no longer practicing at the position. No one asked about that either.

Moments later, after his talk, Paterno was asked if he could recall a most humorous moment with Mills. He stalled as well. "Zack is a very phlegmatic person," he finally said. Then he quoted from *Hamlet* again, this time referencing Polonius's "To thine own self be true" speech.

Inevitably, somebody did ask Paterno about his future. "Ahhh, I get asked all the time. 'Why keep coaching? Why keep coaching? Why keep coaching?' " he responded. "Somebody asked me that Saturday and we just won a football game. Like I told him, 'What the hell am I gonna do? Cut the grass?' " The coach then produced an enormous laugh when, after pretending to put on an imaginary set of headphones, he imitated an old man cutting grass. Then, as if hitting a switch to let the audience know the melancholy portion of the luncheon was about to begin, he turned introspective.

"I'm alive," he said. "I don't want to die. Football keeps me alive."

He talked about how much he loved this team and how badly he felt for Mills and the other seniors who were going to be leaving Penn State, having experienced so much unanticipated failure.

Earlier in the week, he had elaborated even more on the subject to reporters, suggesting that, unlike those classmates who had left the program for one reason or another, these departing seniors at least had given Penn State the full measure of their loyalty. Fourteen of them would be bowing out against Michigan State, including Mills, Wake, Guman, Jefferson, Davis, Gerald Smith, Ryan Scott, and Gould.

"I'm going to miss some of them," he told the press. "I'm disappointed that some of them haven't had the kind of careers that they would like to have had. We're going to try the best we can to send them out of here on Saturday with a win so there is a good taste in their mouth as they leave Penn State. They're a good bunch of kids. . . . I don't think much about the guys that left. They are not believers. The guys that stay is where your obligation is. You try like a dog to make sure they get what they should get out of the program."

Now he told the Quarterback Club audience, "Sometimes I go to sleep at night thinking I could have done a better job for them."

That sentiment had brought Paterno to tears during a practice earlier that week. He had told his players then that he'd be back next year because he was afraid of both living and dying without football. Then, realizing that perhaps the mood he had created was too maudlin, he loosened up on the practice field. When a pair of arguing players exchanged punches, Paterno stepped between them. He told them how stupid it was for two guys in helmets and pads to be fighting, then he put on Tamba Hali's helmet and told the combatants to strike him instead.

Now the audience laughed as Paterno got ready for his wrap-up. Despite everything he had been telling his team, and his season-long denials to the media, no one except the coach and his wife really knew his plans. In fact, there was fresh speculation that week that indicated he was going to step down in a dramatic gesture after the Michigan State game. That way, the thinking went, he would have managed to avoid all the embarrassing farewells and media attention that otherwise would have marked his final season.

As his concluding words sounded surprisingly emotional and valedictory, a confused buzz spread through the room. Maybe the rumors were true.

"Hey, you know what?" he said. "No matter what anyone else says . . . in a lot of ways this has been one of the greatest years I've ever been around Penn State. The crowds have been great, even though we're not fighting for the national championship or anything like that. You folks have shown up every week. You put up with my alibis and excuses and my feeble answers to some tough questions which I don't really want to answer.

"I can only say, from my heart"—he paused to inhale and to gather himself—"it's been a privilege."

With that, he departed with a small entourage and entered the club's elevator. One of his fellow riders was an old College Heights neighbor. Like anyone else stuck awkwardly in an confined space with a casual acquaintance, the coach tried to make small talk.

"It's been beautiful this fall, hasn't it?" he said to the man. "The weather, I mean. Not the football."

• • •

Joe Paterno walked into his weekly radio show the following night, later than normal. He was hungry. He liked to eat with his wife at about 6:15, but on Thursday nights the radio show made that impossible.

"I think she's having some pasta tonight," he said, raising his eyebrows in a look of relish, before going on the air.

Until Paterno arrived, former players Mickey Shuler and Chuck Benjamin had been filling in for their old coach, answering Jones's good-natured questions and defending Paterno whenever the opportunity arose.

"I was on a team here that didn't produce a lot of wins but did produce a lot of great people," said Shuler, a onetime New York Jets tight end, of his 7–5 season in 1976. "It's the same as what's going on now. . . . Players don't get as upset about wins and losses as alums and fans around the country."

Waiting for his cue, the coach kept flexing his right shoulder and grimacing. "I'm going to punch Wake in the mouth," he laughed. "He gave me a shot today in the shoulder."

Thursday's practice had been unusually lighthearted. In what was surely a clue to his level of introspection, Paterno had opened the workout by yet again quoting *Hamlet*, urging his players to cast aside thoughts of this latest losing season and "take arms against a sea of trouble." The old quarterback even threw a few passes. And when he lined up at a wide receiver's spot, the defenders jokingly insisted the linebacker Wake, a graduating senior, cover the coach because they didn't want to precipitate any future reprisals. A subsequent collison with Wake caused the coach's aches.

When regular caller Jerry from Philadelphia came on the line, Paterno noted how sad he was that Jerry's second-favorite team, Temple, was being drummed out of the Big East. "You would hope there'd be some loyalty there," he said in what sounded like an echo from his own situation. "It can't be all business and television and money and all this stuff."

When Mike from Lansdale criticized Penn State's offensive line, the coach, warming to a conversation as he always did, seconded his assessment.

"I agree with you. I think the offensive line's been lousy. I've challenged them. We've had [a lack of] concentration, jumping offsides, holding, not being aggressive. . . . I'll bet we have not gone against an offensive line that has better athletes than ours. I mean that. We've kept the offense as simple as we can and maybe that's a problem. Maybe it's too simple. I really don't know. We have not really dominated the line of scrimmage, and unless you dominate the line of scrimmage you're not really a good offensive team. . . . I think part of the problem is people can be aggressive up front because they don't have to worry about our wideouts."

The conversations had enlivened him. During a commercial break, he was asked if he were surprised that the callers remained so upbeat, positive, and polite.

"Ahhh, who knows?" he answered. "They're being respectful. They might feel like saying, 'That son of a bitch!' Who knows? I don't know. People are up and down. I think they're fair and maybe a little bit condescending. I don't know what kind of radio show you'd get in Texas or someplace else. But it's been pretty consistent here."

It was while answering a question from Dennis of Allentown that Paterno finally gave voice to what he and everyone else around the program seemed to have been denying for months, maybe years.

"What can I tell you," he said. "We're frustrated. You know, we're frustrated. We're frustrated. Frustrated. You know how to spell it? F-R-U-S-T-R-A-T-E-D."

Earlier that Thursday, the Penn State trustees had met again behind closed doors. This session took on a special significance, since it arrived in tandem with the rumor that Paterno was going to resign after the Michigan State game. ESPN had ballyhooed the speculation all that day and Friday, even though the coach's public comments on the subject continued to suggest he'd be back.

Several of the trustees later said Paterno's status never surfaced, either at Thursday's meeting or at the shorter public session a day later. It wasn't on their agenda, they said. And even if it were, there was no established precedent for dealing with a football coach.

"The board is behind Joe," said Chairwoman Cynthia Baldwin, "but his future is not a board issue."

The trustees already had turned the touchy matter over to Spanier, and most were glad to have done so. Those who were keenly interested in football, however, reportedly were assured by Spanier that the uncertainty surrounding the program would not linger indefinitely. Board sources told the *Harrisburg Patriot-News* that a clause in the coach's contract extension mandated that he step down if the losing continued through 2005.

The fourteen seniors' final bus ride from the Lasch Building to Beaver Stadium that Saturday morning was a sentimental journey. Fans, as they always did, lined the route. Some held up signs praising the soon-to-be-departing players. WE'LL MISS YOU, ZACK, read one. Hundreds of the most ardent supporters clustered near the team entrance to the stadium, and they let loose with heartfelt shouts when the players emerged from the bus and began to walk down the tunnel.

"It was very emotional," Mills said of the ride. "It meant a lot to hear that after the up-and-down season I've had. Then, just coming off the bus . . . going into the locker room and you have all those fans screaming."

The final senior to enter Beaver Stadium's field during the pregame introductions before the Michigan State game was Adam Taliaferro. The graduating New Jersey resident, inactive since the day four years ago when, paralyzed, he was carried off the Ohio Stadium field, walked out into the gloomy daylight with only a slight limp.

"People forget he was one of the best freshmen we ever had around here," Paterno said later. "You look back and remember him being carried off the field. Then [a day later] he was on his back and I was there with him, with his mother and father, and we didn't know whether he was ever going to walk again. . . . It is just a great story."

Taliaferro's emotional appearance—he and Mills drew the loudest ovations—appeared to fire up the crowd of 101,486.

Before those introductions, Paterno had walked over to the student section. Yet another "Code Blue" had been declared and the seats had filled in rapidly once the gates opened. Paterno didn't appear to notice a sign there that read, WE WERE . . . PENN STATE. He was searching for five female students who usually occupied the first row. The previous week, they had sent him both a group photo and a note of encouragement, urging the coach to stop by and greet them. So he did.

College students were notoriously fickle fans, and Penn State's were no different. They had been upbeat when the season dawned, but their discontent was sparked early and it accumulated during the losing streak. From the same section where those five girls now sat, angry words had been hurled at Paterno, Mills, and others at the end of several home losses. Now, at season's end, the students, too, sensed a reason for optimism.

"I walk around the campus with kids," Paterno said, "and if they are driving a car or something, they say, 'Hey, JoePa, hang in there.' Kids on the campus come up. I must have fifty letters from kids."

Linebacker Dan Connor said that this would be the Nittany Lions bowl game.

Penn State had entered the Big Ten without a traditional rival. Someone, noting that the schools were the nation's oldest land-grant institutions, decided Penn State and Michigan State should play annually for the "Land Grant Trophy."

Their games tended to be high scoring and, the last two years anyway, one sided. In fact, the 2003 Lions' 41–10 loss at East Lansing was the only game in which Paterno conceded his 3–9 team had been soundly beaten.

The fact that 5–5 Michigan State needed a victory to gain an actual bowl bid, provided a little more incentive in what was otherwise an unattractive matchup.

Erratic Michigan State had averaged 39 points in its previous five games, walloping first-place, fourth-ranked Wisconsin, then leading the Big Ten, a week earlier, 49–10. But against Penn State's increasingly stern defense, the Spartans looked confused.

Phillips intercepted a Spartan pass in the end zone to kill one drive and the two offenses could manage nothing but field goals in a first half that ended with Michigan State ahead, 6–3. Then came the quarter Penn State had been looking for all season.

Hunt's 1-yard run capped a 75-yard drive on the half's opening series and gave the Nittany Lions a 10–6 advantage. Following a Hali interception, it took just one play to make it 17–6, Mills running eight yards to the end zone.

Posluszny, who led the team again that day with fifteen tackles, intercepted another pass, and—again on the first play following the turnover—Mills rumbled 10 yards for a touchdown. Shortly afterward, Donnie Johnson blocked an MSU punt. This time, with twenty-one seconds remaining in the quarter, Mills hit Robinson on a 6-yard TD pass as Penn State's lead exploded to 31–6.

"I wanted the third quarter to go on forever," said Bradley of his defense's play. "Everything was clicking. Guys were making great plays, great drops, great reads. . . . It was really fun to watch."

Mills's scoring pass was the forty-first of his career, tying him with with Tony Sacca and Todd Blackledge as the school's all-time leader. Despite his frequent struggles and relatively weak arm, the quarterback would also end the game as Penn State's career leader in passing yards and total offense. The same fans who had booed him all season screamed, "We love you, Zack!" as the clock wound down on a 37–13 Penn State victory.

As a smiling Paterno ran off the field at game's end, a sideline reporter from ESPN, which had been hinting all weekend that the coach might step down, asked him whether this might have been his last game. Paterno looked as if he had no idea where such a crazy notion might have originated.

"What else am I going to do?" he said for maybe the twentieth time this season. "Cut grass?"

Paterno might have been the only coach in America who could have been greeted with applause as he walked into a news conference following a 4–7 season.

"Holy smokes," he said, gazing up to the balcony area where

season-ticket holders were gathering after the game. "We get two wins and I get that?"

Still, it took only two questions before the subject of his coaching status was raised.

"Have I ever said I wasn't [coming back]?" he said in response to the query. "Was that wishful thinking? No, I'm planning to be back next year. As I've said, I'd like to be able to put together a scenario where I can pick the time I want to leave and have somebody in-house ready to take over. . . . I feel comfortable with the people around me. I'd like to leave when there's a lot of stuff on the table and the next guy can have some success. Rip gave me a great football team. I almost screwed it up my first year, but after that I was OK."

Then how did he explain his behavior all week, so emotional and reflective?

"It's tough to be around a bunch of kids who work as hard as this group has worked and have very little success," he conceded.

It didn't take long before his mood was defiant again. He insisted the constant speculation surrounding his future had been of little concern all season. In fact, he said, he had barely taken note of it. If people thought he was spending time in an armchair, pensively pondering his future, they were mistaken, he said. He implied that, in private, he was just as likely to discuss great literature as football.

"It's really not bothered me at all," he said of all the rumors and criticism. "Someone asked me the other day about my wife and how she takes all the criticism of me. I don't know. We never talk about it. She's in the middle of reading *The Dante Club*. And we're talking about the fact that Dante was gay. And she wanted to know if I knew he was gay. I said, 'Yeah I knew he was gay.' She said, 'Did you know Beatrice in his poem was not a woman, but a man?' I said, 'Yeah I knew that. I read Dante when I was fourteen years old.' Now, I didn't read it in Italian, but I read it. That's what we talk about."

There were some other matters that needed resolving after the celebrations died down. Would Galen Hall be back? Though Hall had signed a three-year contract before the season, it wasn't a crazy question. His offense had been pathetic and there clearly was friction with Jay Paterno.

Hall, confronted by reporters as he exited the field after the Michigan State game, initially shrugged off the inquiries. But a few days later, he revealed that he planned to stay on. "Joe hired me to do a job, and we're going to try to see it through," he said.

He called Jay Paterno "a very bright young coach," but neither he nor the coach's son denied that there had been disagreements. "We bust each other's chops all the time," Jay Paterno said of their relationship. "It's very loose."

Before the process to shut down the facility began at Beaver Stadium that November afternoon, Jay Paterno also was asked if he could foresee a scenario in which his father might not return for the 2005 season.

"Yeah," he said. "If he gets hit by a bus."

CHAPTER 21

THE NEGATIVITY THAT TYPICALLY TRAILS after a losing season like the smoky wake of a dying automobile didn't linger long in Happy Valley. Although Penn State fans had found it necessary to boo and bellyache in 2004, they didn't enjoy it—their native state was reflexive optimism. Confronted by bad news, they preferred to anticipate the next positive development, not dwell on a downbeat past. "I know that in places like Philly or Chicago, sports fans tend to be more critical," said ex–Nittany Lions star Bob Mitinger, several months before his death in 2004. "It seems like they're always looking backward at something that went wrong. But up here, at least when it comes to Penn State football, we tend to always look ahead, always look for the positive."

In Paterno's postseason spin, the 4–7 season very quickly became something to commemorate. On the snowy afternoon of December 12, at the State College Quarterback Club's annual awards banquet, he termed the goal-line stand against Indiana "one of the most inspiring moments in all the . . . years I've been here."

"This team," he continued, "could have folded on several occasions this season. Instead, it turned it all into a demonstration of pride."

At the crowded tables in a Penn Stater Hotel ballroom, middle-aged and elderly couples and their autograph-hunting children and grandchildren applauded the coach's remarks. To unbiased observers of Penn State football, however, the words must have had a dissonant ring. It was great to build character through adversity, but you couldn't sustain a nearly $50 million athletic budget on character alone. Graduation rates and good grooming were nice, but at some point didn't there have to be bowl games and high national rankings again? His Nittany Lions had lost seven times, a record that, even in light of the nine-loss season that preceded it, should have embarrassed Paterno. But the old Lion remained defiantly proud.

His positive words were notable for something else—they indicated that Paterno's career had come full circle. A season after he became Penn State's coach, he had angrily scolded members of the Quarterback Club for attempting to paint a happy face on a close loss to UCLA. Now, nearly four decades later, speaking to the same organization, it was Paterno who was trying to portray a 4–7 season as a Pyrrhic victory.

Even before their coach's brief talk, the departing fifth-year seniors—survivors from a 2000 freshman group more than twice that size—had adopted the same sunny tone. The Nittany Lions had gone 26–33 during their stay in State College. But not long after they and their parents posed for farewell photos with Paterno, they were predicting a bright future. Mills said he sensed a turnaround of the entire program in the last two games. Wake, like Mills an exiting cocaptain, thanked Paterno for "breathing down my neck for five years." He told the gathering of fans and teammates that if he had to do it all over again, "I wouldn't change a thing. . . . You guys are going to be playing on a national championship team before you leave here. I know that in my heart."

Among the 750 attendees at the ceremony, worries about the uncertain offense, Paterno's shortcomings, and the 2004 season in general already had evaporated. While they curiously withheld any applause when Jay Paterno was introduced as a presenter, these fans obviously were enthusiastic about Penn State football's future. The two late victories—which comprised the Lions' first winning streak since late in 2002—and Paterno's frequent hints of recruiting successes had them looking ahead eagerly. The noisy prelunch buzz was filled with talk about 2005's favorable schedule, beginning as it did with home games against South Florida, Cincinnati, and Central Michigan. Paterno would have nine or ten starters returning from the defense that ranked in the top ten nationally in three significant categories— scoring (fourth, 15.3 points per game), pass defense (sixth, 162.3 yards a game), and total defense (tenth, 292 yards a game). And while the offense finished 2004 ranked 105th, most of that unit was back as well. There was experience. There was depth. There was speed. There was hope.

For Paterno himself, the next season also held out the delicious twin prospects of redemption and revenge. Though he never admitted it publicly, he'd been upset by all the criticism. There was nothing he wanted more now than to prove that all the complaints and worries had been misguided. "Don't ever tell Joe he can't do something," his late brother George had said, "because he'll work harder than ever to make sure he does it."

The coach truly believed that, all things being equal, he and his teams should usually, in his favorite phrase, "lick the other guys." That, he knew, was the problem. All things *weren't* equal. Other teams had more talent than Penn State. But to admit that too often in public was to demean his players. It was wiser for him to blame the officiating or inexperience. Yet, in his heart, he understood that the quickest solution to the Nittany Lions' troubles would be to search harder and more selectively for talent.

The more Penn State struggled in 2004, the more he'd become convinced of that. All he needed to compete for a Big Ten title was a couple of game breakers. Even as the clamor about his status and recent record continued to intensify, he had been quietly hunting two of the nation's best.

The two players he had been elliptically referring to for much of the season were Derrick Williams, a six-foot, 190-pound wide receiver/ running back, and Justin King, a six-foot, 185-pound cornerback/wide receiver. Several recruiting Web sites had ranked Williams the nation's No. 1 overall prospect and King the No. 1 defensive back. Both of them could fly. As an eighth-grader, Williams was timed at 4.4 seconds in the 40-yard dash. He got even faster at Eleanor Roosevelt High School. King, meanwhile, ran the 40 in 4.3 while at Gateway High.

Paterno envisioned them as the dangerous wideouts and return men his last few teams had lacked, the breakaway threats who would frighten defenses and win space for his tailbacks and time for quarterbacks. Or, if he decided to keep King as a cover-corner, there were quick-footed defensive backs like senior Ethan Kilmer, junior Jim Kanuch, and freshman Deon Butler who he believed could make the switch to the other side of the ball.

The two scholastic stars had met and become friends at the various football camps they'd attended throughout their highly scrutinized youth. By the start of the 2004 season, they were so close that it was widely assumed they'd attend the same college. In September, it didn't appear that Penn State would be the one. Williams's father, Dwight, had said, without explanation, that the school was "off our list." That list, it turned out, included Florida, Florida State, Tennessee, and Oklahoma, all of whom had enjoyed considerably more recent success than Penn State and each of whom had won a national championship within the last decade.

But when both youngsters and their families visited State College in the fall, they fell under the still potent spell of Paterno. In mid-November, King committed to Penn State.

Still, Williams's indecision remained unsettling. The previous winter Paterno had handwritten a long letter to the youngster. He promised him a personal visit that spring. "Ordinarily, I don't recruit in the spring," Paterno wrote. "But this year . . . the first day we are allowed to be on the road, I'm going to be in Eleanor Roosevelt High School."

He was. And when Williams and his family came to Penn State in late October—a trip that included the obligatory Italian dinner at Paterno's home—they were further impressed by the coach's "humility and generosity." The few dozen Penn State players they spoke with that weekend expressed a deep affection for Paterno, a desire to see his legend restored. "And did you know," Williams's father said in a tone that mixed reverence and amazement, "the coach has a listed telephone number?"

Paterno had been reassuring recruits for a decade that he'd be there throughout their Penn State careers. But for Williams, King, and others, he and his assistants had altered that pitch a little. Now, according to some recruits, youngsters were being sold a two-pronged prospect: If they came to Penn State, they could help Paterno end his legendary career with one final run at a national title, and they could begin a new tradition. The strategy was the clearest sign yet that Paterno would be gone when his four-year extension expired at the end of the 2008 season, just before his eighty-second birthday.

"I'm telling kids that I'm going to hang in there until I think we've got a shot at another national title," he said. "Is that two years? Three years? Or is that wishful thinking on my part? I don't know."

The pitch ultimately worked with Williams. In a nationally televised news conference on December 22, the Maryland phenom announced he'd be joining King on the 2005 Nittany Lions. "That whole state is Joe Paterno," Williams gushed. "It's a great school. The facilities, the people, and the alumni—all of that was great."

That same day, in a Penn State football chat room at *PennLive.com*, a fan whose screen name was Dab824 excitedly tapped out what was on the minds of enthused Nittany Lions fans everywhere: "11–0 in '05!"

Paterno might be old. He might be slowing down. He might have won only seven of his last twenty-three games. But he had just convinced two of the nation's best high-school players to join him. What did that say about a program everyone had written off? What did that say about him?

"When a team is on a down cycle like Penn State and when a coach is old and rumored to be hanging on by his fingernails, how can you not be shocked by Justin King and Derrick Williams both committing to Penn State?" Allen Wallace, publisher of *SuperPrep* magazine, told a Pittsburgh newspaper. "This shows Joe Paterno is fighting as hard as he ever has."

● ● ●

The rush of postseason optimism soon washed away any lingering discontent in State College. Each week, it seemed, brought more evidence of a revived optimism.

There was surprisingly little public outcry when in February Penn State announced a $2–a-ticket increase for 2005 football games. The cheapest nonstudent tickets would now have a face value of $44. It was a rather audacious decision for a program that had plummeted so precipitously from its long-established norm. But, officials insisted, with the state providing an ever-smaller percentage of the university's budget, it was the only way to ensure against an athletic-department shortfall.

The price hike would help compensate for another drop in attendance. The Nittany Lions, who had been second in the nation in average crowds to Michigan in 2001, 2002, and 2003, fell to fourth in 2004, attracting 103,111 per game to Beaver Stadium. Coming on the heels of a decline of nearly 2,000 in '03, this attendance dip of another 2,500 meant there had been an average of 4,171 seats available at each home game.

Another thorny Paterno problem fell away that winter when one of his chief antagonists departed State College. Heather Dinich, the young sportswriter for the hometown *Centre Daily Times* who often criticized and greatly irritated Paterno and his subscriber-relatives, got married after the season and left both the beat and the newspaper. In a subsequent opinion piece she wrote for *New York Newsday*, Dinich got in one last shot at the coach. "Yes, he has graduated 86 percent of his players," she wrote. "But he has lost 86.7 percent of his conference games over the last two seasons. It's clear that Paterno will never leave on his own—not while he can still get down in a three-point stance, be quick with a whistle, and grab players ferociously by their facemasks. And definitely not while he is losing."

Still, the good news kept on coming for Paterno. On January 17, while claiming to raise money for his forthcoming wedding, the anonymous creator of *JoePaMustGo.com* auctioned off his Web site, the electronic gathering point for the coach's critics and a symbol of his diminished stature. The site was purchased by James Arjmand, an eighteen-year-old Penn State freshman. The chemistry major outbid

eighteen others with a bid of $1,010. A State College resident, Arj-
mand immediately shut down the Web site, saying he "wanted to do
something to show appreciation for [Paterno]."

Unlike the previous few off-seasons, Paterno rarely had to deal with
questions about his future. The contract extension and the recruiting
successes had pushed them into the background. Still there were a few
minor headaches, some of which dealt with his secret salary.

Paterno's annual compensation, widely estimated to be one million dollars, was a constant source of frustration and fascination for
journalists across Pennsylvania, primarily because it was so steadfastly
hidden. Efforts over the years to have it made public have failed consistently, in large part because of Penn State's powerful connections in
Harrisburg.

In 1990, Commonwealth Court had ruled that since Penn State
was a "state-related" and not a "state-run" university—even though it
received three hundred milion dollars in state appropriations—it did
not have to open its books to the public.

But in May of 2004, the board of Pennsylvania State Employees
Retirement System—which covered all state workers, including Paterno and Spanier—had decided that its pension records should be
made public. An appeal by Paterno and other Penn State officials was
rejected in November of that year, but the release of the information
was delayed while the university took its pleadings to Commonwealth
Court.

The *Harrisburg Patriot-News* joined in support of the retirement-
board ruling, its lawyers contending that if the data for only Penn State
employees were excluded, the court would be creating a special class
of state workers. Penn State's attorneys insisted there was no compelling reason to release the information, and Spanier said the newspaper's interest was sparked not by any interest in "a manner of
accountability of taxpayers dollars [but by] a curiosity and a feeling of
a right to know." A final decision was expected by mid-summer.

The salary that would be paid to the next Penn State's football
coach also became a controversial topic two months after the season.

At a January 23 trustees meeting, Spanier was asked about the escalating salaries for college coaches.

"The free-enterprise, market-oriented side of me says the market's the market and we have to deal with that," the president began. "On this issue, because Tim [Curley] doesn't have loose change sitting around in his budget and Penn State is not going to be able to get into an arms race in intercollegiate athletics, our philosophy is that our coaches should be paid a fair salary and we think we can pay a fair salary. But we can't go out and be offering one-million-, two-million-dollar salaries to coaches."

That response, not surprisingly, drew enthusiastic applause from professors when it was referenced by Spanier at a subsequent Faculty Senate meeting. But to Penn State's football fans, the university president seemed to be implying that the school wasn't going to conduct a thorough national search to find a successor for Paterno. For those cynics, it appeared to be further evidence that, rather than seek a high-priced, high-profile replacement, they would stay in-house. And that probably meant Tom Bradley, the popular but low-key defensive coordinator whom some alumni felt lacked a big-time coach's presence and reputation.

Spanier was on vacation when an aide telephoned and read him a *Centre Daily Times* column in which Ron Bracken accused him and the school of trying to cheapen the Penn State brand. More criticism followed from other columnists around the state, from radio talk-show hosts and in Penn State chat rooms. Stunned by the reaction, Spanier would respond that his statement had been "a pretty reasonable answer." He labeled his noisiest critics "crackpots who think that I'm here to undermine or ruin or dismantle intercollegiate athletics."

But he did quickly backtrack.

"We're going to continue to go out and hire the best coaches we can," he said, "and we will pay what we have to pay."

When spring practice for the 2005 season began in March, player discipline was not nearly the topic it had been the previous year.

Either Paterno's no-tolerance message had left an imprint on his team, or players were better at hiding their transgressions. There were no underage drinking citations, no assaults, no brawls at parties. In fact, the only embarrassing incident involved a bow and arrow.

Center E. Z. Smith and Mike Southern, a backup linebacker who already had quit the team, were accused of damaging a campus apartment by firing several arrows into its walls during a party there. Smith, who previously had been forced to sit out the 2003 season because of two underage drinking violations, was suspended from the team. He was barred from spring practice and all summer workouts.

Paterno said Smith's status would be reevaluated when he returned for the fall semester, providing he had made restitution for the damage. But once again, he blamed the media for inflating the incident's significance.

"I said to the alumni group this morning, 'You know what, if I hadn't done a couple of things when I was in college, I might have been the first American Pope,' " he noted at the press conference that preceded the April 23 Blue–White Game. "I would love to have everyone of you guys and girls stand up and tell me that you haven't done anything that you would hate like the dickens to have put in the press. I am still dealing with twenty- and twenty-one-year-old kids."

On the field, despite a cry among alumni and sports columnists to make Morelli his starting QB, and despite Paterno's insistence that the youngster was "too good to sit on the bench," it seemed clear that Robinson was going to be Penn State's quarterback at the start of the 2005 season.

Robinson got the majority of the snaps in the storm-shortened Blue–White Game notable as a showcase for the speed of Williams and King. Morelli, meanwhile, continued to perform tentatively.

"I think Michael Robinson has made great progress," Paterno said. "I think he has made really good progress. Jay has worked with him and I think you will see a kid that is a really much-improved passer in his form. You would expect that since that is the only thing he has done. He hasn't had to be playing wideout and running back. You would hope he improved at the one position that you groomed him for. I think he will certainly be a good quarterback. Anthony Morelli, eventually, is going to be a great quarterback. Morelli has a tremendous arm. He has handled a lot of things much quicker than I thought he would. The rap on him was that maybe he wasn't the smartest kid in the world, which has really been unfortunate, because he has accepted things well and does some things well."

On days when the weather prevented him from walking back and forth to his office, Paterno drove his new silver BMW—a much flashier car than he had ever owned previously. In preparation for his fortieth season as Penn State's head coach, he met daily with his assistants— all of whom had returned for '05—and began mapping out the practice routines. They would be much like they always had been:

SUNDAY: Reviewing and breaking down game tapes. Coming up with a preliminary game plan for the next opponent.

MONDAY: Going over the game plan at the various position meetings. Reviewing tapes of the opponents' games.

TUESDAY: Installing the plan during a lengthy, full-pad workout.

WEDNESDAY: Meetings and workouts for 1½ to 2 hours.

THURSDAY: 1–1¼ hours of the same.

FRIDAY: A quick meeting and walk-through.

SATURDAY: Game.

He probably spent more time on recruiting trips than ever before, something he continued to enjoy. "As long as we can walk away from kids we don't like," he said. He chuckled to himself whenever recruits told him "my dad went to Penn State or my grandmother was a cheerleader." Penn State, under siege in its traditional recruiting areas, was in turn trying to extend its geographical reach. Oftentimes, Paterno would fly in a university jet to see three recruits in a single day, each of them hundreds of miles from the others.

Still, even now, at seventy-eight, there was little time for family or vacation. "I am really feeling the neglect of all my grandkids at this stage," he said.

His only extended off-season break from football came when he and other coaches from colleges that had six-figure Nike contracts traveled to Aruba for a combination excursion and meeting. Oddly, given his stance against commercialization, Paterno and Nike chairman Phil Knight had become unlikely friends. At Nike's headquarters in Beaverton, Oregon, employees dropped their children off at the Joe Paterno Child Care Center. Knight spent the Blue–White weekend with the Paternos and was even made an honorary coach of the Blue team in that intrasquad game.

Paterno vowed again to alter his personal workload in ways that would make him a more effective coach. Just as in the year before, when he had delegated some of his nonfootball duties to Fran Ganter, Paterno now continued to shed those old responsibilities. At April's annual coaches' clinic, he was present for only a few onfield drills and he never even showed up for the session's evening social, something he always had attended in the past.

"There are a lot of things that I have gotten caught up in and things that are expected of me that take up a lot of time," he said. "I've been trying to work my way out of [them]. . . . This is going to be a fun year for me. It is, obviously, a big challenge for me personally as well as for the whole program. I kind of thrive on those kinds of things. I have spent an awful lot of time on just trying to be a football coach."

Fifty-five years, in fact. All of them in State College, where the spaghetti sauce has improved over the years, where the homes and the shops and the classroom buildings now spread out to once-unimaginable distances, where his new office is twice as large as his first residence, where his children had been born and had become parents themselves.

"Nobody could have had things go better for them than me," Paterno said after the 2004 season. "I've got my health. . . . I've never missed a practice day in all the years, except when my son was hurt and when my dad died. I've got a great wife, great kids, a great university. I've got everything."

Everything, perhaps, but time.

As another season neared, the old literature major had to be contemplating his mortality. Age was a circumstance all his work, all his past glories couldn't change. "They told me I was everything," King Lear had said. " 'Tis a lie."

He certainly seemed to recognize the urgency of his situation.

Asked during a fund-raiser in Pittsburgh how long he would continue to coach if Penn State did not produce victories, he was surprisingly blunt.

"If we don't win some games," he said, "I've got to get my rear end out of here. Simple as that. We have a team that can go out there and do some things we haven't done in the last few years. I think if we do that, fine. If we don't, I think I have to back away and say, 'Hey, I'm not doing the job.' And it would be easy for me to back away. Well, as far as financially and the whole bit. I'm not a forty-year-old guy trying to create a career for himself."

He was a seventy-eight-year-old guy at the end of one.

Three days before his fifty-fifth Christmas in State College, on the morning that Williams revealed his college choice, Penn State officials said Paterno was relaxing at home. While he might have been at home, it was doubtful he was relaxing.

More likely, he was sitting in his den, watching football videos and drawing up plays, safe again within the crucifix's shadow.

AFTERWORD

FOURTEEN MONTHS AFTER the end of the 2004 season, Joe Paterno still couldn't sleep. Penn State's coach was sitting on a sofa at dawn, restlessly scribbling on a pad of paper. A couple of slices of leftover pizza his wife had reheated for him in their hotel room's microwave sat untouched on a glass coffee table. Sue Paterno slept nearby, worn out physically and emotionally by the triple-overtime Orange Bowl that had ended only hours before, at nearly 1:00 A.M. Elsewhere in the Sheraton Bal Harbour, a posh beachfront hotel that towered over Collins Avenue midway between Miami Beach and Fort Lauderdale, the remainder of the official Penn State traveling party also rested.

Through the room's balcony doors, the light of a new day was becoming visible. A Florida sun, so inflamed that it might have served as the logo for the previous night's Orange Bowl, climbed above the Atlantic Ocean.

Paterno never noticed. All his focus and whatever energy his sleepless body possessed at this hour were directed toward that pad. Nothing else mattered. Not the spectacular sunrise. Not his lingering hunger. Not his weariness. Not his wife. Not his sleeping children and grandchildren, who had been with him in Florida during the long, chaotic run-up to his thirty-second bowl appearance. And certainly not the media, with whom he was scheduled to meet downstairs in a few hours to dissect the previous night's game and, once again, to look ahead.

His surprising 2005 season had just concluded. With its unanticipated victories and its theme of delicious redemption, it was, for Paterno, among the most enjoyable of his forty seasons at Penn State's helm. He'd proved something to his critics. He'd proved something to the media. He'd even proved something to his own school's administration.

Near the end of the miserable 2004 season, AD Tim Curley and president Graham Spanier had gone to Paterno's house hoping to come away with an exit strategy for the aging, beleaguered coach. "I respected their judgment, and literally had asked them if we could sit around and talk about what might be the future for Penn State and Penn State football," Paterno recalled. "[They] thought that maybe the best thing for Penn State would be for me to announce this [2005] would be my last year and I would retire at the end of it. Well, I just didn't think that was the way to do it. And I said, 'No, I don't want to do it that way.' I said, 'Well, let's see what we can get done this year.' "

And though he'd gotten more done than anyone but himself could possibly have anticipated, he wasn't going to gloat. Why pause too long to savor a single moment, a single victory or a single season when there were always more to prepare for? Besides, he was too impatient. Joe Paterno was programmed to look beyond, to tackle the next challenge, to start the next chapter, to answer the newest critic. That's what drove him. Even now, at seventy-nine, he relished those confrontations with the unknown. The allure of the future remained undiminished.

So it was hardly surprising that on this morning, even before the noisy work crews had finished cleaning the debris that 77,773 Orange Bowl fans had left in and around Dolphin Stadium, he had turned toward 2006.

"Ahhh, I was just doodling a little bit," he would say later of that early-morning work session. Actually, he was anticipating the problems that were already consuming his thoughts even though his next game was still eight months away: Could Anthony Morelli replace Michael Robinson at quarterback? If so, how drastically would the offense need to be reimagined? Who would fill the shoes of the seven defensive seniors who had just played their final games? And what about his staff? Could he hold it together for another year?

One subject he didn't need to ponder, not even for an instant, was his future. He'd put those annoying questions to rest. The administration wasn't talking about an exit strategy anymore, were they? Yeah, he'd be eighty at the conclusion of the 2006 season. But who cared? Could a coach who had experienced a season like his be too old, too stubborn, and too out-of-touch?

Like its coach, Penn State had been eager to prove something in 2005. The Nittany Lions tore through the soft opening portion of their schedule. After a slight sputter in a 23–13 season-opening win over South Florida, they routed Cincinnati and Central Michigan in a way that was both encouraging and entertaining. They threw the ball often and they threw it deep to an exciting group of freshmen wideouts. And even though their 3–0 record was exactly what everyone had expected— since all the games were at Beaver Stadium and all against outclassed programs—it was clear on the eve of Big Ten play that the excitement was building again in Happy Valley.

Fans began to look ahead—and back. How could such a daring, offensively appealing team have risen from the ashes of the lifeless 2004 bunch? Suddenly, there were as many theories for Penn State's apparent revival as there had been for its multiseason slump:

- The goal-line stand against Indiana: That dramatic sequence near the end of 2004 had sparked a confidence inside the Nittany Lions' heads.
- Paterno's calm reassurance to players and staff: In the meeting with Penn State administrators he'd convinced those nervous officials that patience was all that was required for a turnaround, then sold that to his players and staff as well.
- The decision to spread the offense in 2004's final game against Michigan State: The resulting offensive outburst served as a successful dress rehearsal for the wide-open attack that would characterize 2005.

- The commitments by stud recruits like Derrick Williams and Justin King: Those signings had not only raised the talent level but reestablished Penn State as a top-flight program.
- The players-only summer tutorials: Robinson bonded with his freshmen receivers throughout the months before the 2005 season, schooling them in the new offense and assimilating them quickly into the team's veteran core.
- Big Ten Media Day: The embarrassment and anger Paterno and his captains felt when they were virtually ignored at the August gathering in Chicago became an important motivator for 2005.

There was some truth to each of these. All together they'd built a positive attitude that nothing in the Nittany Lions' recent past appeared to justify. "We were far away [the last two years]," Alan Zemaitis said. "Inside, the guts of the football team wasn't there. We've done a little surgical work."

When Penn State's chest was cracked, the procedure revealed not just a renewed faith in themselves, but a glowing, red-hot resentment. "I've been telling these guys all summer," Robinson said, " 'if you're not upset about what's being written about us, if you're not upset about how the nation is looking at us, if you're not upset about how people are talking about Coach Paterno, you shouldn't be here. Go home. We don't want you around.' "

A team whose spirit had drifted aimlessly a year ago began to sense its purpose and its opportunity. Togetherness was the Nittany Lions' spring and summer theme. Respect, or rather a lack of it, soon took its place as a rallying cry.

Throughout the summer of 2005, Paterno's players rose early and engaged in their morning rituals with the fervor of a medieval religious sect. It was as if they were seeking collective redemption through self-discipline and focus. By 6:15 A.M., you could see packs of Nittany Lions—silent and stone-faced—jogging reverently through the mountain mist that frequently shrouded State College mornings. Many were dressed only in shorts and sneakers as they ran along the dewy lawns and empty sidewalks of Penn State's slumbering campus. Always at or near the front were the three players who had been elected tri-captains in May: Robinson, Paul Posluszny and Zemaitis. Three times a week Penn State's players would gather, without coaches, for these early-morning runs. On Saturdays, they would start at 8:00 A.M. Twice a week there would be lifting sessions. At 7:00 A.M.

They were preparing themselves, but punishing themselves, too. Convinced by Paterno that any rebirth in 2005 was going to require a new commitment, one that was both spiritual and physical, they were sweating out the guilt and anguish that their dismal 2003 and 2004 seasons had bred.

They had come together for early-morning runs before the previous few seasons, too. And those, it turned out, meant little. But this time they all sensed a different attitude. "We'd have guys saying, 'I don't want to do this, it's early,'" said Posluszny about the summers past. "This year, there's more of an attitude of 'Let's get better. Let's work on winning.'"

In recent summers, said Tamba Hali, Penn State's players had been unable to shake the lingering lethargy that losing created. "[If] we had free time, we just went home and hit the couch," recalled the defensive end. "We watched TV, played video games, slept. . . . Things just weren't stable. We had Mike [Robinson] playing all kinds of positions. We had Zack Mills coming in and out. It just wasn't stable."

Paterno hoped to capitalize as quickly as possible on the new stability. Ignoring both the conventional wisdom and all the evidence the last several seasons appeared to provide, he would tell his players over and over that they were capable of going 11–0. "Coach kept telling us before the season that we didn't come here to go 7–4 or 8–3," recalled Robinson. "He said, 'This is Penn State. We can win every game we play this year.'"

Williams, King and another entering freshman—tight end Francis Claude—graduated early from high school and, like more and more incoming freshmen around the country, turned up on campus in January of 2005. Immediately, in addition to starting classes, they began informal workouts with the returning Nittany Lions and participated in weight-room sessions with John Thomas, the team's strength and conditioning coach. By the time spring practice began in late March and ended with the Blue-White game several weeks later, they were feeling comfortable. This "get them to campus early" trend was sweeping college football and even Paterno, long a vocal advocate of giving freshmen time to find themselves, had acquiesced.

They were schooled by a veteran coaching staff that had endured all the uncertainty surrounding Paterno's job status in recent years. The coach was so certain that 2005 was going to be a memorable season that, once he told the school's administration that he wasn't about to retire, he convinced three assistants to turn down offers elsewhere. "All three were good opportunities," said Paterno, without identifying them. "I think they felt as I did that we had a good bunch of kids. We had worked hard on recruiting. We felt if we all stayed together we could make this a pretty good team. . . . I made sure that they knew I was going to be around. . . . We joined hands and everybody said, 'Let's go to work.' "

Equally important, Paterno finally agreed to step back some in certain areas, becoming more of an overseer than the obsessed, detail-oriented coach he had always been. He gave all his assistants, in particular offensive coordinator Galen Hall, a freer hand. "You have to learn to pace yourself and learn what you do well," Paterno explained. "What I do well is I can critique a practice, I can say, 'I don't like what we're doing,' I can sit there and go through an offensive game plan or a defensive game plan. I still coach a little bit on the field, but in the old days, I had to coach every position."

The long months between the encouraging end of the 2004 season and the start of 2005 built a sturdy camaraderie. And that enabled Penn State to better withstand more of the disturbing off-the-field incidents that had marred previous offseasons.

On January 29, E.Z. Smith, the good-natured center with a taste for beer and a penchant for immaturity, picked up a bow belonging to teammate Tyler Reed and began firing arrows into the wall of the apartment occupied by Reed, Andrew Richardson, and Scott Paxson. No one was injured, but the spree caused $700 worth of damage. In April, Penn State's Judicial Affairs office banned Smith from extracurricular activities until the following fall, meaning the senior anchor of the offensive line would miss all the summer workouts. Reed and Richardson, who apparently had participated as well, plummeted down the depth chart.

Also in April, sophomore linebacker Dan Connor began making crank calls to an aging ex-Paterno aide named Joe Sarra. Sarra, whose mental faculties were somewhat addled even before he stepped aside following the 2004 season, had long been the butt of player jokes. But Connor and at least two other teammates had been making late-night calls aimed at confusing the old coach further, sometimes arranging unwanted pizza deliveries to his house. Connor eventually was suspended for the season's first three games.

More troubling was a case involving Paxson, though details wouldn't surface until long after the 2005 season was over and the defensive tackle's eligibility exhausted. A Penn State coed accused the player of sexually assaulting her in his apartment in December of 2004. Fifteen months later, after the young woman decided to file criminal charges, the university announced that a Judicial Affairs hearing on the incident had cleared Paxson. Subsequent reports, however, revealed that Judicial Affairs initially had recommended a year's suspension, a verdict that was overturned at a second university hearing in the spring of 2005.

Paterno knew all about the Paxson incident. Whether it was his prompting that resulted in the second hearing is not known. The coach later admitted he had been unhappy with how Judicial Affairs had handled some matters involving players, but never got more specific. In any event, he shoved Paxson deep into his doghouse, where he stayed throughout the summer.

The bonding between Robinson and the young wideouts, and the bold new offensive philosophy Hall had sold to Paterno, were both visible early—on the first two plays of a rain-shortened 2005 Blue-White scrimmage.

Robinson hit King on a 35-yard completion to open that game. The quarterback followed that up on the next snap by connecting with Derrick Williams for a big gain. There were still a lot of Penn State fans who wanted to see Morelli at quarterback. But Robinson, who, unlike his experiences in previous preseasons, hadn't been shifted to other positions at all during spring practices, looked poised and confident, completing all six of his throws. "It was a great experience, getting to focus on one position—finally," Robinson, with a wry smile, said afterward.

Those two plays on April 23 were a jolt to the psyche of those who still doubted that Paterno, at seventy-eight, would ever shed his core beliefs. The old coach had rarely allowed freshmen much rein. Now, by calling the numbers of his two prized recruits on the spring game's first two plays, Paterno was tipping his hand for 2005. Williams caught four passes, ran the ball once, and even lined up at quarterback on one play during the scrimmage. King had two catches and two runs and also played defense. And there were two more freshmen wideouts on display—Jordan Norwood, the son of assistant coach Brian Norwood; and Deon Butler, who had been a red-shirted defensive back in 2004. "That was a glimpse of what may happen in the fall," Robinson predicted. "We've got to get the ball in their hands and let them move around."

Just weeks before the 2005 season finally began, members of Penn State's entourage stewed as they flew back to State College from the Big Ten media session in Chicago. Reporters there, for the most part, had ignored them, assuming the Nittany Lions were headed for another season near the bottom of the conference standings. And on those rare occasions when they did have a question for Paterno or Robinson or Posluszny, the interviewers' attitudes tended to be condescending and patronizing.

"That really bothered us," Posluszny recalled. "We were out there and we felt like we didn't get very much respect at all. Maybe we didn't deserve it because of the way we played the past couple of years . . . but we came home a little bit angered about that. I still can remember one reporter. He said to Michael [Robinson], 'Since Penn State and Illinois have kind of been in the same boat these past couple years, are you really looking forward to that game as one of the biggest of the year?' "

That snub fired them up. So did Paterno's more passionate demeanor. The spark that occasionally had been missing from the coach's behavior in recent years was back. Alone with them, he talked and acted as if he believed they could go undefeated. He sensed something in his players that outside observers couldn't detect. "He kept believing in us," said Paxson. "Even when nobody else did, he kept believing."

Part of it could be explained by the coach's emotional connection to this team. Paterno liked their attitudes and their personalities. There didn't seem to be as many egos. He liked to tell the story of Hali's hair. When he was recruited, the New Jersey lineman had long cornrows. Paterno frequently told recruits they'd need to get a haircut before they arrived in State College. But for some reason he hadn't mentioned it to Hali and, as a result, would have been willing to put up with his long hair. But Hali sensed his coach's feelings and showed up with a short haircut anyway. "That tells you something about Tamba," said Paterno, "and this whole team is like that. It's a great team to be around. It's fun to be around them."

When Penn State's new freshman students arrived in State College for the fall semester in late August—a week before the Nittany Lions' season opener—Paterno addressed them at a campus gathering. "He was eloquent," said Penn State president Graham Spanier. "He received two standing ovations. He's as energized and determined as I've ever seen him. His passion for this season is great."

That passion grew, week by week through the 3–0 start. On September 23, when Paterno accompanied his team to Illinois for the following day's game at Northwestern, he was as eager to play a Big Ten opener as anyone could remember. He was convinced this team possessed something different from their immediate predecessors. Presented with an opportunity late in a game, he was sure they would seize it. "So many of the games we have lost in the last couple of years," Paterno said, "came down to one play."

As if on cue, one play would determine the Northwestern game— and ultimately their season.

All through the spring and summer, and even into the season, Paterno had been focusing on one of his favorite drills. Near the end of practices, he would line up the offense, instruct a student-manager to crank up the simulated crowd noise on the sound system, and call out specific game situations. "OK," he'd yell, "it's fourth-and-nine," or "third-and-seventeen," or "fourth-and-twelve."

That Saturday, with just 1:39 left in the fourth quarter, Penn State, having battled back from 23–7, was trailing Northwestern, 29–27. The situation confronting the Nittany Lions was even more dire than Paterno's practice scenarios. It was a fourth-and-15. On Penn State's own 15.

In the huddle, Robinson, growing in stature as a leader each day, calmly assured his teammates that they were going to get the first down. "We had lost yards on the previous two plays," he recalled. "But for some reason there was no doubt in my mind that we were going to make it. I don't know why. It just seemed like practice." Butler said he and his fellow freshmen, getting their first taste of big-time college pressure, were relaxed by their quarterback's words and demeanor. "Mike was so calm," he said. "It was like it was first-and-ten on the first play of the game."

Robinson told tight end Isaac Smolko they'd be running a play that always clicked in practice: the young wideouts would take off down the edges, leaving plenty of room in the middle for Smolko. "Smolko has probably got the most reliable hands on the team," said Robinson. The ball was snapped and Williams and Butler took off on the wings. The free safety moved toward Williams. Smolko ran just past 15 yards and turned. Robinson's pass, whizzing through a picket fence of raised arms, was there when he did. "People used to question his throwing ability," Butler said. "All I know is whenever the game is on the line, his percentage is 100 percent."

The 20-yard gain sustained the desperate drive. Moments later, Williams caught his first touchdown pass and Penn State had a 34–29 conference road win, its most significant victory in three seasons. "That fourth-down play . . . was probably when we knew this was going to be a special season," said linebacker Tim Shaw.

Paterno was elated afterward, though his public comments to reporters were weighed down with the thick caution that had long been the hallmark of his pre- and postgame interviews. "You have to make those kinds of plays if you are going to be a really good football team," he said. "You have to make them over not just one game. You have to do it over a period of a couple of games at least, three or four. Then you have a good football team. Right now we are a decent football team, but we are a project yet."

But a truer measure of the coach's inner joy was his decision to allow some of his freshmen to speak with reporters after the game. ("I owe you guys that," he said to reporters—though just days later he would cancel the players' regular weekly interviews.) King, Williams and Butler clearly were ecstatic after their first significant collegiate triumph. It was left to Robinson to rein in the postgame enthusiasm. "There's one quote I live by from Frederick Douglass: 'There can be no progress without struggle,' " the QB said. "And that's how this team thinks. We stuck together. But, you know, this isn't the Rose Bowl. This is our first Big Ten win. We've got to move on from here."

Back at home the following Saturday, Penn State thrashed eighteenth-ranked Minnesota, its senior-laden defense stifling Gophers tailback Laurence Maroney. Now Paterno, with his unbeaten team having just entered the top 25 at No. 16, had to prepare his players for what he knew would be their season's biggest test—a nationally televised nighttime home game against No. 6 Ohio State the following week.

Penn State's students needed no preparation. Not long after the Minnesota game ended, they'd begun camping outside Beaver Stadium's student entrance to ensure themselves the best seats for the Ohio State game. The population soon swelled to several hundred students and nearly as many tents. The local Wal-Mart and Dick's sporting goods stores quickly sold out of tents. This mini-village acquired a predictable name—Paternoville. Students brought portable generators and miles of extension cords to power the space-heaters, laptops, and TVs that transformed the tents into virtual motel rooms. ESPN dispatched its *Cold Pizza* and *College GameDay* crews to State College to report on the village of Nittany fans. Several players and assistant coaches stopped by the tent city as did Paterno, after much prodding from his staff. Paterno asked Lou Prato, who heads the university's sports museum, where "Paternoville" was located. "Not far from your statue," Prato said.

Most of Penn State's students had never witnessed a pregame buildup like this. "I don't know whether I would put it in the category you would put it in," Paterno said to reporters who asked where this excitement ranked. "Whether it's a Category Five hurricane, Category Four hurricane or Category Three hurricane, when it hits you, it hits you. You don't look up and say, 'Is that Four, Five or Three?' "

When it came, at the end of a gray, rainy Saturday, the Ohio State game, played before the third largest crowd in Penn State history (109,839), validated the return of Paterno's program to national prominence. The exclamation point came with 1:21 left, and the Nittany Lions leading, 17–10. Hali sacked Buckeyes quarterback Troy Smith near midfield. Paxson scooped up the resulting fumble and Beaver Stadium, cobbled together in various expansions during the decades like a giant erector set, shook and rumbled beneath the joyful writhings of the reborn. "That," said Butler, "was pure pandemonium."

No one looked more relieved than Paterno, wet and weary on the sideline. "I was scared to death the whole time," he admitted after the narrow victory. "One play. That's all it would have taken." With his team at 6–0, and back in the top ten (No. 9) after a prolonged absence, Paterno had to face an avalanche of questions about how he had managed to pull such a successful season out of his well-worn hat. "I never really felt like we were far away," he said over and over.

A week later, Penn State's players stood in Michigan Stadium at dusk and wondered if someone were going to wake them from their nightmare.

Robinson's 3-yard touchdown run with fifty-three seconds remaining had given Penn State a 25–21 lead. What followed that fleeting joy was twenty hours' worth of regret and frustration.

With no time left on the clock, Michigan QB Chad Henne connected with Mario Manningham on a game-winning, 10-yard touchdown pass. Paterno was kicking himself. He hadn't told Kevin Kelly to squib the kickoff that followed Robinson's score, or at least to keep the ball away from dangerous returner Steve Breaston. "We talked about [a squib]," he said. "We probably should have power-kicked it to the other side of the field from that kid." Breaston made him pay, returning it 41 yards to Michigan's 47.

On the drive that followed, there were two plays that induced flashbacks to the controversial calls that had gone against the Nittany Lions during their multiseason slump—including a few at Michigan Stadium. One was a 17-yard pass-reception on which Jason Avent appeared to have been out of bounds. The other came immediately afterward. The scoreboard showed twenty-eight seconds remaining following Avent's catch. But Michigan coach Lloyd Carr called a timeout and complained to the officials that the clock should have stopped with thirty-two seconds left. The officials compromised and added two seconds.

Every pessimist in Happy Valley knew those two seconds would end up costing Penn State the game. When the decision to add the time was explained to the Penn State coach, Paterno's response was "Ah, baloney." Sure enough, those two seconds left Michigan with just enough time for the winning play; when Henne lined up over center for that final snap, there was one second left.

Immediately following the loss, cyberspace hummed with the fury of Penn Staters convinced that, for a second time in four seasons, the officials had stolen a Michigan Stadium victory from their Lions. "I am glad the refs learned some new and interesting ways to [cheat] us out of a win in Ann Arbor," read one post to a Fightonstate.com chat room. "They have spent their playbook on us." In an e-mail to a local newspaper, another fan wrote: "Personally, I feel that if the Super Bowl champions were to play Michigan at their stadium, they, too, would lose."

Things didn't get any better for the Nittany Lions. They soon learned that Williams had broken his arm on a late kickoff and would be lost for the season. Then a mechanical problem delayed their flight home for more than three hours. They got back to State College at 2:30 A.M. "It's tough," linebacker Dan Connor said of the sudden disappointments. "It kind of kills you inside. . . . But it's like when we beat Ohio State. You think about it for twenty-four hours and then you've got to turn the page. There are a lot of other good teams in the Big Ten. We want to win the rest of them. So we've got to stop thinking about all that, stop worrying about all that."

A week's worth of worrying ended with the Nittany Lions' 63–10 blowout victory at Illinois. Robinson was phenomenal, throwing for four touchdown passes and running for two more before exiting with less than two minutes left in the first half and the Lions ahead, 56–3. The QB was beginning to attract national attention. Those getting their first look at him wondered why Paterno had waited until his senior season to hand him the offense. The coach, who wasn't about to start comparing the relative attributes of Robinson and Zack Mills, didn't have an answer. But it was clear he'd been impressed too.

"I think Michael Robinson has been the heart of the football team and hasn't gotten anywhere near the notoriety nationally that he should have," said Paterno. "He does it all. Every game we've played, in the clutch, he's done the things that had to be done to win the game. Even at Michigan, he took us down the field at the end of the game. . . . He went through a lot of, 'I'm a quarterback. I'm a wideout. I'm a running back. I'm this, that and the whole bit.' Finally, when he had his chance just to be the guy that runs the show, he has done just a great job."

With Robinson going increasingly to Butler on big plays and Tony Hunt's running providing an effective offensive counterweight, the Nittany Lions finished off their final three Big 10 opponents—Purdue, Wisconsin and Michigan State—by a combined score of 99–51. Their 7–1 conference record left them tied with Ohio State, but because the Lions had beaten the Buckeyes, they were official Big Ten champions for the first time since 1994.

In the meantime, there was plenty to keep the good times rolling in Happy Valley. Hali and Posluszny were named first-team all-Americans. Posluszny, who admitted he was thinking of leaving Penn State for the NFL before his senior season, won both the Butkus and Bednarik Awards as the nation's top linebacker. Robinson, who broke Kerry Collins's single-season school record for total yardage by accumulating 2,687, was named the Big Ten's Offensive Player of the Year (though, curiously, Northwestern's Brett Basanez was named first-team all-conference quarterback).

Meanwhile, Paterno not only garnered a slew of Coach of the Year awards for his study, but he also helped land another sensational class of freshmen recruits, including five-star running back/defensive back A.J. Wallace of Pomfret, Maryland.

When Florida State upset Virginia Tech in the ACC title game and Texas and USC finished unbeaten, Penn State's bowl fate was set. For countless fans, it turned out to be a disappointing scenario. Two-loss Ohio State, whom the Nittany Lions had beaten, got the sexy Fiesta Bowl matchup with Notre Dame. Penn State got an Orange Bowl berth opposite Florida State, a team with four losses and a No. 22 ranking. "Of course, we'd like to have two undefeated teams," said Phil Smith of the Orange Bowl committee. "But we think it's great that we have the champions of the Big Ten and the champions of the ACC."

Clearly, the matchup needed a hook.

"I feel like driving to State College and drown my sorrows at the Rathskeller," wrote a contributor to a Penn State football blog, the 50-Yard Lion Blog. "Is the ghost of Richard Nixon haunting us? If we beat FSU, which I hope we do, the pundits will say we beat a nobody. If we lose, it just keeps the misperception there is no such thing as Eastern football."

Promoters tried to sell the January 3 game as a duel between its legendary septuagenarian coaches, Paterno and Bobby Bowden, a strategy that seemed to irritate Paterno. The Penn State coach frequently appeared determined to highlight the differences unpleasantly. While Bowden was his usual "aw-shucks" avuncular self in advance of the game, Paterno was confrontational and just plain grouchy.

When reporters from all over Pennsylvania—not to mention Orange Bowl officials from Miami—descended on State College December 7 for what had been billed as "Orange Bowl Media Day," the last opportunity to talk with Penn State players before game week, they were stunned. Paterno had not allowed his team to attend.

"You know, they've got exams. They've got to go to school,"

Paterno tried to explain to an angry group of reporters. "We've got final exams next week, and right now, Friday and Saturday, we've got to practice; and I'm not crazy about practicing Friday and Saturday. Sunday we have the senior banquet, and then Monday we start exams. We've got thirty-five kids with exams on Monday. OK? I could care less—I'll be very upfront with you—I could care less about you guys."

The words echoed a theme that Paterno had raised earlier in the season—he no longer related to the people who covered him and his team. "I can't trust you guys anymore," he had said in September, lamenting the vanished camaraderie between him and Penn State's beat writers. "I am just being honest with you. It's no fun. I don't like you guys anymore."

Obsessed with all the potential distractions, Paterno decided to bring his team to Florida on December 20, a day before his seventy-ninth birthday. Not only would that give them two weeks in Florida, but it meant his coaches and players would be away from home on Christmas. In Florida, once the two-a-day practices beneath a hot sun began, the coach soon recognized he'd made a mistake. Two weeks of single-minded focus was probably too much to ask of college kids. It only added to his irritability.

Penn State hadn't been to an Orange Bowl since 1986. They'd been to three between 1969 and 1974, and that's the era Paterno used as a measuring stick. Back then, the game was played in Miami's Orange Bowl, instead of at Dolphin Stadium in Miami Gardens. Because his team had played there so often, Paterno knew the organizers well and they were glad to accommodate him and his team. But things had changed substantially in the intervening decades. The old crowd was gone. The demands had increased enormously. There were early-morning news conferences, afternoon beach parties, photo shoots during practices, and sponsors, fans and alumni to be appeased. Though the media was headquartered in Fort Lauderdale, Penn State stayed in Bal Harbour and Florida State in Hollywood Beach. That meant the two coaches had to be driven—with a police escort—to Fort Lauderdale for the news conferences. Despite the fact that he had 6 1/2 weeks to get ready for Florida State, Paterno complained that his obligations were costing him preparation time. At the opening news conference, he cut off an official who was merely trying to introduce him and lay down some ground rules for the interview.

"Let's go, we don't need a speech. I got to get out of here in a half-hour. . . . Is this the Miami Bowl or the Fort Lauderdale Bowl?" he asked, though no one had the nerve to tell him it was neither. "I don't know in God's name why you [media] guys are up here and we're down there. It took me thirty minutes with a police car to come up here."

Paterno would complain often that week about his schedule, as if the Orange Bowl appearance were a punishment instead of a reward that would bring the school a multimillion-dollar payout.

"I get instructions from the BCS, 'This is what you gotta do,' " Paterno said. "In the old days, I used to work with the Orange Bowl Committee. They'd tell me, 'This is what you gotta do.' I'd say, 'Ah, baloney. Change it around a little bit.' . . . I go from here back to my hotel. I go from there to a lunch in Miami Beach. I go from there to a rally and . . . hey, you know, it's in the contract. You gotta stay where they tell you to stay. We used to pick our own hotel and the whole bit. So I don't like the whole thing. I love the old way. But I'm a dinosaur."

But all that was just "inside baseball" between Paterno and the media. It was another ill-advised—and probably misunderstood—comment on another subject that once again raised the debate about Paterno's age and attitudes. It came after Florida State linebacker A.J. Nicholson had been sent home. A nineteen-year-old woman had accused him of sexual assault in the player's hotel room.

"It's so tough," Paterno began when asked about the incident. "There are so many people gravitating to these kids. [He] may not even have known what he was getting into. A cute girl knocks on the door, what do you do? Geez, thank God they don't knock on my door. . . . But that's too bad. You hate to see that."

By the time Penn State returned home from the game, women's groups in Pennsylvania were decrying the coach's insensitivity and calling for his resignation. Paterno ignored the criticism and the controversy soon evaporated. But for Penn State officials, his comments and his Orange Bowl behavior were a couple of more warnings about the dangers of employing an increasingly cantankerous coach who was nearing eighty.

All the unpleasant rancor was forgotten in the wake of a wildly exciting—though not particularly well-played—Orange Bowl. The game stretched on through 4 1/2 hours and three overtimes, ending at 12:58 A.M. Penn State finally won it, 29–26, when freshman kicker Kevin Kelly, who had missed two potential game-winners earlier in the marathon, connected on a 29-yarder not long after Florida State's kicker bounced a field-goal try off an upright.

Fittingly, that winning field goal followed a convoluted bit of strategy. When, on a second-and-9 at Florida State's 12-yard line, Paterno sent out the field-goal unit for what would turn out to be Kelly's game-winner, he wanted a fake. Robinson hated the call and begged for another shot or two at the end zone. Paterno, though unyielding, called a timeout. With the call, the coach appeared either to be protecting his young kicker, who already had missed from 29 and 38 yards, or to have lost confidence in him. When the snap came to holder Jason Ganter, the son of Paterno's longtime offensive coordinator, at the 19, he didn't like what he saw. He called off the fake. Kelly's game-winner split the uprights.

Perhaps the most significant event in Paterno's record twenty-first bowl victory occurred late in regulation, when Posluszny tore two ligaments in his right knee and left the game. Surgery would be required, a development that caused the junior linebacker to withdraw his name from consideration for the 2006 NFL draft.

Hunt also was injured, on Penn State's second offensive play. In his place, junior Austin Scott, long a habitue of Paterno's doghouse, finally displayed the form that had allowed him to set numerous Pennsylvania high school records. He carried the ball twenty-six times for 110 yards and a touchdown. Ethan Kilmer, a senior who had transferred from Shippensburg and walked on, caught six passes, including one for a TD.

"What a way to end a career," said Robinson. "That was an unbelievable game. I don't think anyone who played in it will ever forget it."

As players, fans and workers setting up an on-field stage for a postgame ceremony scrambled all around them, Paterno and Bowden came together for a midfield embrace. "You know, Bobby," Paterno said, "we're getting too old for this stuff."

It was after 1:30 A.M. when Paterno, his hair unusually disheveled, and walking with a slight limp after spending nearly five hours pacing the sideline, emerged from a locker room in the basement of Dolphin Stadium and headed for the postgame news conference.

Sue Paterno, carrying a cane that helped her walk following a bad fall several months earlier, was sitting outside the door waiting to congratulate him. "Joe!" she yelled to no response when she saw him. "Joe! Joe!" Finally, her husband spotted her in the crowd. When they hugged, he seemed to fall wearily into her arms. "It's late," the coach said.

Surrounded by dozens of people—all of whom looked to be a half-century younger than Penn State's first couple—the Paternos made their way to the crowded interview room. Stepping gingerly onto the podium, Paterno glanced at his watch. "Geez," he said, "I've usually been in bed a couple of hours by now."

The questions came and it didn't take Paterno long to revive himself. Soon he was dissecting the game, sparring and joking with the writers, teasing the players who sat alongside him. The transformation from the old man who had limped out of the locker room minutes before was astounding. This is what kept Joe Paterno young.

"Coach Paterno has gone through a lot of criticism," Robinson said. "People wanted him to leave. I can't believe people wanted him to leave."

AUTHOR'S NOTE

WRITING AN UNAUTHORIZED BOOK on Joe Paterno is a lot like being a linebacker defending against one of those sweeps his Nittany Lions love to run: You've got to keep your head up at all times, fight off wave after wave of interference, and never take your eyes off the target, no matter how well-protected and untouchable he might seem.

A culture of secrecy looms over Penn State. For decades, journalists, civic groups, and even its own faculty members have fought unsuccessfully to open up the university's budget and files. That mentality is reflected in Paterno's program. Much to the annoyance of generations of authors, sportswriters, fans, and NFL scouts, he has constructed a nearly impenetrable wall around Penn State football. He emerges from behind it only long enough to perform his weekly media and public-relations duties. His assistant coaches are off-limits during the season. His players are even harder to reach.

Though Paterno finally relented in the days just before and after the 2004 season ended—granting me a lengthy interview and access to his radio show, and allowing me to accompany him to his normally off-limits Quarterbacks Club appearance—I was forced to spend the previous months shadowing him and his team from a safe distance. Wherever the old coach went—to games in Minneapolis, Boston, or Bloomington, to banquets in Pittsburgh, Valley Forge, or State College, to news conferences in Beaver Stadium's posh media room or a storage shed beneath Indiana University's Memorial Stadium—I was there, watching and listening.

As a result, many of the Paterno quotes in this book came from my being present at his weekly teleconferences, postgame press conferences, radio shows, and public appearances. Players were interviewed by phone or in chaotic postgame settings when a dozen or so were brought into a room and beset by scores of news-starved journalists. I often had to rely on my colleagues' published accounts of their interviews with players I could not reach in the precious few moments we were allotted.

Curiously, while Paterno rarely grants one-on-one interviews with reporters who regularly cover Penn State football during the season, he is more willing to find a few minutes for those from national newspapers, magazines, and Web sites. Consequently, I scoured daily as many of those as I could find for fresh Paterno tidbits. The most helpful newspapers in providing daily insights into Paterno, the 2004 season, and the culture of Penn State football were the *Centre Daily Times* in State College and the student-run *Daily Collegian*. In addition, in this age of new technology that Paterno has yet to grasp or acknowledge, several Web sites offered a look at how Penn State fans reacted from week to week. They included BottleofBlog.com, GoPSUsports.com, PennLive.com, and PSUPlaybook.org. Also, thanks to Paul Dyzak and his colleagues at the Penn State University Archives, I was able to review the university's massive collection of Joe Paterno–related material, including a newspaper clippings file that dates back to his arrival in State College in 1950.

Jeff Nelson, Penn State's assistant athletic director for communications, was as helpful as he was able to be in assisting me with credentials, directing me to the right ex-player or administrator, and answering all sorts of inane questions.

Penn State president Graham Spanier, athletic director Tim Curley, retired vice president for finance Bob Patterson, and a host of ex-players, including Denny Onkotz, John Shaffer, John Capelletti, the late Bob Mitinger, and Lydell Mitchell, were generous with their time.

Among the books on Paterno and Penn State that were extremely helpful and provided glimpses into games, seasons and players long gone were Ken Denlinger's *For the Glory* (St. Martin's Press, 1989); *Joe Paterno: Football My Way* by Joe Paterno, Mervin D. Hyman, and Gordon White (Macmillan Co. 1971); *Joe Paterno: In Search of Excellence* by James A. Paterson and Dennis Booher (Leisure Press, 1983); *Joe Paterno: The Coach of Byzantium* by George Paterno (Sports Publishing, 1997); *Lion Country: Inside Penn State Football* by Frank Bilovsky (Leisure Press, 1982); *The Nittany Lions: A Story of Penn State Football* by Ken Rappoport (The Strode Publishers, 1980); *No Ordinary Joe: The Biography of Joe Paterno* by Michael O'Brien (Rutledge Hill Press, 1998); *Paterno: By the Book* by Joe Paterno with Bernard Asbell (Random House, 1987); *Penn State: An Illustrated History* by Michael Bezilla (Penn State University Press, 1985); and *Road to Number One: A Personal Chronicle of Penn State Football* by Ridge Riley (Doubleday & Co., 1977).

I'm also eternally grateful to Gene Foreman, my old managing editor at *The Philadelphia Inquirer* who now teaches journalism at Penn State. Gene generously allowed me the use of his State College apartment for several days a week throughout the football season.

Lastly, I'd like to thank the boys and girls on the bus—the Penn State beat writers whose minds I picked, whose media guides I borrowed, whose patience I tested, and whose complaints about access I shared. They include Mark Brennan of *Blue White Illustrated*, Jerry Kellar of the *Wilkes-Barre Times Leader*, Rich Scarcella of the *Reading Eagle*, Ray Parrillo and Bill Lyon of *The Philadelphia Inquirer*, Dave Jones and Bob Flounders of the *Harrisburg Patriot-News*, Neil Rudel of the *Altoona Mirror*, Heather Dinich of the *Centre Daily Times*, Jenny Vrentas and Wade Malcolm of the *Daily Collegian*, Neil Geoghegan of the *Daily Local News*, Chico Harlan of the *Pittsburgh Post-Gazette*, and Rob Biertempfel of the *Pittsburgh Tribune-Review*.

This book came about because of the energy and efforts of my agents, Venture Literary's Frank Scatoni and Greg Dinkins, and the massive and incredibly helpful insights of Gotham Books editor Brendan Cahill.

And, of course, nothing would have been possible without the love and patience of my dear wife, Charlotte, who wouldn't know a blitz from a blintz.